Consumer Lending in France and America

Credit and Welfare

Why did America embrace consumer credit over the course of the twentieth century, when most other countries did not? How did American policymakers by the late twentieth century come to believe that more credit would make even poor families better off? This book traces the historical emergence of modern consumer lending in America and France. If Americans were profligate in their borrowing the French were correspondingly frugal. Comparison of the two countries reveals that America's love affair with credit was not primarily the consequence of its culture of consumption, as many writers have observed, nor directly a consequence of its less-generous welfare state. It emerged instead from evolving coalitions between fledgling consumer lenders seeking to make their business socially acceptable and a range of nongovernmental groups working to promote public welfare, labor, and minority rights. In France, where a similar coalition did not emerge, consumer credit continued to be perceived as economically regressive and socially risky.

Gunnar Trumbull is the Philip Caldwell Professor of Business Administration at Harvard Business School. He received his AB from Harvard College in 1991 and his PhD in Political Science from the Massachusetts Institute of Technology in 2000. He has served as a Jean Monnet Fellow at the European University Institute in Florence, Italy, and a Research Fellow at the Brookings Institution in Washington, DC. His research focuses on consumer politics in Europe and America. His previous books include *Consumer Capitalism: Politics, Product Markets and Firm Strategy in France and Germany* (2006) and *Strength in Numbers: The Political Power of Weak Interests* (2012).

Consumer Lending in France and America

Credit and Welfare

GUNNAR TRUMBULL
Harvard Business School

CAMBRIDGE
UNIVERSITY PRESS

CAMBRIDGE
UNIVERSITY PRESS

32 Avenue of the Americas, New York, NY 10013-2473, USA

Cambridge University Press is part of the University of Cambridge.

It furthers the University's mission by disseminating knowledge in the pursuit of education, learning, and research at the highest international levels of excellence.

www.cambridge.org
Information on this title: www.cambridge.org/9781107693906

First published 2014

Printed in the United States of America

A catalog record for this publication is available from the British Library.

Library of Congress Cataloging in Publication Data
Trumbull, Gunnar.
Consumer lending in France and America: credit and welfare / Gunnar Trumbull, Harvard Business School.
pages cm
Includes bibliographical references and index.
ISBN 978-1-107-01565-4 (hardback) – ISBN 978-1-107-69390-6 (paperback)
1. Consumer credit – United States. 2. Consumer credit – France. 3. Bank loans – United States. 4. Bank loans – France. 5. Public welfare – France. 6. Public welfare – United States. I. Title.
HG3756.U54T78 2014
332.7′43 – dc23 2013042457

ISBN 978-1-107-01565-4 Hardback
ISBN 978-1-107-69390-6 Paperback

For Thor and Taj

Contents

Figures and Tables

Figures

Tables

1

Introduction

At the beginning of the twentieth century in America, small household loans were both commonplace and a source of general concern. Social reformers fought to limit the economic and social impact of small lenders they decried as loan sharks; reputable businesses steered clear of sales credit because of the questionable consumers they worried it would attract. By the 1970s, credit in America had been reimagined as a legitimate tool of household finance that was understood to have broad social and economic benefits. This transformation in the moral economy of credit accompanied a revolution in lending technologies and the regulatory treatment of credit. Ultimately, these changes allowed American households to amass unprecedented debt – debt that eventually precipitated the worst financial crisis of postwar America. To understand the origins of that crisis, we need to understand not just the shifting habits of consumers but also what happened to lenders as the public moved from opposing credit to embracing it. This book traces how that transformation occurred.

Research into the origins of America's enthusiasm for credit has primarily focused on household demand. Historians have emphasized the role of credit in providing financial discipline, the ability to meet real material needs during economic downturn, and the role of credit in meeting goals of social aspiration.[1] Behavioral economists have noted a pervasive tendency of consumers to favor near-term consumption. Because credit allows us to move consumption forward in time, humans seem to be hardwired to want to borrow.[2]

[1] Lendol Calder, *Financing the American Dream: A Cultural History of Consumer Credit* (Princeton: Princeton University Press, 1999); Louis Hyman, *Debtor Nation: The History of America in Red Ink* (Princeton: Princeton University Press, 2011).

[2] Richard Thaler and Cass Sunstein, *Nudge: Improving Decisions about Health, Wealth and Happiness* (New Haven: Yale University Press, 2008); Dan Ariely, *Predictably Irrational: The*

Sociologists have argued that the flattening of real wages and the decline of welfare programs in the 1970s drove households to rely more on credit for their everyday needs.[3] Whatever the precise mixture of causes, household demand for credit seemingly has always been high. Rare indeed are lender complaints about a lack of consumer demand for credit. Less scholarly attention has been applied to how that demand has historically been met: on the supply of credit, companies that competed to provide it, regulators who wrote the rules for the sector, and a range of nongovernmental groups that came to see access to consumer credit as a means to achieve their own societal goals. This does not imply that the reasons for consumer borrowing were unimportant. Lenders and their supporters have always told stories about why consumers borrow. Such accounts mattered less for their rigorous grounding in fact than for their impact on policymakers and social reformers who sought to reimagine consumer credit as economically and socially legitimate.

In addition to the overwhelming focus on credit demand, most accounts of the origins of American consumer credit have also focused on the U.S. experience in isolation. Single-country case studies have their virtues, but they do not allow the observer easily to differentiate what is unusual about the U.S. case from what is common even to countries with very different credit practices. To provide this sort of comparative leverage, this book pairs the U.S. consumer lending experience with that of France. The French case is informative in part because its lenders were highly capable. The largest consumer lender in Europe, Cetelem, emerged and consolidated in early postwar France. Cetelem's success was attributable in large part to its rapid adoption of cutting-edge lending technologies – most borrowed directly from U.S. lenders. Yet, despite similar technology, U.S. and French credit outcomes differed dramatically. American households and regulators embraced credit as a virtue. Their French counterparts warned of the dangers of credit and endorsed restrictions on lending. We observe the impact of these different approaches in the level of household borrowing in the two countries. In 2007, at the height of consumer credit extension, French households still held less debt, measured as a share of disposable income, than American families did almost two generations earlier, in 1950. This book seeks to explain why.

Indebted America, Frugal France

Like the United States, France was an early mover in consumer credit. It boasted one of the first large-scale consumer credit registries – created by the

Hidden Forces that Shape our Decisions (New York: Harper Collins, 2008), 145; David Laibson, "Golden Eggs and Hyperbolic Discounting," *The Quarterly Journal of Economics* 112/2 (1997), 443–477.

3 Monica Prasad, *The Land of Too Much: American Abundance and the Paradox of Poverty* (Cambridge, MA: Harvard University Press, 2012), 235–238; Waltraud Schelke, "In the Spotlight of Crisis: How Social Policies Create, Correct, and Compensate Financial Markets," *Politics and Society* 40/1 (2012), 3–8.

Administration Dufayel in 1882 – which by the end of the century had amassed records for 3.5 million French households. The 1920s saw a boom in French auto lending companies – both industry captives and independent lenders – that paralleled the rise of the General Motors Acceptances Corporation and other non-captive auto finance companies in the United States. Following World War II, however, patterns of credit use in France and the United States diverged. Across every measure, American families out-borrowed their French counterpart by large margins. Indeed, France has consistently had among the lowest levels of consumer indebtedness of European countries with well-developed financial sectors.

In the immediate wake of World War II, as credit-driven consumption boomed in the United States, French families faced credit rationing. In 1949, the first year for which we have reliable comparative data, consumer credit represented nearly 10 percent of gross domestic product (GDP) in the United States, but just 0.2 percent of GDP in France.[4] Even as rationing was relaxed, however, French consumer lending remained low. Between 1955 and 1985, American households consistently carried consumer (non-mortgage) debt equal to 15–20 percent of their disposable income.[5] During the same period, French household debt rose gradually from 1 percent to 3 percent of disposable income. Household debt levels rose in both countries with financial deregulation in the early 1980s, but still France's lending deficit persisted. At its peak, in 2005, U.S. consumer debt had risen to 30 percent of disposable income, compared to 11 percent in France.[6] (See Figure 1.1.)

A similar pattern emerges when we consider the share of families that carried debt in the two countries. In the United States, surveys conducted in the 1950s found that between 45 percent and 60 percent of families reported outstanding consumer debt.[7] Interestingly, that share did not rise significantly even with the run-up of credit use in the 1990s and 2000s. A nationwide survey in 2008 found

4 Cetelem Historical Archives (CHA), Paris, France. UFB, "Notes sur le Financement des Ventes à Crédit aux États-Unis," December 1952, 1–2. These uncataloged archives were accessed at the Cetelem offices in Paris in 2008. They were later incorporated into the archives of BNP Paribas. Some of the documents used in this research were, at the time of publication, no longer accessible.

5 Early estimates of consumer indebtedness were measured against GDP. By the 1960s, observers began reporting indebtedness as a share of household disposable income. Where possible, I report debt as a share of disposable income.

6 The U.S. figure for household indebtedness includes home equity extraction used either for new consumption or to pay off consumer debt. Alan Greenspan and James Kennedy, "Sources and Uses of Equity Extracted from Homes," *Oxford Review of Economic Policy* 24/1 (2008), 120–144.

7 Marius Allègre, "Étude du Crédit à la Consommation," *Conseil Économique*, March 4, 1954, 267–279; Jean Chicoye, "Les Achats à Crédit," *Revue de l'Action Populaire* 140 (July–August 1960), 787; Richard L. D. Morse Papers (RLDM), Consumer Movement Archives, Kansas State University Department of Special Collections, Manhattan, Kansas. Collection name box 58, folder 8; V. Alonzo Metcalf and Lorene S. Wilson, "Consumer Credit – A Commodity," Publication of the University of Missouri, Extension Division, 1960, 3; George Katona, consumer credit surveys.

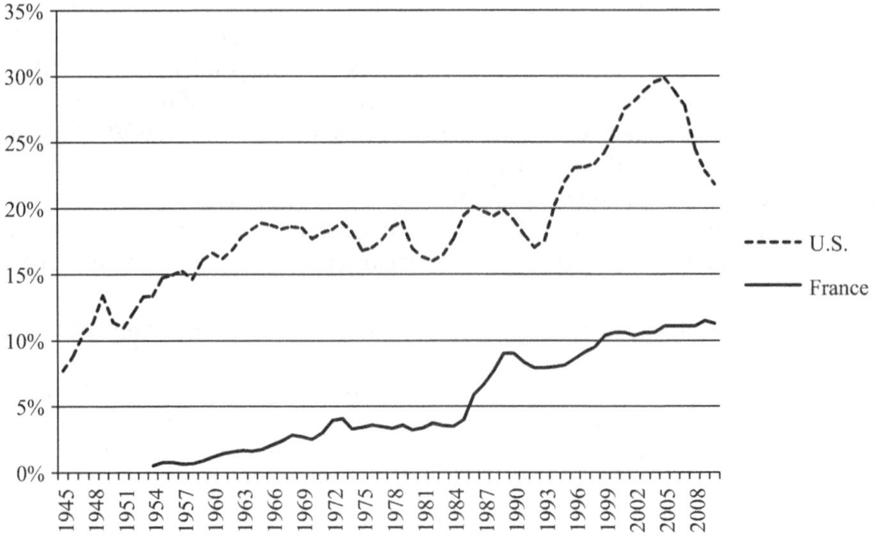

FIGURE 1.1. Household Non-Mortgage Debt in France and the United States, 1945–2005 (Share of Disposable Household Income)[8]

that 61 percent of U.S. households reported non-mortgage debt.[9] In France, a lower share of households relied on credit. A series of surveys conducted between the early 1950s and late 1970s all found that between 20 percent and 25 percent of surveyed families reported holding non-mortgage debt.[10] With financial deregulation, the share of households carrying debt increased somewhat. Surveys conducted in the 1980s and 1990s found that roughly a third of all families carried non-mortgage debt.[11] These results suggest that roughly half as many French households relied on non-mortgage credit at any given moment than did American households.

These data are consistent with information we have on the share of sales that were made on credit in each country. Surveys from the 1950s show that roughly 60 percent of all consumer durable sales in the United States were

[8] U.S. data from 1994 to 2008 have been adjusted to include equity extraction that took the form of consumer credit, as calculated by Alan Greenspan and James Kennedy. This includes the share of home equity loans and cash-out mortgage refinancing that went to consumption, including home renovation, and the discharge of existing consumer debt. At its peak, in 2005, home equity extraction for consumption accounted for an additional 5 percent of consumer credit as a share of disposable household income, over conventional consumer credit.

[9] Retrieved from http://emergingminds.org/Poll-Unpaid-Credit-Card-Bills-Worrying-American-Families.html (accessed August 14, 2009).

[10] Serge Jeanneteau, "La Vente à Tempérament," *Économie*, September 20, 1956; *Les Échos*, May 28, 1973; *Maintenant*, May 7, 1979.

[11] *La Croix*, May 20, 1988; Paul Defourny and Josette Bienfait, *Données d'Image sur le Crédit* (Paris: Cetelem-BVA, 1992); Hubert Balaguy, *Le Crédit à la Consommation en France* (Paris: Presses Universitaires de Paris, 1996), 23.

made on credit.[12] For cars, the share was as high as 85 percent.[13] In France, credit sales as a share of total retail sales were significantly lower. Surveys in the 1950s and early 1960s show that roughly 20–30 percent of all consumer durable sales were on credit.[14] For automobiles, the share increased from about 20 percent in the early 1950s to around 40 percent in the mid-1960s.[15] By the 1990s, the proliferation of revolving credit accounts had made it difficult to distinguish which particular products were being sold on credit. Nevertheless, the broad cross-national pattern of credit sales seems to have been the same. In 1995, 22 percent of all household goods, durable and perishable, were being sold on credit in the United States, compared to 9 percent in France.[16]

Although the French relied less on consumer credit than did their American counterparts, this does not seem to have reflected a disproportionate objection to buying on credit. In fact, French households were surprisingly open to using credit. When the founders of one of France's early credit cards, the Carte d'Or, surveyed the French public in 1968, 60 percent of respondents said that they would appreciate access to credit.[17] Three of four Renault workers surveyed in 1969 reported viewing consumer credit favorably.[18] In the United States, where credit was more pervasive, consumer opinion of credit was, if anything, slightly more negative. A survey in 1954 found that half of American households thought buying on installment credit was a good idea, versus 37 percent who opposed it.[19] A survey of farm-operator families in 1959 found that only 54 percent thought it was acceptable to buy household equipment on credit.[20] It would be a mistake to place too much weight on such surveys, given differences in exposure to credit in the two countries. Nonetheless, they suggest that the French had no greater moral, ethical, or religious objection to the principle of consumer credit than did Americans.

12 CHA, UFB, "Notes sur le Financement des Ventes à Crédit aux États-Unis," December 1952, 1–2; François des Aulnoyes, "Le Crédit à la Consommation," *Combat*, January 30, 1954; Michel Drancourt, *Une Force Inconnue: le Crédit* (Paris: Hachette, 1961), 26.

13 Union Fédérale de la Consommation, *Bulletin Mensuel d'Information* 29 (1955), 48; Michel Drancourt, *Une Force Inconnue: Le Crédit* (Paris: Hachette, 1961), 26.

14 André Malterre, "Problème du Crédit à la Consommation," *Journal Officiel* 20, August 11, 1961, 770; "Le Crédit à la Consommation en France," *Agence Économique et Financière*, June 9, 1959.

15 Marius Allègre, "Étude du Crédit à la Consommation," *Conseil Économique*, March 4, 1954, 269; Gerard Constant, "La Vente à Crédit," *Les Cahiers Français*, April 1965, 18.

16 Hubert Balaguy, *Le Crédit à la Consommation en France* (Paris: Presses Universitaires de Paris, 1996), 22.

17 Maurice Roy, "La Guerre des Cartes est Déclarée," *L'Express*, March 4, 1968.

18 Michael Seidman, *The Imaginary Revolution: Parisian Students and Workers in 1968* (Wilmington: University of North Carolina Press, 2004), 264.

19 Jan Logeman, "Different Paths to Mass Consumption: Consumer Credit in the United States and West Germany during the 1950s and 1960s," *Journal of Social History* 41/3 (2008), 544.

20 RLDM, box 152, folder 32, Robert L. D. Morse, "Credit and its use: Attitudes and practices of Kansas farm-operator families, 1955," draft article, May 14, 1959.

As they looked across the Atlantic, French observers seem to have been both fascinated and repelled by the American credit culture. They noted the popularity in the United States of wallets with a large number of slots for credit cards, but also coveted the elaborate kitchen equipment that even middle-class American families purchased on credit. For opponents of credit liberalization in France, the United States stood as a cautionary tail. A labor union representative to France's National Consumer Council, arguing against the liberalization of consumer credit, admonished his colleagues in 1954: "We are not from across the Atlantic, where people are born on credit."[21] Although French accounts of American credit culture were frequently exaggerated, it was hard to overstate the extent of credit use in the United States. A 1957 survey of Kansas farm-operator families showed that 5 percent of those who had children did in fact use credit to pay for the birth.[22]

Such anecdotes point to the place of credit in a broader policy discourse in the two countries. In France, where the government provided costly social services such as medicine and a minimum income support, the high interest rate associated with consumer credit came to be seen as an additional burden on the working class and poor. In the United States, where such social services were not generally available, credit allowed the working class and poor to gain access to social services even if they could not at the moment afford them. Credit attitudes also emerged against a backdrop of different postwar economic models in the two counties. In France, a focus on promoting exports led policymakers to view consumer credit as risky because domestic demand could drive inflation that would hurt sales abroad. In the United States, growth focused on serving large and largely unmet domestic demand made the liberal use of consumer credit look like a reasonable way to stimulate demand, increase scale, and raise wages.

These economic and social dimensions of consumer credit are important for understanding how the French and U.S. credit markets emerged, and diverged, in the postwar era. They made it possible for Americans to imagine that borrowing was useful, and for French to view it as a risky indulgence. But they are not sufficient to explain why American lenders offered credit so generously, and why policymakers and other societal actors allowed them – indeed encouraged them – to do so.

Two broad classes of theories have most commonly been evoked to explain differences in lending behavior, both across time and across countries. Liberal theories have focused on the role of deregulation and credit scoring in

[21] Archives of the Conseil National de Crédit (CNC) of the Banque de France, Paris, France, 1427200301, box 283, Comité national du Crédit, Comité du Crédit à Court Terme, December 1953–June 1961, Meeting of the Comité du Crédit à Court Terme, January 9, 1954, 13.

[22] RLDM, box 152, folder 32, "Proposed Testimony of Richard L. D. Morse, at the Hearings on S.2755, before the Subcommittee on Production and Stabilization," Committee on Banking and Currency, April 13, 1960, 4.

promoting lending. Sociological theories have emphasized the link to a culture of consumerism and the idea of credit as a form of private-sector welfare. Yet these accounts, described in more detail in the next section, do a poor job of accounting for the postwar trajectory of consumer credit in the United States and France. The research presented in this book points instead to the causal importance of policy coalitions that shaped what both lenders and policymakers considered legitimate small lending.[23] In France, a coalition of lenders and regulators came to emphasize goals of consumer protection over credit access. In the United States, a coalition of lenders and nongovernmental organizations emphasized goals of credit access over consumer protection. The remainder of this book examines how those coalitions emerged and evolved, and the impact they had on both lenders and policymakers.

We should note that this research focuses specifically on non-mortgage consumer credit. Consumer credit includes a range of loan types: personal loans, installment sales loans, secured auto loans, and revolving credit of the sort offered by credit cards. It does not include home mortgages, for two reasons. First, mortgages are distinct from consumer credit in that they represent real investments. In acquiring a mortgage, new homeowners save on future rent payments. Mortgages are, in this way, far closer to business loans, for which the economic logic of borrowing is less ambiguous. Second, the market for mortgages has been driven overwhelmingly by government policies that have insured, securitized, and subsidized them. Although the political drivers behind these policies are of great interest, they obscure rather than clarify the link between credit and other economic transformations in American society.

Theories of Consumer Credit

Existing accounts of consumer credit have rested on either liberal or sociological foundations. Liberal theories of consumer credit treat these markets as emerging naturally, subject to conditions of supply and demand. Given the seemingly stable and high demand for consumer credit, the liberal approach has mainly focused on the impact of new lending technologies and the loosening of credit market regulations to explain the growth in credit supply. Among technological drivers, academic attention has focused on the growth of firm-level credit scoring and the sharing of lending data via independent credit rating agencies. The theoretical roots of this explanation date to a theory propounded by economists Joseph Stiglitz and Andrew Weiss, in which they argued that lenders would ration credit to risky borrowers even if those borrowers are willing to pay a premium for the risk.[24] Unable to

[23] Gunnar Trumbull, *Strength in Numbers: The Political Power of Weak Interests* (Cambridge, MA: Harvard University Press, 2012).

[24] Joseph E. Stiglitz and Andrew Weiss, "Credit Rationing in Markets with Imperfect Information," *American Economic Review* 71/3 (1981): 393–410.

distinguish between risky-but-honest borrowers and others who accepted the requirement to pay a high interest rate because they never intended to repay, lenders would hold back from making higher-interest-rate loans. In empirical tests of the Stiglitz-Weiss thesis, researchers have found that the presence of credit rating bureaus – which allow lenders to measure credit quality independent of price – has a positive effect on credit extension in cross-national comparisons.[25]

The pattern of credit rating in the United States and France fits with the pattern of credit extension in the two countries. Postwar America boasted hundreds of local credit bureaus. By the 1970s, these had consolidated nationally and computerized their records. By the 1980s, many advanced industrialized countries had converged on a system of centralized credit rating that mirrored the American system. But French lenders eschewed centralized credit data. In fact, the French government banned consumer lenders from sharing positive credit rating information, such as outstanding loans and loan applications. In its place, the Banque de France ran a more limited "black" list of borrowers that had already defaulted on loans. The logic of the ban focused on concerns about data privacy. But the lack of centralized, positive credit data also made it hard for new lenders to break into the market, and this earned it support from the majority of French lenders.

Although the focus on credit rating is fruitful, such institutions have not always been historically decisive for lenders. In both the United States and France, successful early lenders developed a range of alternative strategies for managing consumer nonpayment. Morris Plan Banks, which made small loans in the interwar period in the United States, relied exclusively on cosigners to ensure repayment. Installment lenders in early postwar France relied primarily on their retail partners to assess the creditworthiness of their customers. In both cases, repayment rates were unusually high.

A survey of company financial accounts reveals that borrower nonpayment during these periods was an important but relatively low-priority cost for lenders in both countries. Far more important for their bottom line were the more mundane administrative costs associated with registering new loan contracts, tracking those contracts through to their duration, managing bill

[25] Tullio Jappelli and Marco Pagano, "Information Sharing in Credit Markets," *Journal of Finance* 48/5 (1993), 1693–1718; Tullio Jappelli and Marco Pagano, "Information Sharing, Lending and Defaults: Cross-Country Evidence," *Journal of Banking and Finance* 26/10 (2002), 2017–2045; Akos Ronas-Tas, "Consumer Credit in Transition Economies," in Victor Perez-Dias, ed., *The European Experience in Comparative Perspective* (London: Berghahn Books, 2009); Bruce G. Carruthers and Barry Cohen, "Noter le Crédit: Classification et Cognition aux États-Unis," *Genèses* 79 (2010), 48–73; Alya Guseva, *Into the Red: The Birth of the Credit Card Market in Postcommunist Russia* (Palo Alto: Stanford University Press, 2008); Peter L. McCorkell, "The Impact of Credit Scoring and Automated Underwriting on Credit Availability," in Thomas A. Durkin and Michael E. Staten, eds., *The Impact of Public Policy on Consumer Credit* (Boston: Kluwer, 2002).

mailings, and processing timely follow-ups in case of late payment. Accordingly, those technologies that most transformed the supply of credit came not primarily from centralized credit scoring, but from computerization, innovations in telecommunications, and back-office mechanization. Successful consumer lenders in both France and the United States invested heavily to stay at the forefront of new information technologies.

The second driver of lending in the liberal account was the degree and kind of government regulation, and deregulation, of consumer lending. Without question, the liberalization of lending regulations in the 1980s caused an increase in lending volumes at the time in both France and the United States. Most significant in the United States was the relaxing of state usury laws triggered by the 1978 *Marquette v. First of Omaha* Supreme Court ruling. In France, regulators in the early 1980s relaxed restrictions both on credit volumes and on the down payment and repayment period for installment loans. In both cases, liberalization was followed by credit growth.

But the broader pattern of consumer lending in the two countries fits poorly with the liberalization thesis. In the United States, consumer borrowing expanded most rapidly during the 1950s, at the peak of small loan regulation. U.S. states at the time applied highly restrictive usury caps, even as interest rates went largely unregulated in France. Prior to deregulation in the 1980s, American credit markets were arguably *more* regulated than their counterparts in France. Nor can we treat regulation as fully independent of societal perceptions of credit. In France, for example, the experiment with credit deregulation in the 1980s generated a heated public debate about the social costs of overindebtedness. This debate in turn caused a backlash that led policymakers to significantly reregulate the sector. Any meaningful account of credit regulation must also explain differences in public perceptions of the benefits and risks associated with liberal household access to credit.

A second, sociological set of theories attributes the development of financial markets to underlying societal institutions and norms. In the case of consumer credit, these sociological arguments have taken two broad forms. The first interprets consumer credit as an outgrowth of American consumerism. These accounts emphasize the role of early installment credit as a means to "push" consumption, stabilize demand for mass-produced products, and attract and retain customers.[26] The mass marketing of early household equipment and automobiles clearly depended on credit.[27] Credit was also useful for the consumers of mass-produced goods. Foremost, it allowed purchasing without first saving. Equally important, by providing a monthly bill that had to be paid,

[26] Donncha Marron, *Consumer Credit in the United States: A Sociological Perspective from the 19th Century to the Present* (New York: Palgrave, 2009); Martha L. Olney, *Buy Now, Pay Later: Advertising, Credit and Consumer Durables in the 1920s* (Chapel Hill: University of North Carolina Press, 1991); Rowena Olegario, *A Culture of Credit: Embedding Trust and Transparency in American Business* (Cambridge, MA: Harvard University Press, 2006), 35.

[27] Isabelle Gaillard, "Télévisions et Crédit à la Consummation: Une Approche Comparative France-Rfa 1950–1970," *Entreprises et Histoire* 59/2 (2010), 102–111.

credit promoted a kind of budget discipline that helped consumers rationalize their purchases.[28] French sociologist Jean Baudrillard has argued that it was in part credit that made the newly emerging culture of mass consumption, with its lure to excess, compatible with the parallel culture of hard work and self-discipline.[29]

The problem with this link between credit and consumerism is that the causal direction is difficult to detect. Did liberal access to credit make Americans' consumerist culture possible? Or did a pre-existing culture of consumerism make credit seem acceptable and even attractive? Given the challenge of disentangling the causal thread, attributing high levels of consumer debt to the impact of a consumerist culture seems like a tendentious claim. At the very least, we would want to understand in greater detail how one translated into the other.

A second form of sociological argument has focused on the link between credit and social class. Historians have tended to emphasize a relatively benign relationship between credit and class. Louis Hyman argues in *Debtor Nation* that credit allowed poorer American families in the 1950s and 1960s to look like wealthier families. By expanding access to the trappings of suburban consumerism, credit promoted social integration and a blurring of class lines.[30] Lizabeth Cohen notes in *A Consumers' Republic* that the struggle by women and urban blacks in the 1960s and 1970s to gain access to credit served as a productive vehicle for pursuing social justice.[31] Others have tended to view the link between credit and class more critically. A range of scholars have noted the role that credit seemed to play in the United States as an ersatz welfare policy.[32] In these accounts, U.S. wage stagnation and welfare retrenchment beginning in the early 1970s drove a growing wedge between family incomes and expenditures.[33] As consumers relied on credit to fill the gap, credit scores

[28] Lendol Calder, *Financing the American Dream: A Cultural History of Consumer Credit* (Princeton: Princeton University Press, 1999).

[29] Jean Baudrillard, *The Consumer Society: Myths and Structures* (London: Sage, 1970), 81.

[30] Louis Hyman, *Debtor Nation: The History of American in Red Ink* (Princeton: Princeton University Press, 2011), 172.

[31] Lizabeth Cohen, *A Consumers' Republic: The Politics of Mass Consumption in Postwar America* (New York: Random House, 2003), 383.

[32] Elizabeth Warren, "The Vanishing Middle Class," in J. Edwards, M. Crain, and A. L. Kalleberg, eds., *Ending Poverty in America: How to Restore the American Dream* (New York: The New Press, 2007); Monica Prasad, "The Credit/Welfare State Tradeoff: Toward a Demand-Side Theory of Comparative Political Economy," *SSRN Working Paper*, December 16, 2010; Monica Prasad, *The Land of Too Much: American Abundance and the Paradox of Poverty* (Cambridge, MA: Harvard University Press, 2012); Waltraud Schelke, "In the Spotlight of Crisis: How Social Policies Create, Correct, and Compensate Financial Markets," *Politics and Society* 40/1 (2012), 5; Jan Logemann, "From Cradle to Bankruptcy: Credit Access and the American Welfare State," in Jan Logemann, ed., *The Development of Consumer Credit in Global Perspective: Business, Regulation, and Culture* (New York: Palgrave, 2012).

[33] Raghuram Rajan, *Fault Lines: How Hidden Fractures still Threaten the World Economy* (Princeton: Princeton University Press, 2010); Robert Reich, *After Shock: The Next Economy and America's Future* (New York: Knopf, 2010); Hyman, *Debtor Nation*, 219; Herman

became a new indicator of social status, and household indebtedness, especially at the lower end of the economic spectrum, grew.[34] For some observers, the displacement of welfare and wages by credit reflected a fundamental failure of American economic and social policy.[35] But for a new generation of politicians that took power in the 1980s and 1990s, the idea that access to credit could create an economic buffer and promote social mobility became one pillar of a new "third way" welfare politics that embraced markets and reduced government largesse.[36]

There are two main problems with the credit-as-welfare thesis. First, it does a poor job of explaining historical and cross-national patterns of credit use. In the United States, expansive use of credit preceded the period in the early 1970s when income stagnation and welfare retrenchment began. In fact, American workers were relying heavily on consumer credit already in the 1950s, during a period in which their wages were rising and welfare benefits were being enhanced. U.S. household credit use did begin to increase again beginning in the 1980s, but by then average wages had already been stagnant for a decade. Nor was credit-as-welfare a distinctly American idea. When U.S. welfare reformers at the beginning of the twentieth century began looking for ways for the poor to help themselves, they borrowed ideas about charitable credit that had been operating in France for more than a century. These French institutions – charitable pawnshops and municipal credit unions – were so well accepted that they were later incorporated into the formal welfare state.[37]

The second problem with the credit-as-welfare thesis is that it overemphasizes the role of relatively poor borrowers. Especially in the wake of the 2008 financial crisis, sociological arguments linking credit to welfare were deeply influential in analyzing the causes of the crisis. For the political left, they offered an explanation of the crisis that linked the crisis to economic inequality. As wages had diverged, lower-income Americans were forced to rely more heavily on credit to keep up. The answer to the crisis, in other words, was higher wages.[38] For the political right, overindebtedness reflected state-led efforts to extend credit to the poor as an ersatz welfare transfer. The particular culprit was government regulation in credit markets, including the Equal Credit

Schwartz, *Subprime Nation: American Power, Global Capital, and the Housing Bubble* (Ithaca: Cornell University Press, 2009), 208; Robert H. Frank, *Luxury Fever: Money and Happiness in an Era of Excess* (Princeton: Princeton University Press, 1999), 45.

34 Marion Fourcade and Kieran Healy, "Economic Categories in Neoliberal Society." Paper presented at the Annual Meeting of the American Sociological Association, Las Vegas, August, 2011.

35 Greta R. Krippner, *Capitalizing on Crisis: The Political Origins of the Rise of Finance* (Cambridge MA: Harvard University Press, 2011).

36 Iain Ramsay, "Comparative Consumer Bankruptcy," *University of Illinois Law Review* 2007, no. 1 245.

37 Gunnar Trumbull, "Credit Access and Social Welfare: The Rise of Consumer Lending in the United States and France," *Politics and Society* 40/1 (2012), 9–34.

38 Robert Reich, *Beyond Outrage: What Has Gone Wrong with our Economy and our Democracy, and How to Fix It* (New York: Random House, 2012).

Opportunity Act (1974), the Community Redevelopment Act (1977), and the Bankruptcy Reform Act (1978). What both of these views share is an interpretation of the 2008 financial crisis that places the blame on overborrowing by the poor. Although it is true that poorer American families increased their use of credit beginning in the early 1980s, the lowest two income quintiles nonetheless represented only a small share of total outstanding credit.[39] Moreover, there would seem to be a deep injustice in laying the blame for financial crisis on those with the least resources and who were least prepared to handle the resulting economic disruption.[40]

The Politics of Markets: Credit, Coalitions, and Legitimacy

The account in this book attributes the emergence and divergence of U.S. and French consumer credit to the ways in which the sector was transformed into a legitimate economic activity. Lenders have always been sensitive to public perception of their business. At the beginning of the twentieth century, societal attitudes toward credit in both France and the United States were mainly negative. Small lending was closely associated with criminality – a charge based partly on the reality of aggressive collections tactics and partly grounded in anti-Semitism and the cultural stereotype of the Jewish moneylender. A broad coalition of social reformers, welfare advocates, religious puritans, labor organizers, and employers at the time saw the small-loan sector as a threat to individual morality and social order. Although credit's general disrepute did nothing to reduce consumer demand, it did make reputable businesses wary of lending or selling on credit. This was especially true for retailers, who feared the stigma that accompanied credit sales, and for commercial banks, whose reputation in related lines of business could be threatened by engaging in an activity that was perceived as ethically marginal.

By the end of the twentieth century, the popular perception of lending in the two countries had been remade. Lenders were perceived as serving societally useful goals. But differences had also emerged in the two countries. For the United States, credit had become synonymous with opportunity. Access to credit, interpreted as something akin to a right, was perceived as a means to achieve social mobility. Credit cards endowed social status; credit ratings became a proxy for economic standing. Consumer lenders, once marginalized, emerged as some of the most profitable companies in the financial sector. For France, public perceptions of consumer lending also changed, but in a different direction. As in the United States, consumer credit became widely available,

[39] Andrea Ryan, Peter Tufano, and Gunnar Trumbull, "A Brief Postwar History of US Consumer Finance," *Business History Review* 85/3 (2011), 461–498.

[40] For more on this tradition, see: Judith Treas, "The Great American Recession: Sociological Insights on Blame and Pain," *Sociological Perspectives* 53/1 (2010), 3–18.

borrowing on credit mainly lost its stigma, and reputable firms engaged in lending. But the sector was also seen as risky, especially for poor and working-class borrowers, who could be lured into a spiral of debt and economic exclusion. Like other risky markets, consumer credit remained the focus of intensive regulation, including interest rate caps. Access to credit was not a right, as in the United States, but a risky luxury to which access could legitimately be restricted.

How was the business of consumer lending transformed over the course of the twentieth century? And why were the outcomes in France and the United States so different? The chapters in this book elaborate a political account of credit market extension that emphasizes the central role of societal coalitions that supported the legitimacy of consumer credit markets. The book finds that different coalitions that emerged in support of consumer credit in the United States and in France in turn drove different trajectories of consumer lending.

In the United States, the supply of consumer credit was supported by an evolving coalition between progressive activists and consumer lenders. The groundwork for abundant consumer credit was laid in the 1910s and 1920s, when credit access was supported by progressives as a salve to the emerging working class, and by powerful industrialists as an alternative to expansive welfare of the kind that was spreading in Europe. In the 1950s and 1960s, consumer credit became an element of the postwar productivity coalition, in which organized labor supported credit to the working class and manufacturers encouraged credit both to drive new demand and as a bulwark against communism. Credit seemed to create a virtuous cycle, with new credit purchases driving scale in manufacturing, the resulting productivity increases enabling increases in wages. By the 1970s, credit market access became a consensus issue of women's and welfare rights campaigns. These groups reconceived credit access as a right of citizenship and a means to economic equality. These evolving lender-activist coalitions laid the groundwork for a "third way" politics of the 1990s that portrayed credit access as a means to bring opportunity to the poor.

The evolving legitimacy coalitions that sustained support for consumer credit over time rested on a shifting discourse about the rationale for consumer credit. Consumers in the 1910s and 1920s were seen to be relying on credit as a form of insurance in case of injury, unemployment, birth, or any other shock to income or expenses. During the 1950s and 1960s, both returning soldiers and a whole generation that had grown up in the shadow of war were seen to be borrowing to furnish their newly acquired houses. Consumption that had been postponed during World War II could now be unleashed. During the 1970s, credit became a symbol of economic equality for women and blacks. It also, coincidentally, provided many middle-class Americans with a hedge against the rising costs of everyday goods that was driven by the first oil shock. By the 1990s, household borrowing was being portrayed as an investment, grounded in the notion of an ownership society in which credit access drove social and economic mobility.

As the case for credit use evolved, past arguments in its favor did not entirely disappear. Rather, they became layered in an increasingly dense discourse that portrayed consumer credit as a salve to a range of societal problems. The core of that discourse was an equation of social welfare to liberal access to credit markets.

In France, the legitimation of consumer credit took a different path. Unlike in the United States, France had few activists pushing credit as a tool of social welfare. This meant that a different kind of legitimacy coalition emerged, one that emphasized the interaction of dedicated consumer finance companies with the state. For economic policymakers, excess consumer borrowing risked driving inflation and exchange-rate appreciation, crowding out industrial investment, and countering effective monetary policy. Politically, a coalition of interests on the left and right came to agreement around the potential social ills of borrowing. The Catholic right expressed traditional religious concerns about usury and the potentially exploitative nature of debt contracts. The labor left interpreted consumer credit as an illegitimate claim on workers' income, with the potential to de-radicalize union membership. For consumer lenders, whose economic futures depended largely on the discretion of government regulators, these concerns led them to emphasize low cost and responsible lending practices. Legitimate consumer lending was modest, disciplined, and focused on financing household necessities.

By the early 1980s, as deregulation and new telecommunications and computing technologies transformed the economics of consumer lending, France's government-lender coalition evolved. Rising household debt levels triggered a public debate about the social and economic costs of overindebtedness. France's regulatory response did not follow the American pattern. Unlike their American counterparts, French policymakers never embraced the idea of credit access as a societal right. In bankruptcy reform, for example, French policymakers were deeply resistant to offering debt forgiveness, even for families that risked being permanently marginalized by excessive debt. Regulators also blocked the creation of centralized positive credit databases for consumers. Their opposition was based partly on concerns about data privacy, but they also felt such databases would unfairly distribute proprietary lender information.

For French policymakers, consumer credit entailed responsibilities, including the responsibility to develop a good record in order to gain access to credit, and the responsibility to repay that credit under virtually any circumstance. France's consumer finance companies reinforced this view. They embraced usury ceilings, which kept new high-rate competitors out of the market and limited the riskiest classes of loans. And they blamed commercial banks, which had only recently entered the consumer lending sector, for precipitating the overindebtedness crisis by offering irresponsible loans. For the French, credit markets were merely markets, not a form of social policy. They brought advantages and disadvantages, and they had to be regulated.

The Business of Credit

The evolving credit coalitions in each country drew in a range of economic and social actors, but three in particular were critical: commercial banks, retailers, and organized labor. These groups came to opposite views about the role and desirability of consumer credit. Their interests, in turn, drove patterns of public policy that tended to reinforce their perceived interests.

Commercial banks and retailers were the major postwar lenders. Both kinds of lenders played important roles in the rehabilitation of credit as a legitimate line of business. Retailers provided most of the early innovations in consumer lending. U.S. retailers in particular were highly creative. They developed not only the physical form of the credit card, but also the technology of revolving credit in which multiple products could be charged to a common credit account. Although such credit was expensive to administer – the small transactions amplified the administrative costs of lending – it was extremely popular. For American retailers, revolving credit allowed them to attract and retain customers with a flexible credit plan that did not require frequent credit applications and approvals.

The surprise is that French lenders did not adopt a similar approach to credit. France's largest sales finance company, Cetelem, launched the country's first revolving credit account in 1965. It then quickly abandoned it. The reason had to do with the organization of France's retail credit system. Unlike in the United States, retail credit was offered primarily by independent finance companies such as Cetelem. Because they did not directly benefit from profit on sales of merchandise, and their total volume of lending was set by government regulators, these French lenders were more sensitive than their American counterparts to the profitability of their loan portfolios. What Cetelem quickly discovered was that revolving credit accounts were expensive to administer and offered a correspondingly low financial return. Under constant financial pressure, Cetelem and other lenders abandoned their early revolving credit products and did not reintroduce them until the mid-1980s.

In terms of public and policymakers perception of credit, the role played by commercial banks was also important. In the United States, where banks moved aggressively into consumer lending prior to World War II, they pushed for regulatory policies that favored the sector. In France, by contrast, banks opted to steer clear of consumer lending until the late 1980s. This difference in timing would prove consequential. A key element in modern consumer credit was the link between a universal payment card and a revolving credit facility. This package, embodied in the American-style credit card, allowed the customer to use a single credit card to pay virtually any vendor. More importantly, any payment made this way was potentially a loan, subject to later repayment decisions by consumers. In the United States, where banks were already making small loans prior to the growth of card payment systems, those systems could easily merge the payment function with a credit facility.

These hybrid payment-credit cards, which emerged in the United States in the 1950s, were not offered by banks in France until a generation later.

One obstacle was that French banks were engaged in the profitable industrial investment sector, backed up by government industrial planning that virtually guaranteed handsome rewards for those investments. This kind of guided lending left national banks relatively unsophisticated, and their experience managing loan risk was narrow. When they did experiment with consumer lending, first in 1962 and then again in 1972, high nonpayments led to disappointing financial results. Moreover, these banks relied on their good name for continued government support. Moving into relatively high-interest-rate lending to poor and marginal consumers posed a special risk for them, should they be cast as usurers or worse. And because France's big commercial banks did not have significant exposure to consumer credit markets, they were perfectly willing to accept a high degree of regulatory restriction on the sector.

In the United States, the early pioneers in consumer lending tended to come from legal backgrounds. Edward Clark, a former lawyer who had worked for the law firm that sewing-machine manufacturers Isaac Singer had previously hired to settle a patent dispute, designed and launched the Singer installment-selling plan in the 1850s.[41] Both Arthur Morris, inventor of the early Morris Plan installment lending certificates of the 1910s, and Ralph Schneider, cofounder of the Diners' Club travel card, had been practicing lawyers before launching into consumer credit. This common base of legal expertise reflected the legal challenges of offering consumer credit within the constraints of state usury laws that set interest rates at unrealistically low levels. And, because successful lenders pursued continual legal innovation to evade usury restrictions, they operated in a perpetual legal grey zone.

For both France and America, the reality of consumer credit the 1950s and 1960s was that few, if any, lenders were earning meaningful profits on the basis of interest payments on consumer loans. Even the most successful lenders faced lean years in the 1950s and 1960s. For most of the first decade and a half of its existence, Cetelem had the lowest profitability of all the affiliates of the Groupe Bancaire.[42] In America, Diners' Club came to the brink of bankrupcty – despite charging an 8 percent retailer transaction fee – until it was saved by the introduction of an annual membership fee. Many of the U.S. banks that launched consumer credit in the late 1950s quickly pulled back as they became weighted down with losses. Most European banks that experimented with making personal loans in the 1960s also quickly stepped away.[43] Consumer lenders that were able to survive this lean period did so through a combination of

[41] Robert A. Lynn, "Installment Credit Before 1870," *Business History Review* 31/4 (1957), 419.

[42] CHA, Résultats de l'Évaluation de Cetelem et les Hypothèses de Travail qui en Ressortent, May 21, 1969, Annex VII.

[43] The notable exception was automobile lenders, for which the large size of each loan made administrative costs relatively less burdensome.

severe cost containment, investment in automation, and a variety of stratagems that spread some of the cost and risk to manufacturers and retailers.[44]

Despite the poor chances of earning a return, U.S. banks nevertheless persisted in consumer lending. In part, it proved a creative way to get around legal restrictions on interest rate competition in a highly fragmented banking context. The large number of U.S. banks – 15,000 in the early postwar period – meant that even small towns experienced intensive competition among local "unit" banks for deposits and loans. Restricted by Regulation Q under the Federal Reserve Act from enticing new depositors with higher interest rates, they resorted instead to gifts, including the now-proverbial free toaster offered by some banks to new account holders. What they also quickly discovered was that new depositors could be lured in with the offer of revolving credit accounts. Further, agreements with retailers about accepting revolving payment were often accompanied by new inventory or development loans. For many American banks, making consumer loans, even at a loss, was an investment in growth.

Welfare and Consumer Credit

For labor and welfare rights advocates, consumer credit has always posed a conundrum. On the one hand, access to credit offered the possibility of self-sufficiency. With credit to bridge periods of financial difficulty, families could stay off of the public dole. On the other hand, misuse of credit could lead to a cycle of debt that would result in permanent exclusion from the benefits of economic and social citizenship. In general, American trade unions and worker advocates tended to emphasize the benefits of credit access while de-emphasizing the potential costs. In France, nearly the opposite pattern emerged. Unions worried that the high interest charged on consumer credit led workers to reduce the amount of money they had available to spend on necessities. How labor and other welfare rights groups came to understand the role of credit in turn had implications for the broader supply and regulation of credit.

From its origins in the mid-nineteenth century, modern consumer credit embodied both the aspirations and the fears of the emerging working class. On the one hand, access to credit seemed to offer a route out of poverty; on the other hand, the burden of repayment imposed a constant new strain

[44] The problem of low profitability for consumer loans appears not to have been limited to France. Speaking at the 1961 annual meeting of the Association of European Bankers, German economics minister Ludwig Erhard noted: "Even if personal credit constitutes for the bank an annoying and costly service, one must show good faith for... among the obligations of the banker, one must include this: an individual should be able to approach him to borrow several hundred marks without having to mortgage his house and all of his possessions." André Malterre, "Problème du Crédit à la Consommation," *Journal Officiel* 20, August 11, 1961, 761–776.

on the family budget. The early sewing machine credit plans, led by Singer in the 1850s and quickly copied by their French counterparts, embodied the Janus face of consumer credit. For pieceworkers, who produced in their homes, purchasing their own sewing machines allowed them to command a higher price and escape the constraints of selling to a single buyer. In France, sewing machine retailers indirectly assisted their customers in finding such work by selling their customer lists to clothes manufacturers, who approached recent buyers about producing piecework. But it also imposed new burdens. The regular repayment schedule for the installment loan matched poorly with the irregular market cycle for clothing. Sewing machines were frequently pawned during down times, with the loan used to cover the installment payments.[45] Many households that bought sewing machines on credit to produce their own clothes found that they needed to make additional clothing for sale in order to meet their monthly payments. Historian Judith Coffin captures the social logic of the credit purchase for the early working class borrower: "The price of independence... was indebtedness."[46]

Traditional consumer credit was primarily term credit: debts accrued over time were repaid in a lump sum. Two types of term credit were widely available at least back to the Middle Ages: pawn and open-book store credit. Both were used to smooth the seasonal fluctuations in work and income that most small artisans, farmers, and household businesses faced. They allowed families to match regular expenses, such as food and heating, with irregular income. Modern installment credit had a different logic. It was from its origins primarily working-class credit, tailored to the stable income, material aspirations, and periodic economic shocks that faced modern wage earners. Borrowed as a lump sum and repaid in tranches, it allowed salaried workers to match one-off expenses – whether the purchase of expensive durables or unforeseen medical costs – to their stable, predictable year-round salary.

The stability of income enjoyed by the modern salaried worker made it possible to offer longer-term loans on the installment plan to even modest borrowers.[47] Early installment credit was targeted primarily at the poorer working classes – those that had low wages but a regular salary. This fact gave installment lending a stigma for upper-middle-class households. The stigma began to erode only with the introduction of expensive consumer goods such as the automobile, for which even more affluent families might require credit.[48] Still, economist Gottfried Haberler, writing in 1942, observed that installment

[45] Public pawn shops were preferred, because these often allowed women to use the machine in the pawn shop as a means of earning money to pay off their loan.

[46] Judith G. Coffin, "Credit, Consumption, and the Images of Women's Desires: Selling the Sewing Machine in Late Nineteenth-Century France," *French Historical Studies* 18/3 (1994), 755–756.

[47] Ronald Aminzade, "French Strike Development and Class Struggle: The Development of the Strike in Mid-Nineteenth-Century Toulouse," *Social Science History* 4/1 (1980), 69–70.

[48] David Caplovitz, "The Social Benefits and Costs of Consumer Credit," in Royston Miles Goode, *Consumer Credit*, United Kingdom Comparative Law Series 3 (1978), 127.

credit served "mainly the lower income classes."[49] Because of their working-class focus, early consumer lending companies emerged not in the financial capitals of their countries, but where their customers were, in the hearts of industrial regions. In the United States, Household Finance Corporation, which was later acquired by the Hong Kong and Shanghai Banking Corporation, was founded in 1878 in Minneapolis-St. Paul. Other early U.S. consumer lenders operated in Atlanta, Chicago, Milwaukee, and throughout the industrial Midwest. France's Cetelem, although headquartered in Paris, opened its first retail lending offices in the industrial towns of Marseille and Lille. A similar pattern is found in other countries. Provident Clothing and Supply, the door-to-door lender that came to dominate postwar working-class credit in England, was founded in 1880 in the industrial town of Bradford. That many of these lenders continued to operate in the deindustrializing towns of their origins was a testimony both to the unorthodox financial culture in the consumer lending sector and to the enduring importance of low wages and rent for what had long been a low-margin sector.

Despite their shared roots, consumer credit and the working class enjoyed a complex, contentious relationship. Labor representatives were torn by the opportunities and challenges permitted by modern installment plans. Three sorts of tensions became especially evident in the post–World War II era. First, consumer credit was fundamentally regressive in its cost structure. A big part of the cost of consumer lending was administrative, including new client subscription, recordkeeping, and billing. Most of these were fixed costs that did not change with the size of the loan. This meant that smaller consumer loans were relatively more expensive to administer, implying a higher interest rate. A survey of U.S. consumer lenders in 1952 found that the fixed administrative costs for consumer loans included $2.50–$3.50 to evaluate a loan application, and $0.20–$0.30 per month to cover billings and collections.[50] For a six-month loan of $100, administrative costs alone translated into an annual percentage rate (APR) of 24 percent, even before the cost of capital and provisions for nonpayment were included. A study by France's national credit council in 1961 estimated that the average cost of (larger) commercial loans came 75 percent from interest and 25 percent from administration, whereas the average cost of (smaller) consumer loans came 45 percent from interest and 55 percent from administration.[51] Quite apart from the risk of nonpayment – which was traditionally very low for carefully administered loans – the poor paid more for credit. That gave consumer credit a built-in bias against lower-skilled, lower-paid workers.

49 Gottfried Haberler, *Consumer Instalment Credit and Economic Fluctuations* (New York: National Bureau of Economic Research, 1942), 26.

50 CHA, UFB, "Notes sur le Financement des Ventes à Crédit aux États-Unis," December 1952, 19.

51 CNC, 1427200301, box 283, Comité National du Crédit, Comité du Crédit à Court Terme, December 1953–June 1961, Meeting of the Comité du Crédit à Court Terme, June 19, 1961, 21.

Two further features of consumer credit made it a double-edged sword for labor. First, access to sales credit allowed workers to weather strike actions. But labor leaders also noticed that workers with outstanding debts tended to be more reluctant to organize and strike in the first place. Indeed, for America's industrialists of the 1920s, working-class access to consumer credit on reasonable terms was seen as a means of pacifying the domestic workforce at a time when their European counterparts were moving toward socialist and communist ideologies. Second, consumer credit could work to counteract union gains in wage negotiations. Whether credit raised or lowered purchasing power seemed to depend highly on historical context. On the one hand, high interest rates charged to wage earners reduced their purchasing power over time, as a greater share of their income was dedicated purely to interest payments. On the other hand, manufacturers in the 1950s and early 1960s credited consumer borrowing with dramatically increasing demand, creating economies of scale in manufacturing that allowed producers to lower the prices of their goods and increase wages.

The ambiguity of credit for organized labor became a key point of division between France and America. French unions were systematically opposed to credit extension. They worried that credit was reducing workers' purchasing power and observed that debt obligations tended to de-radicalize the workforce. American unions eventually came to similar conclusions in the late 1960s, but by then policymakers were not paying attention. Initially, between the 1930s and 1950s, they had argued vociferously in favor of worker access to credit. They opposed Regulation W – a set of down payment and repayment restrictions on consumer credit imposed by the Federal Reserve Board during the Korean War in order to limit sales credit extension – and favored state laws that raised usury caps for small loans. They justified these positions by emphasizing the importance of consumer credit for maintaining manufacturing jobs. They also were aware that many union members relied heavily on consumer credit to sustain themselves through long and difficult strike actions. This early division between the views of French and American organized labor set different trajectories for consumer credit policy.

Organization of This Book

The eight empirical chapters of this book are divided between studies that focus primarily on lending industry practice and those that focus on politics and government policy. Together, they trace the sources of national differences, both in the regulation of the sector in the early postwar period and in the deregulation of the sector from the late 1970s.

The first four chapters provide comparative case studies of postwar consumer lending practice in France and America. Chapter 2 traces the origins of American commercial banks' early move into consumer lending. That move had its origins in charitable campaigns during the interwar period to extend legal, inexpensive credit to the working class. By linking credit to charity, these reformers made it possible for banks to enter the sector without damaging their reputations. Following World War II, American banks embraced consumer credit and the credit card payment system as a means to compete in an intensely fragmented banking sector. Chapter 3 explores the role of retailers in promoting a vision of consumer credit as economically legitimate and socially benign. Critically, American retailers invented and embraced revolving credit as a tool for attracting and retaining customers. By the early 1960s, American banks were offering revolving credit to the broad public via credit cards that were accepted at most national retailers and service providers.

The next two chapters explore why similar innovations did not take hold in France until the late 1980s. Chapter 4 traces the resistance of French banks to offering small loans. Faced with strong returns from bank-funded industrial investments and persistent apprehension about the legitimacy of consumer lending, French banks left the small loan business to France's dedicated consumer lenders. When, in the 1960s, these consumer finance companies began launching American-style credit cards, France's banks countered with a payment card, Carte Bleue, which was specifically not tied to a revolving credit facility. Chapter 5 focuses on France's largest consumer finance company, Cetelem, in order to explain France's delayed embrace of revolving credit. Intent to find profit in a business with notoriously low margins, Cetelem experimented with a revolving credit plan – and then set it aside over concerns about expense and the need to control credit volumes.

The next four empirical chapters trace the evolution of French and American consumer credit regulation. Chapters 6 and 7 offer comparative studies of national restrictions on the quantity and price of credit offered. They explore how U.S. policymakers struggled to make state-level interest rate caps compatible with the liberal provision of consumer credit, and how French policymakers emphasized quantitative restrictions on credit as a tool to limit the impact of consumer credit use on industrial investment and inflation. Chapters 8 and 9 then trace the politics of credit deregulation. In America, social movements promoting the rights of women and blacks in the 1970s cast the credit debate in terms of broad rights of citizenship that paved the way for deregulation. In France, a backlash against credit liberalization in the 1980s led to new policies that narrowed the possibilities for greater credit extension. More generally, liberal American access to credit was legitimated by a coalition between social activists and consumer lenders. French restrictive treatment of consumer credit was legitimated by the perception that the French state had to step in to limit the negative economic consequences of liberal financial markets. The result was a surprising reversal of roles, in which the French state restricted credit access on the grounds that it was economically inefficient, and the American state promoted credit access on the grounds that it would promote social welfare.

2

Commercial Banks and Consumer Credit in the United States

One feature distinguished the consumer loan sector in the United States from that in every other advanced industrialized country: the early entry of commercial, deposit-taking banks into consumer lending.[1] In France, commercial banks made brief and unsuccessful forays into personal lending in the early 1960s and again in the early 1970s, then waited another decade before reentering the sector for good. This left the French consumer loan sector dominated by dedicated consumer finance companies that offered credit to finance the sales of autos and other products. American banks, by contrast, began to experiment with dedicated personal loan departments in the 1920s and 1930s. Banks were not the leaders in the consumer sector. For most of the postwar period, sales credit offered by auto lenders and national retail chains such as Sears and JC Penney accounted for the largest share of outstanding consumer debt. Nonetheless, bank engagement in the consumer loan sector had a profound impact both on the regulation of consumer lending and on consumer perceptions of borrowing. Because banks were seen as legitimate financial institutions, their engagement in consumer lending offered a seal of approval that made policymakers – and probably also households – more accepting of consumer credit. Moreover, because commercial banks were already making loans when new card payment technologies emerged, banks themselves became strong advocates for a new hybrid credit-payment card system that came to distinguish the American consumer credit system from that in other advanced industrialized countries.

Commercial banks faced two major obstacles to making consumer loans. First, banks relied heavily on reputation, and small loans in the early twentieth

[1] A single exception was Barclay's Bank in the United Kingdom, which launched the Barclay Card in 1958.

century were widely perceived as disreputable. Second, the fixed costs of small loans tended to make them unprofitable unless banks invested heavily in new kinds of automated loan-processing technology – technology that was not required for standard commercial loans. American banks quickly overcame these obstacles. Their early move into consumer lending is in large part a story of accident and opportunism.

Why would banks enter a sector that had so recently been viewed as either openly corrupt or at least disreputable? The project to make lending safe for banks began outside of the banking sector, at the confluence of a variety of social experiments intended to offer fairly priced credit to workers and the poor. These experiments – charitable pawn, credit unions, the Russell Sage Foundation-sponsored small-loan laws, and the Morris Plan banks – all had their roots in a response to the social costs inflicted by the financial crises of 1896 and 1906. Although they employed different strategies, all shared a common insight that access to credit on fair terms could help needy families to help themselves. The Russell Sage small-loan laws were especially influential. By making legitimate lending profitable within a clear legal framework, the small-loan laws pushed out the more egregious high-rate lenders that had long sullied the sector's reputation. But it was also in part the restrictions imposed by the small-loan laws that made it possible for commercial banks – which fought and won a battle to be exempted from the small loan laws – to best dedicated consumer finance companies and take over the sector.

Even as the reputation of the small-loan sector was rehabilitated, banks faced a second obstacle to consumer lending. The high costs and low profitability of this line of business were, for commercial banks in most countries, a fatal detraction. The problem was one of scale. So long as the loans were relatively large, as for auto loans or other large consumer purchases, the fixed costs of making the loan could be covered comfortably by interest charged. As U.S. banks moved to offer smaller personal loans in the 1920s and 1930s, and especially revolving credit beginning in the 1950s, the cost of managing these administration-intensive accounts made them, on average, unprofitable. Many banks nonetheless opted to accept these early losses. The main motivation related to the competitive context of early U.S. banking. At a time when banks were restricted from competing on deposit rates, and takeovers were restricted, credit cards became a means to attract new depositors. By the early 1980s, as technological and regulatory changes made consumer lending profitable, American banks were already positioned to capitalize on the profits.

American bankers' move into consumer lending had its roots in the interwar period. The first commercial bank opened a dedicated personal loan department in 1924. By a decade later, when the U.S. government began insuring banks for unsecured personal loans targeted at home improvement, thousands of banks had moved into small lending. The Federal Reserve recorded 13,000 registered consumer lenders in the United States in 1934. Some were finance companies and retail lenders, but the bulk of them were state-chartered banks. In order to make profitable small loans, banks had to find means to work around strict state usury caps. These interest ceilings, which typically ranged from 6 percent to 8 percent per year, were far too low to make small personal loans economically viable. Banks that succeeded in making small loans were forced to rely on legal contrivances that brought them into formal compliance. These evasions were ethically murky, however, and banks that operated in this gray zone risked their reputations. Nonetheless, by the 1960s, banks had taken over the small lending business from dedicated consumer finance companies and were competing directly with retailer chains to offer consumer credit for their purchases. How and why this happened is the focus of this chapter.

Inventing Credit as Welfare

American families at the turn of the twentieth century relied on small loans to bridge periods of unexpected need. Those loans came in the form of sales credit from retailers or as loans from pawnshops or from consumer finance companies. Rates on these loans were typically 3 percent per month for pawn, and up to 20 percent per month for unsecured small loans. Not only were these loans expensive, they also subjected the borrower to potential harassment and were often accompanied by abusive collections techniques. Social reformers concerned about the social cost of high-interest-rate lending decried what contemporaries called "the loan shark problem." They nonetheless recognized that many of those who were driven to borrow from loan sharks had a genuine need for extra funds. In the absence of government-sponsored social-insurance programs, workers faced with loss of work, sickness, childbirth, or other unanticipated financial shocks relied on small loans to cover the costs. By providing legitimate, low-cost loans to needy families, they hoped to meet these real needs and also push abusive loan sharks out of business.

The first nationwide effort to provide credit as a form of welfare was a set of nonprofit charitable pawnshops offering small loans secured against household articles. The first and largest was the Provident Loan Society in New York, created in 1894 in the wake of a financial panic. Modeled explicitly on the French mont-de-piété (see below), Provident was not a conventional charity. It offered loans at the lowest rate that was "consistent with sound business principles."[2] Provident Loan raised capital by issuing bonds that were purchased by New York philanthropists. Returns on these bonds were capped at 6 percent, with any excess profit going to charitable causes.[3] Loans were

[2] Archives of the Russell Sage Foundation (RSF), Rockefeller Archive Center, Sleepy Hollow, New York, box 24, folder 186, Document of the Provident Loan Society, c. 1939.

[3] RSF, box 24, folder 186, Letter from Arthur Ham, Provident Loan Society, to John M. Glenn, March 6, 1939.

smaller than those available from conventional small lenders, ranging from $1 to $50, and charged an interest rate of 1 percent per month. Unlike conventional pawnshops, the Provident Loan Society was explicitly borrower friendly: standards for pawn were generous, debts could be repaid in installments, and excess earnings from auctioned pawn were returned to borrowers. The institution was so successful that similar institutions soon emerged in cities across the country. In 1909, a National Federation of Remedial Loan Societies was established, and in 1915 it had forty member organizations.[4] By 1917, the remedial loans societies across the country had made a total of 6 million loans totaling $205 million.[5]

The success of the charitable loan societies emphasized the extent of demand for legitimate loans on a business-like basis. It also revealed the limited ability of charitable organizations to provide an adequate supply of credit. In 1910, two initiatives emerged to meet the need: the Morris Plan banks and the Russell Sage Foundation's draft small-loan law. Both saw small loans as a valuable response to the welfare needs of workers and the poor. Both envisioned a role for legitimate private lenders in meeting that need. And both projects would, by the 1930s, transform small lending into a legitimate business that linked credit to social welfare. But any effort to meet that demand ran into the obstacle of state usury laws. With interest rate ceilings set at 6 percent or 7 percent per year, serving the small-loans market was simply not profitable. The key was to make the case that higher interest rates were in the public interest.

The first to make the case was Arthur Morris, a lawyer from Norfolk, Virginia, who foresaw both social and financial benefits to offering small loans "on mutually advantageous terms." The Morris Plan banks attacked the usury problem through a combination of moral suasion and legal legerdemain. The legal strategy was to amplify the interest charged by not crediting installment payments to the principal of the loan. In Morris's patented approach, weekly installment payments went to the purchase of a deposit certificate that would, at the end of the loan period, be used to repay the loan in full.[6] This allowed Morris to advertise a 6 percent interest rate, but effectively charge double that rate on the declining balance of the loan. He also added a 2 percent processing fee, which, when combined with the interest charged, generated a total effective

[4] Shelly Tenenbaum, *A Credit to Their Community: Jewish Loan Societies in the United States, 1880–1945* (Detroit: Wayne State University Press, 1993), 97.

[5] RSF, box 25, folder 191, Letter from Robert W. De Forest to Clark Williams, president, Industrial Finance Corporation, March 27, 1917.

[6] Morris seems to have stolen the idea from David Stein, a former client, who later sued Morris. The court found against Stein, arguing that the mutual structure of Stein's loan company was substantially different from the ownership structure of the Morris Plan banks. Arthur J. Morris (AJM) papers, Library of Congress, Washington, DC. box 5, Industrial Finance Corporation, 1913–1916, Letter from Randolph Hicks to Arthur J. Morris, July 19, 1915; *Stein v. Morris* (Virginia 1917), 91 S. E. 177; *Stein and Others v. Morris and Others*, Supreme Court of Virginia, January 11, 1917.

interest rate of more than 19 percent.[7] Morris justified this approach by arguing that he was creating a habit of savings. The Morris Plan encouraged borrowers to continue to invest in deposit certificates even after their loans were paid off. "The purpose," explained one advocate of the Morris Plan, "is to create the habit of thrift through systematic investment usually in the first instance as a condition of a loan advanced by us, and afterwards and permanently, for investment."[8]

Two other features of the Morris Plan emphasized its societal benefits. In order to ensure repayment, new applicants were required to bring two "endorsers of good character," who took joint responsibility for the loans.[9] This system proved highly effective at assuring repayment, and defaults averaged less than 0.5 percent in all Morris Plan banks. But Morris's mantra that "character is the basis of credit" also served to link debt to the virtues of trust and responsibility. Small lending was, in this formulation, a public service. Moreover, the Morris Plan banks, which did not take deposits, sought funds by issuing bonds that they advertised as an aid to public welfare. Like the Provident Loan bonds, their return was capped at 6 percent. The bonds were marketed by personal reference to community leaders and industrialists. For these affluent investors, Morris's message was about class peace and, over time, explicitly anticommunist. Writing in 1914, Morris explained:

> If the industrial worker no longer has to humiliate himself by entering a pawnshop, or trafficking with a loan shark . . . but finds himself the welcomed customer of a bank that extends credit to him at the same rates that are charged the business man, he will feel less hostile, and perhaps not at all so, toward the people who, having acquired capital, put their savings at his disposal on mutually advantageous terms.[10]

By 1930, 142 licensed Morris Plan banks were operating in 31 states.[11]

During the time when the Morris Plan banks were consolidating, a second approach to socially beneficial small lending was also spreading. Under the influence of (and considerable lobbying by) the Division of Remedial Loans of the Russell Sage Foundation, state legislatures began adopting a uniform small-loan law that gave lenders reprieve from strict usury caps in exchange

[7] In the original Morris Plan loan, a borrower would purchase a $100 certificate that was held by the bank, receive $92 in cash, then repay the bank $2 every week for fifty weeks. The $8 taken out of the loan included a 6 percent discount and a $2 administration fee. RSF, box 25, folder 191, Letter from Clark Williams, president of Industrial Finance Corporation, to Robert W. De Forest, vice president of Russell Sage Foundation, May 28, 1917.

[8] RSF, box 25, folder 191, Letter from Clark Williams, president of Industrial Finance Corporation, to Robert W. De Forest, vice president of Russell Sage Foundation, May 28, 1917.

[9] For details on the Morris Plan banks, see: *The Morris Plan of Industrial Loans and Investments* (New York: Industrial Finance Corporation, 1915); Michael Easterly, "Your Job Is Your Credit: Creating a Market for Loans to Salaried Employees in New York City, 1885–1920," PhD Dissertation in History, University of California, Los Angeles, 2008, 206–244.

[10] *The Independent*, February 23, 1914, 281.

[11] *New York Times*, April 27, 1930.

for embracing borrower-friendly lending practices.[12] Under these laws, states raised their usury cap to 3.5 percent per month (42 percent per year). In order to take advantage of the higher rate, lenders agreed to advertise real effective interest rates (on the declining balance, and including any fees), not to raise rates on outstanding loans, and to allow early repayment without penalty.[13] As states took on the new legislation, many consumer finance companies that had previously operated at the legal margins discovered that they could lend profitably and entirely legally under the new framework. These "42-percenters" frequently gained market share by acquiring departing "high raters." One of the lenders that thrived under the small-loan legislation was the Household Finance Corporation, and it became a close ally of Russell Sage in fighting for small-loan laws in new states.[14] State-level legislative battles typically pitted Russell Sage and a collection the allied 42-percenters against a coalition of high-raters and religious conservatives who shared an interest in keeping usury caps low. Gradually, Russell Sage and its allies won. By 1935, twenty-six states had adopted versions of the Russell Sage small-loan law.[15]

Russell Sage and the Morris Plan banks shared a common vision of commercial credit as a tool for self-help. This vision helped link small loans for needy households to ideas about welfare and self-reliance. They also gradually pushed the most egregious high-rate loan sharks out of business. By the 1930s, small lending had largely been rehabilitated as a legitimate economic activity with social welfare benefits.

Yet this was also the moment at which both the Morris Plan banks and consumer finance companies operating under the small-loan laws became vulnerable. For the Morris Plan banks, the problem started with the Great Depression. Because they did not take deposits, the Morris Plan banks did not suffer the financial distress that led to the closing of so many American commercial banks. But the market for the bonds they issued to raise capital virtually dried up. By the mid-1930s, most former Morris Plan banks had transformed themselves into deposit-taking commercial banks in order to secure funds for lending out. For America's consumer finance companies, the transparency required under the small-loan laws increasingly placed them at a disadvantage to commercial

[12] The Russell Sage Foundation's Small Loan Law is discussed at length in other works. See: Elisabeth Anderson, "Experts, Ideas and Policy Change: The Russell Sage Foundation and Small Loan Reform: 1909–1941," *Theory and Society* 37 (2008), 271–310; Bruce G. Carruthers, Timothy W. Guinnane, and Yoonseok Lee, "Bringing 'Honest Capital' to Poor Borrowers: The Passage of the U.S. Uniform Small Loan Law, 1907–1930," *The Journal of Interdisciplinary History* 42/2 (2011), 393–418.

[13] RSF, box 28, folder 216, "Memoranda of Information Requested by Trustees' Committee on Small Loan Question," April 28, 1943, 24.

[14] Their motivation was at least in part to improve their public image on the eve of their public offering of stock, in 1929.

[15] RSF, box 24, folder 186, Letter from Shleby M. Harrison, RSF, to Jeremiah Milbank, president of the Provident Loan Society of New York, April 25, 1935.

banks that, because they fell outside of the small-loan laws, could advertise apparently more favorable interest rates. Many copied the practices of the Morris Plan banks, reporting interest as a "discount" on the total amount of the loan, rather than on the declining balance. Doing so allowed them to significantly underreport the true cost of borrowing. Consumer finance companies, now bound by the small loan laws, could not copy this practice.

The very strategies that had made consumer lending socially acceptable had also made the early lenders in those sectors vulnerable. The small-loan sector was ripe for takeover – all that was needed was a boost from the federal government.

Government Support for Small Loans

In 1934, with the economy still mired in the Great Depression, Title I of the new Federal Housing Act provided for government backing to secure loans intended for house modernization and the purchase of household equipment. Title I home improvement loans were conceived to create jobs in the construction and contracting sectors while also rehabilitating a decaying housing infrastructure.[16] They also represented the first foray for most participating banks into unsecured personal loans for working-class clients. Of $265 million in Federal Housing Administration (FHA) – insured home improvement loans made in the first two years of the program, $191 billion were made by banks. And although $60 million of that went to purchase machinery and equipment, the lion's share went to pay contractors: for installing central heating, masonry and carpentry, and roofing, plumbing, painting, and plastering.[17] Bank of America, for example, reported that one-quarter of its FHA-insured home improvement loans went to equipment.[18] To make these loans attractive for participating banks, the FHA insured up to 20 percent of their home improvement portfolio. Bankers' responses were enthusiastic.

In its first year, the FHA registered 11,945 financial institutions to accept insurance under Title I, including roughly 100 new finance companies created by household goods manufacturers to provide financing for their products.[19] Roughly half of the banks that registered for FHA insurance actually reported making home improvement loans.[20] The Title I program clearly increased bank lending to households and consumers. Whereas only a handful of banks in the 1920s had personal lending departments, by 1940, 5,000 banks were

[16] Carter McFarland, "An Economic Evaluation of FHA's Property Improvement Program," *The Journal of Land and Public Utility Economics* 23/4 (November 1947), 399.
[17] *Wall Street Journal*, January 17, 1936.
[18] *Bankers' Magazine* 132/5 (May 1936), 485.
[19] *Bankers' Magazine* 132/5 (May 1936), 406.
[20] Carter McFarland, "An Economic Evaluation of FHA's Property Improvement Program," *The Journal of Land and Public Utility Economics* 23/4 (November 1947), 403.

making Title I and other personal loans.[21] In its first 12 years, the FHA program supported more than 6 million home improvement loans.[22]

Banks participated in the Title I program for a combination of reasons. In the depths of the recession, a fall in business lending left banks with ample deposits to invest. For these banks, and especially those for which state banking laws restricted out-of-state investments, consumer lending in their own communities was an attractive option.[23] Banks had also not shed employment during the Depression – a move banks feared would be seen as a signal of financial weakness. This staff surplus meant that the considerable overhead involved in making small loans would impose few additional labor costs and create tasks for some of their unoccupied employees. Banks that held mortgages saw the home improvement loans as a means to help preserve their existing mortgage investments.[24] So attractive was the new business that bank associations lobbied repeatedly to have the FHA Title I program extended – first to include structures owned by nonprofit civic associations, then to small business structures.

The Title I program was less important for the volume of credit it provided than for the impact it had on commercial banks. In its first four years of operation, Title I loans represented only 2–3 percent of outstanding consumer debt.[25] What Title I does seem to have done was introduce American bankers to the practice of making small loans. First, the fixed interest rate on these loans, along with the government-insured absence of risk, meant that banks could focus on just one variable – reducing cost – to increase profitability. They invested heavily in automation, and over time began to hire industrial engineers to streamline their processes.[26] Inspired by time-motion studies in manufacturing, they worked to introduce similar process and flow efficiencies in their personal banking divisions. Banks also learned plenty about consumer borrowers. They learned that consumers would repay loans, even in difficult times. Default rates on Title I loans rose to 3 percent during the depths of the Great Depression and fell to 2 percent by the early 1950s. By setting aside reserve funds to cover potential losses, banks discovered that they could lend profitably, even outside of the FHA insurance. One industry observer noted in 1937: "Banks realize today that even in the absence of a Government guarantee

[21] William Trufant Foster, *Painless Debtistry* (Newton, Mass.: Pollack Foundation for Economic Research, 1933), 6; Carl A. Dauten, *Financing the American Consumer* (St. Louis, MO: American Investment Company of Illinois, 1956), 66–70.

[22] Carter McFarland, "An Economic Evaluation of FHA's Property Improvement Program," *Journal of Land and Public Utility Economics* 23/4 (November 1947), 399.

[23] Harry T. Rohs, "Buying 'On Time,'" *Wall Street Journal*, October 30, 1944.

[24] L. A. Chambliss, "Modernization Loan Program of the Federal Housing Administration Should Be Continued," *Bankers' Magazine* 134/1 (January 1937), 32.

[25] L. A. Chambliss, "Modernization Loan Program of the Federal Housing Administration Should Be Continued," *Bankers' Magazine* 134/1 (January 1937), 32.

[26] Harry T. Rohs, "Buying 'On Time,'" *Wall Street Journal*, October 30, 1944.

they can finance loans such as are eligible for insurance under FHA Title I with safety and at a good profit."[27]

Observers have tended to attribute the rapid growth in bank-based consumer lending to loans issued under Title I, but the role of Title I is more nuanced. Even before the launch of the program, hundreds of U.S. banks had already created consumer lending departments.[28] National City Bank of New York was running a large and profitable small-loan business, and its success was widely touted in the banking community. By the late 1920s, hundreds of banks were reportedly contacting it to find out about its experience.[29] The network of Morris Plan banks had also proved highly successful. And although the FHA loans were smaller than average commercial loans, they were larger than the typical consumer loans handled by consumer finance companies. The Title I loans written by National City Bank, for example, averaged $525 and were repaid in installments over twenty months.[30] Because larger loans were less costly and less technically challenging to administer, they were also more profitable.

The inspiration for the FHA Title I program itself seems to have come from successes in the consumer finance sector. Albert L. Dean, a former vice president at the General Motors Acceptance Corporation (GMAC), was appointed to head the National Recovery Administration, and GMAC's defaults in the early years of the Great Depression remained below 1 percent. Moreover, the Johns-Manville Company, a provider of (asbestos) insulation and other construction materials, had already begun in 1924 to experiment with unsecured home improvement loans to finance purchase of their products. After early failed attempts, it relaunched the program successfully in 1931, offering loans at 24 percent interest.[31] Although the plan was not profitable by the time the FHA lending program was introduced, it was at least breaking even, and was taken by legislators as a template for the Title I program.

Perhaps the greatest impact of the FHA loan insurance program was the legitimacy that government support provided for banks to enter a sector that had long been tainted by accusations of excessive interest charges and aggressive collections techniques. First, the FHA promoted the Title I program through extensive outreach to local communities. They sent representatives around the country to provide information on the program to women's groups,

[27] Morris Bernhard, "Personal Loan Departments in Banks," *Bankers' Magazine* 134/4 (April 1937), 320.

[28] William Trufant Foster, *Painless Debtistry* (Newton, MA: Pollack Foundation for Economic Research, 1933, 6; Carl A. Dauten, *Financing the American Consumer* (St. Louis, MO: American Investment Company of Illinois, 1956), 66–70.

[29] John Walker Harrington, "Big Banks and Small Personal Loans," *Bankers' Magazine* 116/6 (June 1928), 900.

[30] *Wall Street Journal*, September 11, 1934.

[31] U.S. Congress, Senate, Committee on Banking and Currency, Hearing on S. 3603, 73rd Congress, 2nd Session, May 16, 1934, 293.

including local home improvement clubs, labor unions, civic associations, and farm associations.[32] The FHA's Industrial Sales Committee also sponsored specially designed trucks, called the Better Homes Caravan, to travel the country and advertise new household equipment of the sort that could be purchased with Title I loans.[33] A second benefit of the Tile I program was the legal protection it afforded, especially from strict state-level collateral and usury laws. Given the questionable value of housing assets, the FHA called on banks to make Title I loans without collateral. Making uncollateralized loans was unfamiliar to most banks. Most states also passed legislation exempting federally insured loans from all interest-rate restrictions. Third, the FHA loans taught many banks that consumer loans could be made profitably. FHA Administrator Stewart McDonald would later recall: "The big thing in this has been to educate the banks to do this kind of business."[34] In 1937, when the Title I program was stopped, Morris Bernhard reported in *Bankers' Magazine* that "the personal loan department... has risen from the position of just another banking service to one of the important sources of revenue for banks located in our industrial and commercial centers."[35]

Perhaps the most unexpected impact of the Title I program was the legitimacy these loans gave to banks' practice of pricing consumer loans in terms of a "discount." Almost from the moment they began making personal loans, many commercial banks had adopted the practice of posting their interest rates as the difference between the amount borrowed and the amount repaid, referred to as the discount. For a $95 loan at a 5 percent discount, the borrower repaid $100 over many weeks or months in equal installments. Because the regular payments reduced the balance of the loan over time, the effective interest on the declining balance was twice the discount rate, or 10 percent. The practice of discounting was attractive in part because it allowed banks to post rates that, if deceptive, at least appeared to fall below state usury caps. The draft Title I bill had defined interest in what would eventually become the conventional way: at 5 percent "on the declining balance," plus additional fees provided for credit investigation, collection, and loan supervision that, taken together, pushed the interest rate toward 10 percent.[36] In consultation, banks lobbied for Title I interest rates to be expressed as a discount, with no fees, and this

[32] *Washington Post*, April 28, 1935.

[33] P. Bradley Nutting, "Selling Elegant Glassware during the Great Depression: A. H. Heisey & Company and the New Deal," *The Business History Review* 77/3 (2003), 466.

[34] Joseph D. Coppock, *Government Agencies of Consumer Instalment Credit* (Washington, DC: NBER, 1940), 22.

[35] Title I was restarted again in 1938, but with banks contributing to a common insurance fund to cover loan losses. Morris Bernhard, "Personal Loan Departments in Banks," *Bankers' Magazine* 134/4 (April 1937), 320.

[36] Federal Housing Administration, *The Amended Modernization Credit Plan* (Washington, DC: Government Printing Office, 1935), 13; U.S. Congress, Senate, Committee on Banking and Currency, Hearing on S. 3603, 73rd Congress, 2nd Session, May 16, 1934, 15.

formula was adopted in the final legislation. This seemingly arcane pricing rule signalled the beginning of a generation-long fight over how bank interest rates would be reported. By lending government legitimacy to reporting interest as a discount rate, the Title I program reinforced a practice that allowed commercial banks to advertise rates that were significantly lower than those advertised by competing consumer finance companies bound by the Russell Sage small loan laws. Ultimately it was part of what allowed banks to supplant consumer finance companies in the small loan sector.

Banks versus Consumer Finance Companies

As more banks began to enter the consumer lending sector under the FHA Title I insurance scheme, the Russell Sage Foundation began contemplating legal provisions that would do for banks what the Uniform Small Loan Law had done for consumer finance companies. In its initial studies into the loan shark problem, Russell Sage had lamented the lack of personal loans by banks. Rolf Nugent, the influential head of its small-loan department, explained that "one of the reasons for prevailing anti-social lending practices was the unwillingness of banks to make consumer loans in small sums on undesirable collateral."[37] They assumed that new laws that raised the legal rate of lending for commercial banks could lure them into the sector. Initially, the American Bankers' Association (ABA) was receptive to the proposal. It collaborated with Russell Sage through the 1930s to design a uniform law that would cover banks. Individual banks were also interested in the idea. Through the 1930s, the early wave of banks to launch personal lending departments maintained close ties with Russell Sage, which worked with them to collect and analyze personal lending data from at least 60 commercial banks. They sought advice on their lending programs from Russell Sage, and supported the idea of usury reform. This arrangement lasted until 1940, when the ABA took over small loan reporting, and when its stance toward usury shifted. Two years later, it launched an all-out struggle to shield commercial banks from small lending laws that would bring banks under the same truth-in-lending standards applied to consumer finance companies.

For Russell Sage, acceptance of the bank practice of discounting had always been a necessary evil. It embraced the early Morris Plan banks, whose pricing scheme concealed the full costs of borrowing, in part because they seemed to address genuine worker needs for access to credit. But discounting and other means of hiding lending costs also opened borrowers to potential abuse. First, discount rates did not include additional fees for processing, late payment, or insurance. Because such fees could be imposed late in the contract, the real cost of the loan might increase over time. Second, borrowers who paid off

[37] RSF, box 28, folder 216, "Memoranda of Information Requested by Trustees' Committee on Small Loan Question," April 28, 1943, 7.

their loans early were typically not rebated the excess interest they had been charged at the beginning of the loan. In cases of early prepayment, effective interest rates could quickly become very high. While consumers were alert to such practices when dealing with consumer finance companies, Russell Sage worried that they were unlikely to expect it from reputable commercial banks. Finally, as small lending by banks grew, it became clear that their exemption from transparent pricing practices was giving them an advantage over consumer finance companies. In order to defend the success of their small loan legislation, Russell Sage concluded that similar provisions would have to be extended to banks.

Initially, the greatest challenge to bringing bank lending under a legal and transparent regulatory framework seemed to emanate from the dual system of state and national banks in the United States. In 1935, Russell Sage began a close collaboration with the superintendent of banks in New York to draft a bill that would allow banks to charge up to 12 percent on the unpaid principle, so long as they stated their charges in "simple interest," including all fees. The banks opposed it.[38] As with subsequent state efforts to legislate interest rates and open the way for banks to make small loans, the proposed New York legislation ran into the problem of nationally chartered banks. Whereas New York could clearly regulate state-charted banks, these would be at a disadvantage to their nationally chartered counterparts unless those were also bound by the state regulations.[39] But the extent to which federal law would permit states to regulate the behavior of nationally chartered banks remained unclear. In the case of New York, state bank regulators were given to understand that James O'Connor, the powerful comptroller of the currency under President Franklin Roosevelt, was opposed to any state regulations that would subject nationally chartered banks to different regulations across the different states in which they operated. When the New York Bank Law passed, in 1936, its small loan provisions had been stripped away, allowing both discounting and the addition of administrative and late fees.

This objection to a small-loan law for banks turned out to be mainly illusory. Although most states would eventually alter their bank regulations to allow banks to make small loans at a profitable rate by permitting discounting and the use of various fees, one state did not. In 1941, Nebraska passed a small-loan law that imposed the same interest rate and transparency standards for all lenders, including finance companies, banks, and installment sales companies.[40] The effect was to put banks and finance companies on an even playing field.

[38] David H. Rogers, *Consumer Banking in New York* (New York: Columbia University, 1974).

[39] RSF, box 28, folder 216, "Memoranda of Information Requested by Trustees' Committee on Small Loan Question," April 28, 1943, 9.

[40] In an unusual move, the state banking regulator was charged with administering the law. Nebraska Laws, 1941, L. B. No. 282; Harold Johnson, "Nebraska Has No Loan Shark Problem Today," *Law and Contemporary Problems* 19/1 (1954), 45; Clyde William Phelps, "Monopolistic and Imperfect Competition in Consumer Loans," *The Journal of Marketing* 8/4

In a letter of June 21, 1941, Comptroller of the Currency O'Connor wrote to Wade R. Martin, director of banking for the Nebraska state government, objecting to the restriction on national banks, arguing that it would cause "unwarrantable and undue interference with the exercise of the functions of the national banks."[41] The Nebraska attorney general affirmed that national banks fell under the law, with certain restrictions on enforcement – including a ban on entering national bank premises. A group of eight nationally chartered banks in turn sued in federal court for an injunction on the grounds that the regulation infringed on the National Banking Act.[42] The Nebraska State Banking Department responded, successfully, that the states had "police powers" that extended to regulating banks, so long as they did not directly conflict with the provisions of the National Banking Act.[43] The Nebraska exception held until 1953, when a new amendment to the state banking law allowed banks to circumvent the state usury cap by charging additional insurance and administrative fees.[44]

The Nebraska defeat signaled a new confrontational stance between banks and consumer finance companies over usury and the reporting of interest rates. Banks, whose loan pricing practices had always been in a legal grey zone, came to see reforms like that imposed in Nebraska as a threat to an increasingly important line of business. Beginning in 1940, the Consumer Credit Division of the ABA began to move away from any plan that would require banks to report the cost of consumer loans as simple interest.[45] The ABA now roundly denounced any deal that would trade higher legal interest rates caps in exchange for truth in lending. Instead, it urged all state banking associations to fight simple interest bills by introducing bills that explicitly allowed discounting.[46] Banks had long argued that their lending practices were already in compliance with state usury laws, and worried that the new legislation would cast doubt on their previous lending practices. There was, in Nugent's words, a "gradual crystallization of opinion among banks in favour of adopting the Morris Plan techniques, largely because they feared the public reaction to the admission of a high interest rate."[47]

(April 1994), 393; F. B. Hubachek, "Progress and Problems in Regulation of Consumer Credit," *Law and Contemporary Problems* 19/1 (1954), 10.

41 "Nebraska Rules on National Banks," *Personal Finance News* (December 1941), 7, 11.

42 *Wall Street Journal*, November 26, 1941.

43 RSF, box 28, folder 217, Preliminary Draft of a Uniform Law to Regulate Installment Selling, November 1, 1940, 13.

44 Nebraska Laws, 1953, L.B. 280. Ironically, it was a Nebraska bank, First National Bank of Omaha, that in 1978 appealed successfully to the U.S. Supreme Court for the right to offer credit cards in neighboring Minnesota at an interest rate that exceeded *that* state's usury limit.

45 RSF, box 25, folder 191, Letter from Rolf Nugent to F. B. Hubachek, December 30, 1943.

46 RSF, box 28, folder 217, Preliminary Draft of a Uniform Law to Regulate Installment Selling, November 1, 1940, 11.

47 RSF, box 28, folder 216, "Memoranda of Information Requested by Trustees' Committee on Small Loan Question," April 28, 1943, 10.

In reality, the legal case for the banks' pricing practices had always been tenuous. As one observer acknowledged, the principle of the state usury laws clearly prohibited the discount method: "If the usury statutes are to be adhered to in the spirit, as well as in the letter, no legal sanction is to be found for a charge of higher than 7 per cent per annum, computed on the principal of a loan."[48] Yet bank were nervous about supporting special legislation that traded higher usury caps for greater transparency, for two reasons. First, state usury laws were popular. Pushing for higher rates would make banks look bad. Second, reporting simple interest rates would force banks to reveal a number that was significantly higher than borrowers were accustomed to seeing. As the banker acknowledged, "Borrowers would be on our necks if we quoted simple interest rates."[49] Further, banking observers warned that *any* reform would "reinforce in the public mind such doubt and confusion as has been created, by propaganda, with regard to whether or not bank charges are usurious."

Behind this concern about reputation lay a difficult economic reality. A combination of factors – fewer loans, higher cash holdings, and a move by companies toward direct debt issuances – combined to push down bank profitability at the time. A survey of New York banks found that their loan-to-asset (cash plus Treasury bills) ratio fell dramatically over the course of the 1930s, from 1.8 in 1931 to 0.6 in 1934, and then to 0.25 in 1940.[50] The lower leverage hurt their profitability. By 1940, U.S. commercial bank profitability had dropped to a record low (6 percent return on equity), a dip in profits that was matched again only by the financial crisis of 1987.[51] Amid this bleak landscape, the burgeoning small loan business had become one of the few banking bright spots. Banks complained that Russell Sage was trying to block them from making small loans precisely at the moment when the traditional lines of business were no longer making "adequate earnings."[52]

As bank small loans grew in importance in the late 1930s, Russell Sage became increasingly critical of new practices intended to insulate banks from state usury laws. One prominent case involved the Vee Bee Service Company, a loan insurance provider. In 1939, the accountant Vernon Buchman of Memphis, Tennessee, founded the eponymous Vee Bee System. In this scheme, banks offering loans required lenders to pay an additional 5 percent for "surety collateral" beyond the typical 8 percent discount on the loan. Sixty percent of

48 Tom E. Savage, "Banks and Consumer Credit," *Bankers' Magazine* 146/3 (March 1943), 197.

49 Tom E. Savage, "Banks and Consumer Credit," *Bankers' Magazine* 146/3 (March 1943), 7, 212.

50 Charles W. Calomiris and Berry Wilson, "Bank Capital and Portfolio Management: The 1930s 'Capital Crunch' and the Scramble to Shed Risk," *Journal of Business* 77, no. 3 (2004), 425.

51 Mark W. Nichols and Jill M. Hendrickson, "Profit Differentials Between Canadian and U.S. Commercial Banks: The Role of Regulation," *Journal of Economic History* 57, no. 3 (1997), 676.

52 *Bankers' Magazine* 141/5 (November 1940), 411.

this fee went to an account held by the bank at Buchman's American Surety Company; the remainder went straight to American Surety. American Surety agreed to use the funds held in the account as surety collateral to cover any loan defaults.[53] By separating out the cost of insuring against default from the interest rate charged by the bank, the Vee Bee System allowed banks to make small unsecured loans at high interest rates while still conforming to state laws governing both usury and collateral.[54] This scheme, and others like it, proved popular. By 1944, fifty-two banks had subscribed to the Vee Bee System.[55] In 1940, in response to a written complaint from the Russell Sage Foundation, the office of the Comptroller of the Currency launched an investigation into the Vee Bee system for "promoting high interest rates."[56] Rolf Nugent of Russell Sage submitted written testimony that the Vee Bee system was deceptive for borrowers.[57] The Vee Bee Service Corporation responded by suing Russell Sage for libel, slander, and conspiracy. The case was thrown out by a New York State appellate court, upholding the recommendation of a court referee, which found that the Vee Bee system "operated to place upon the borrowers charges which in effect were usurious."[58]

The Vee Bee affair helped to sour relations between banks and Russell Sage. Particularly concerned were the Morris Plan banks, which in the 1920s had worked closely with the Russell Sage Foundation in their campaign against loan sharks. By 1940, many of the Morris Plan banks had transformed themselves into deposit-taking banks, and these increasingly felt threatened by attacks on loan pricing arrangements that were not too different from their own loan certificate scheme. Writing in 1942, Myron R. Bone, executive secretary of the American Industrial Banker Association, which represented the Morris Banks and other so-called industrial lenders, sided with the ABA against adopting simple interest disclosure. He explained: "Morris Plan banks and other industrial banking institutions were created for the purpose of helping necessitous persons to get *out* of debt.... You tell him the exact cost in dollars and cents. He makes repayment in dollars and cents. Neither is a complicated and variable interest computation. It is honest, simple and easily understood." He warned the Morris lenders that the "petty money lenders" were issuing ever larger loans that made them direct competitors with the Morris banks. The consumer finance companies, with support from Russell

53 Anthony L. Styskal, "Usury Law – Evasions Through Exactions Other than Interest – Discounted Interest as Usury," *Southern California Law Review* 18 (1944–1945), 276.

54 RSF, box 25, folder 191, L. Lawrence Green, Referee's Report and Opinion, *Vee Bee Service Company v. Household Finance Corporation*, Russell Sage Foundation, Byrd Henderson and Rolf Nugent, New York Supreme Court, Index No. 19404, 1941.

55 *New York Times*, October 22, 1944.

56 "Sage Foundation Raps Vee Bee System," *American Industrial Banker*, August 1940, 19; *Bankers' Magazine* 141/5 (November 1940), 411.

57 *Business Week*, June 19, 1940, 42.

58 *Vee Bee Serv. Co. v. Household Fin. Corp.*, 51 N.Y.S.2d 590, 597–598, affd 269 App Div 772; *New York Times*, October 22, 1944.

Sage, "have chosen this critical period as the time in which to launch their assault."[59]

As in the earlier anti-loan shark campaigns, the Household Finance Corporation again took a central role in the campaign to fight what it perceived as the unfair advantage enjoyed by banks. Since the early 1930s, Household had been pushing for new legislation in Wisconsin that would govern small loans by banks – legislation that the Wisconsin Bankers Association opposed.[60] By 1942, the struggle between Household and the banks had gone nationwide. The ABA warned its members that Household was introducing bills in state legislatures across the country that would require banks to report simple interest.[61] Household responded reassuringly that "no well-informed person questions the propriety or desirability of banks conducting a small loan business."[62] But it also argued that banks were reporting interest in a way that was intentionally deceptive: "The reason for concealing the true rate is that it enables the lender to avoid admitting that he charges more than regular rates."[63]

To offer assistance, Russell Sage in 1942 sent every state banking commissioner a copy of a model bill it had developed that would bring banks into its small-loan provisions. When a version of the Russell Sage model bill was proposed in Wisconsin, the president of the Wisconsin Bankers Association warned banks to oppose it "to avoid the odium upon banks which would follow its enactment."[64] State banking associations began arguing that a "simple interest" standard for quoting the cost of loans that was used by small-lending companies was not transparent to buyers. In a typical pamphlet on the topic, the Missouri Bankers Association argued: "At the bank, [the borrower] is told what the cost will be in dollars and cents, and that amount is deducted at once. No guessing there.... At the small loan company he is told that the cost will be so much per month on his reducing balance. 'How much does that make in money?'"[65] Speaking to a group of bankers in 1943, the president of the Wisconsin Bankers Association argued that the simple interest approach "makes it virtually impossible for the average borrower to figure out the actual cost of his loan at the time he gets his loan."[66]

59 Myron R. Bone, "Discount Plan Being Assailed," *The Industrial Banker* 8/6, December 1942, 9.

60 RSF, box 28, folder 216, Letter from Wall G. Coapman, Wisconsin Bankers Association, to the Trustees of the Russell Sage Foundation, May 28, 1943.

61 *ABA Bulletin*, February 1942.

62 Household Finance Corporation, Annual Report, 1942, 14.

63 Household Finance Corporation, Annual Report, 1942, 12.

64 "Percent per Month Bills Appear," *Industrial Banker*, February 1943, 9.

65 RSF, box 28, folder 217, Missouri Bankers Association Pamphlet, "Candor or Camouflage," c. 1943.

66 RSF, box 28, folder 216, G. O. Thorpe, "The Fair Way to Quote Charges on Installment Loans," summary of an address at the Meeting of the Dane County Bankers Association in Madison, Wisconsin, March 30, c. 1943, 4.

In 1943, Frank Hubachek, attorney for Household Finance, wrote to Rolf Nugent, former head of Russell Sage's Credit Research Department who was now working in the U.S. Office of Price Administration. Hubachek wanted Russell Sage to reconstitute its small-loan group, which had recently been closed down due to the war, and mobilize around new small loan legislation for banks. He warned that, although the small-loan laws of the 1920s had virtually eliminated loan sharks, legitimate small-lending business now "received a heavy blow" from the growth of small loans from banks, promoted by their practice of reporting interest on a discount basis. He warned of a "shift toward deception and oppression."[67] Nugent clearly shared Hubachek's concerns. Breaking with neutrality, Nugent lambasted the banks: "It is not that simple interest calculations are strange or restrictive or costly or undignified for banks, but simply that the acknowledgement of an interest charge higher than the conventional rate is believed to be harmful to them."[68] His attack drew a quick response. Testifying before the Wisconsin Bankers Association in 1943, Kenton Cravens, chairman of the ABA's consumer credit council, came close to accusing the Russell Sage Foundation of treason: "It is my conviction that any one... responsible for the introduction of any legislation of a non-essential character which provokes controversy and divides us at the time of our greatest national peril is guilty of an act unworthy of a patriotic citizen. The philosophy of our enemies is simply one of division, friction, distrust, and discontent."[69]

By late 1943, the legal battle for the future of small lending had been won by the ABA and commercial banks. Consumer finance companies that had prospered under the 42 percent usury ceiling imposed by state small loan laws, and that had been central players in reimagining small lending as a legitimate line of business, now faced the reality that those same laws put them at a disadvantage to banks. Some consumer finance companies responded by attempting to *become* banks. Two major nationwide finance companies, Commercial Investment Trust and Commercial Credit, sold their local offices and attempted to buy local banks. They were blocked by state banking regulators.[70] Nugent suggested that the entire small loan project might have to be abandoned if consumer finance companies were to survive. Writing in 1943 to the board of trustees at Russell Sage, he warned: "If banks are to escape the principles of the Uniform Small Loan Law, these requirements must be avoided by the small loan business as well."[71] But the small loan laws were popular in most states, and state legislatures did not act to remove them. With the exception of auto

[67] RSF, box 25, folder 191, Letter from F. B. Hubachek to Rolf Nugent, December 24, 1943.

[68] Rolf Nugent, "Why Not Candor in Small Bank Loans?" *Survey Graphic*, March 1943, 6.

[69] RSF, box 28, folder 216, Kenton R. Cravens, "In Support of the Argument for Discount and Fees," testimony delivered before the Wisconsin Bankers Association, January 21, 1943.

[70] AJM, box 9, The Morris Plan Co. – New York, 1940–1950, Memo from Ralph Ridelberger, November 5, 1943, 3.

[71] RSF, box 28, folder 216, "Memoranda of Information Requested by Trustees' Committee on Small Loan Question," April 28, 1943, 25.

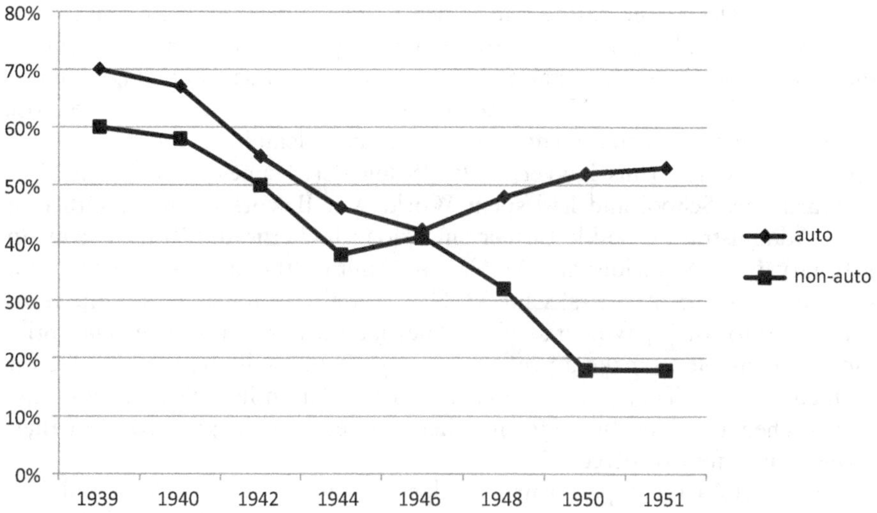

FIGURE 2.1. Consumer Finance Company (Non-Bank Financial Firm) Share of Auto and Non-Auto Consumer Lending in the United States, 1939–1951[72]

lending, where consumer finance companies continued to dominate, World War II marked the decisive turning point for their experiment in offering business-like credit to the American public.

Paying with Plastic

Commercial banks moved into consumer lending by building on the practices and legitimacy that had been created by consumer finance companies. Their move into card payments was similarly opportunistic and built on early non-bank innovators of general-purpose payment cards. The first nation-wide payment cards were issued by Western Union in 1914, followed in the 1920s by hotel cards issued by major chains and gas cards issued by the oil companies.[73] These cards were limited in the kinds of products they covered. The first general-purpose payment cards appeared only at the end of World War II. The earliest and most prominent of these was Diners' Club, launched in 1950.

Diners' Club founder Frank McNamara liked to say that the idea for Diners' Club came to him when he forgot his wallet while dining out in Manhattan. A more reliable account suggests that McNamara, who owned a small-loan company, got the idea from a client. One of his credit customers had set

[72] CHA, UFB, "Notes sur le Financement des Ventes à Crédit aux États-Unis," December 1952, Annex F.

[73] Richard Rutter, "Consumer Credit Heads for a Peak," *New York Times*, May 10, 1959; Steve Worthington, "Affinity Cards: A Critical Review," *International Journal of Retail and Distribution Management* 29/11 (2001), 486.

up a small sales credit business in which he lent out retail charge plates – a precursor to retail credit cards – to neighbors, paid the retailer at the end of the month, then collected installment payments – presumably at a high interest rate – from his neighbors. He was borrowing from McNamara to finance those loans. When the scheme went wrong, the man defaulted, and McNamara referred the case to his lawyer, Ralph Schneider. Schneider was trained at Harvard Law School and had spent World War II working in the Office of Price Administration beside former small loan law crusader Rolf Nugent. In February 1950, Schneider and McNamara built on the failed shopping credit scheme and created Diners' Club.[74] They initially charged restaurants a 10 percent fee for their payment service. (They later lowered it to 7 percent.) Still, they were unable to make a profit until they introduced a $5 per year fee for each customer.[75] They put 20,000 cards in circulation in their first two years and reached 1 million by 1959. Retailer fees represented 70 percent of their revenue, user fees 30 percent.[76]

The Diners' Club experiment was closely watched, and quickly emulated. Some of the entrants were new entrepreneurs. In 1951, Portland, Oregon, businessman Edwin L. Mays created National Credit Card Inc. to provide a universal payment card targeted at traveling businessmen. Unlike Diners' Club, National Credit Card added a "budget plan" that allowed customers to extend the terms of repayment beyond thirty days. But, as for so many others, making small loans proved financially unprofitable, and the new card filed for bankruptcy in 1954.[77] Others were expansions of existing programs. In 1953, the Universal Air Travel Plan, a cooperative payment card created for the airline industry, began extending its scope to include auto rentals. Both the Sheraton and Hilton hotel chains, which already had their own affinity cards, began in 1958 to expand them to a variety of retailers dealing in "demi-luxe" products. Hilton's Carte Blanche became one of the three big competitors in the general travel and entertainment card business.

American Express was among the last to enter the travel and entertainment card fray. Initially focused on shipping, American Express had already, in the 1800s, launched two private payment systems: a money order that was independent of the U.S. Post Office, and the traveller's check. In 1958, in a bid to catch up with the growing universal payment card market, American Express sent 8 million credit card applications to potential customers.[78] Its model exactly replicated Diners' Club, combining a retailer charge (7 percent) with an annual fee to the cardholder.

What made these cards so attractive, and initially so successful, was the highly fragmented American banking system. In 1950, the United States had

[74] Irwin Ross, "The Credit Card's Painful Coming-of-Age," *Fortune*, October 1971, 108.
[75] *Washington Post*, November 4, 1964.
[76] Michel Schlosser and Gérard Tardy, *Les Cartes de Crédit* (Paris: Dunod, 1971).
[77] *Wall Street Journal*, March 24, 1954; *Chicago Daily Tribune*, June 15, 1952.
[78] Michel Schlosser and Gérard Tardy, *Les Cartes de Crédit* (Paris: Dunod, 1971).

14,000 banks. This proliferation had been encouraged by state laws that restricted branch banking and, in many cases, limited banks to a single office (so-called unit banking). For travelers, and businessmen in particular, the patchwork of local banks meant that it could be hard to find a bank branch to cash out-of-state checks. Short of carrying cash or traveler's checks, the travel and entertainment cards offered one of the only good payment alternatives. These were first and foremost payment cards, not sources of credit.

Not all businesses were happy with the new payment cards. Two groups in particular were difficult to convince to accept card payment: restaurants, which had thin margins and little access to capital, and large retail chains that already had their own affinity payment cards. Resentment was especially strong among restaurants, for which the standard 7 percent credit card fee represented a significant inroad into profits. So long as payments were being made by the traditional "travel and leisure" customer, namely traveling businessmen, restaurants accepted the cards as a way to bring in new customers to whom they would not normally have had access. In a survey of restaurants in 1959, *Restaurant Magazine* found that restaurants that accepted credit cards experienced a mild increase in customers. Customers who paid with cards spent between 18 percent and 32 percent more than those who paid cash.[79] The concern was that once too many customers began paying on cards – the industry group Restaurant Association put the threshold at 20 percent – the cost of fees would eat into profits. For many restaurants, accepting credit card payment meant that they also had to borrow to cover the cost of accounts receivable until they were reimbursed by Diners' Club or American Express.[80] For smaller restaurants, this meant taking on debt.

By 1959, restaurants across the country had begun to rebel. Initially, they fought for lower card fees. Only Hilton responded to their requests, lowering fees on its Carte Blanche to between 4 percent and 4.5 percent – a move that probably precipitated its subsequent decline. When American Express and Diners' Club refused to follow suit, restaurants resorted to alternative means. In some cities, smaller restaurants banded together to form their own dining cards. Seattle restaurants launched a concerted campaign to get Diners' Club to reduce its charge from 7 percent. In November 1958, in preparations for their negotiations, the city's restaurants jointly agreed to raise the price for customers using credit by 5 percent.[81] When Diners' Club refused to reduce their rates, twenty-seven Seattle restaurants formed a cooperative group, Select Restaurants of Washington, that issued 10,000 payment cards to their own local clients. The initial charge per transaction of their new card was 3 percent. Although they continued to accept Diners' Club, participating restaurants applied a 7 percent surcharge to those purchases. Similar payment card programs emerged in Portland, Oregon, across the whole state of Wisconsin, and

[79] "Credit Cards," *Restaurant Management*, October 1959, 69.

[80] *Restaurant Magazine*, October 1959, 110, 114.

[81] *Washington Post*, November 23, 1958.

among a group of restaurants in Florida and Georgia.[82] Oregon's Preferred Restaurant Card even created a reciprocal agreement with the Seattle plan. At least one national restaurant chain, Fred Harvey, began providing its own credit rather than relying on Diners' Club or American Express.

Other restaurants experimented with charging differential prices for credit clients. In Wisconsin, for example, the Restaurant Association recommended that all of its members charge 5 percent to anyone buying on credit. The justification for the charges was fairness: "There is a time and place for credit in the industry, providing those who secure the credit follow the American custom of paying for it. Only in this manner can the restaurant owner protect his cash customers and avoid discriminating against them."[83] Restaurant owners quickly backed away from these plans, in part because they drove away credit clients, who reported feeling stigmatized, and in part because it was increasingly leading cash customers to request discounts for paying in cash. In Milwaukee, local restaurants took out newspaper advertisements opposing the imposition of credit surcharges. Capitalizing on the discontent with credit card fees, the Rozee Bonus Card Club allowed subscribing members ($5 per year) to receive a 10 percent discount at participating hotels and restaurants when they paid in cash. By May 1959, the Rozee Club had 220,000 members (200,000 had been offered for free as a start-up promotion).[84] None of these plans lasted long, but the resistance to the high vendor fees associated with travel and leisure cards created an opening for bank-sponsored credit cards to make inroads.

Bringing Credit and Card Payments Together

Initially, commercial banks were slow to respond to the challenge of these national payment cards. Having built their expertise in making small loans, most banks focused on launching local sales credit schemes that allowed small retailers to compete with credit plans offered by national chains (see Chapter 4).[85] In one way, this distraction proved fortuitous. It meant that banks mainly sat on the sidelines as Diners' Club, American Express, and others took the heat for pushing their new universal payment cards – and the fees associated with them – onto retailers and restaurants. By the time banks moved to take over the national card payments system, the struggle for acceptance of payment cards and their associated fees had already been fought and won.

The early bank sales credit accounts that emerged following World War II generally offered payment via specialized bank checks. In 1951, the Franklin

82 These credit card revolts remain poorly documented. See William R. Clabby, "Credit Card Revolt," *Wall Street Journal*, June 11, 1959.

83 "Credit Cards," *Restaurant Management*, October 1959, 118.

84 Charles Grutzner, "Answer to the Credit Cards," *New York Times*, May 3, 1959.

85 *New York Times*, May 1, 1952.

National Bank of Long Island became the first bank to offer sales credit via a plastic card.[86] Through the mid-1950s, hundreds of banks, mainly located in the Northeast, launched local credit check and card payment systems in which the bank took responsibility for securing payment. Unlike the travel and leisure cards, which had to be repaid in full at the end of the month, the new bank sales credit programs allowed consumers to purchase with retailers and then repay their own banks over time.

Banks initially marketed their sales credit to smaller retailers, arguing that accepting bank credit would allow them to compete with large chain retailers that already offered in-house credit plans.[87] Small retailers that agreed to accept bank credit had to pay a fee to banks that ranged from 4 percent to 7 percent. Although banks argued that credit customers spent more than cash customers, the new credit plans seemed to force stores to choose between higher sales volume and a higher sales margin. Many retailers tried to split the difference. They accepted the new bank credit cards but also took measures to limit their impact on profits. Some stores that accepted cards offered discounts for paying cash. Others offered their own credit to customers who could show that they had qualified for a bank credit card. Another common practice was to honor credit cards on regularly priced items, but not on designated "sales days."[88] Partly because of this sort of retail resistance and partly because of high administrative costs, the first wave of bank-sponsored retail credit plans struggled to make a profit. By 1958, all but twenty-seven of the hundreds of early bank credit experiments had failed.[89]

Undeterred, banks launched a second wave of sales credit plans in 1958. Banks that had previously provided installment loans and secured personal loans began offering more flexible revolving accounts that could be used for a wide variety of purchases. The primary incentive was to provide credit for expenditures on services that, by their nature, involved no collateral. Branded variously as Borrow-By-Check, Ready Money, or even Instant-Manu-Matic, these accounts gave customers a set of special credit account checks that could be used to pay for any expense. Some banks linked these accounts to credit cards, and these became more common over time. Modeled on existing retail credit cards, most bank revolving accounts charged 1 percent per month on outstanding balances, plus typically a twenty-five-cent fee for processing each check or card payment. Qualifying customers were given a credit limit equal to a month's salary, and borrowers were required to repay at least one-twelfth of that credit limit each month, or pay down the account entirely.[90]

86 Irwin Ross, "The Credit Card's Painful Coming-of-Age," *Fortune*, October 1971, 109; Timothy Wolters, "'Carry Your Credit in Your Pocket': The Early History of the Credit Card at Bank of America and Chase Manhattan," *Enterprise and Society* 1/2 (2000), 325.

87 Richard Rutter, "Consumer Credit Heads for a Peak," *New York Times*, May 10, 1959.

88 Richard Janssen and James McDonald, "Credit Slowdown," *Wall Street Journal*, April 6, 1960.

89 Michel Schlosser and Gérard Tardy, *Les Cartes de Crédit* (Paris: Dunod, 1971), 7.

90 Richard Rutter, "Consumer Credit Heads for a Peak," *New York Times*, May 10, 1959.

Banks often advertised these programs by direct mail.[91] Unlike department stores, which created their new revolving credit accounts for customers whose creditworthiness did not qualify them for the more prestigious thirty-day charge accounts, banks launched the new revolving accounts as a premium product. This approach was influenced in part by their assumptions about the economics of revolving credit. Because they were not secured against any underlying property, as were personal or installment loans, banks subjected revolving accounts to a higher standard of creditworthiness. Some banks targeted promotional mailings specifically at more affluent parts of town. Others got the mailing lists of professional associations, as for doctors and dentists. Banks also made special arrangements with their local credit agencies to track revolving customers over time. Any change in creditworthiness would prompt a warning to the bank holding their account.

Bank credit card plans grew from 27 in 1958 to 40 in 1959, 160 in 1960, and 200 in 1961.[92] Among these were small regional and local bank cards, but also some of the largest banks in America. On the West Coast, Bank of America launched its Bank-Americard in 1958 in Fresno, California. On the East Coast, Chase Manhattan issued its Chase Manhattan Credit Plan (CMCP) in the same year. Bankers who had predicted quick profits from their card programs faced a basic dilemma. Consumer credit, like mass manufacturing, enjoyed powerful economies of scale. But any bank that expanded its card base without sufficient care risked heightened repayment woes. Many of the early card issuers succumbed to these contradictory pressures. In 1960, Bank of America sent 700,000 credit cards through the mail to people who had not requested them and who had not been screened for repayment risks.[93] Such excesses led to a period of reconsideration and retrenchment. Due both to a combination of failure and acquisition, the number of bank-issued credit card plans fell again, from 200 in 1961 to 80 in 1964.[94]

Consumer finance companies also saw the new credit cards as a means to get back into the sales credit business. Many began offering their own payment cards tied to lines of credit. These suffered the same fate as the early bank lenders. The most concerted attempt came in 1959 when Seaboard Finance, the third-largest U.S. sales finance company, launched the International Charge Inc. (ICI) credit card. It launched the program by issuing 1.5 million cards to its past and present borrowers in 39 states. ICI's format copied bankcard programs that were emerging at the time, charging 18 percent on revolving credit plans with a 6 percent fee on sales from retailers.[95] It continued to expand in 1960 with rapid acquisitions of charge accounts from smaller

91 Cyril J. Jedlicka, senior vice president, City National Bank and Trust Company, "Revolving Credit Plans," *1959 Consumer Credit Symposium*, New York: Consolidated Reporting Company, 1960, 126–127.

92 Richard Janssen and James McDonald, "Credit Slowdown," *Wall Street Journal*, April 6, 1960.

93 Michel Schlosser and Gérard Tardy, *Les Cartes de Crédit* (Paris: Dunod, 1971).

94 Michel Schlosser and Gérard Tardy, *Les Cartes de Crédit* (Paris: Dunod, 1971), 10.

95 "Living on the Cuff," *Consumer Reports*, September 1959, 490.

retailers, including the Barker Brothers department store chain and furniture retailer W. & J. Sloan. In November 1960, they took over the credit card business of First Western Bank and Trust Co. By the end of the year, ICI boasted 289,000 active card users and 34,000 participating merchants.[96] By early 1961, it was operating in twenty-three states. But, like so many of the early efforts to take over the credit card business, ICI was unable to keep costs sufficiently low to make revolving credit accounts profitable. With the majority of its business in bulk sales contract discounting, auto finance, and consumer consolidation loans, Seaboard had relatively little experience managing smaller consumer loans. When ICI reported a net loss of more than $1 million in the first nine months of 1961, it began the process of closing offices and severing customer contracts.[97] By 1962, it had only 90,000 customers in California, and in September of that year Seaboard shut down ICI entirely.[98] Seaboard stock fell from a height of $1.02 to $0.44 in the wake of the credit card failure.[99]

The Bank Card Network

Given the dismal record of the first and second waves of bank credit cards, the surprise is that any banks would decide to try again. But they did. The third and largest wave of bank credit cards launched in 1965. By 1967, an estimated 1,500 banks were offering credit cards, and an estimated 11–13 million of these were in active use.[100] From their early forays into credit card lending in the late 1950s and early 1960s, sober bankers understood that they were unlikely to make significant profits on their new credit card lines. Their goal appears to have been to use the new revolving credit facility as a loss leader: an attractive service that would draw in new customers to the banks who would open savings accounts, make deposits, and potentially become clients for other banking services. Many of the customers who were not approved for the new credit card accounts were directed toward personal loans that were both secured and more profitable.[101] As an added benefit, banks found they were able to attract additional commercial business from retailers with whom they made arrangements for credit card sales.[102]

The resurgence of interest in credit cards was driven by a perception that America was moving to a "cashless" society, embodied in the early success of

96 *New York Times*, August 25, 1959; *New York Times*, November 1, 1960.

97 *Wall Street Journal*, September 8, 1961.

98 *Wall Street Journal*, May 2, 1962.

99 "Seaboard Writes Off Its Mistake," *Financial World*, November 7, 1962, 6.

100 RLDM, box 35, folder 4, E. J. Kersting, *Credit Cards: Thirty Days to Reality*, August 1967.

101 Cyril J. Jedlicka, senior vice president, City National Bank and Trust Company, "Revolving Credit Plans," *1959 Consumer Credit Symposium*, New York: Consolidated Reporting Company, 1960, 129–131.

102 "Living on the Cuff," *Consumer Reports*, September 1959, 490.

Diners' Club and American Express, coupled with a fear that Bank of America was on track to take over the U.S. payments and credit market entirely. By 1966, the BankAmericard had reached 1.25 million users and had registered 45,000 participating sellers.[103] Regional branch banks around the country responded with their own ambitious credit card plans. Typical of these was First National City Bank in New York, which acquired a 50 percent stake in Carte Blanche from Hilton, and also created its own card, the Everything Card. Others followed suit. New entrants included Mellon Bank and Pittsburgh National in Pennsylvania, Seattle First National, First Wisconsin National, and Citizens' Bank and Southern Bank in Georgia. Hundreds of local and regional banks also began new card programs.

Aspiring credit card programs competed simultaneously on two fronts: for new individual customers, and for new retailer affiliates who would accept their cards as payment. To attract new individual customers, banks aggressively marketed their cards. Mass mailings of unsolicited active credit cards again became a common practice. And although pushing credit cards out the door like this was effective at increasing the number of cards in circulation, it also abetted corruption. Chicago in particular became a hot spot for credit card fraud. In 1966, the Midwest Bank Card launched with a mass mailing of active cards to 5 million people in the Chicago area just before Christmas. The results were disastrous. Consumer credit default rates in Chicago for 1967 rose to 5.7 percent, compared to the average U.S. rate of 2 percent.[104] In March of 1967, the mafia intercepted a mailing of activated Diners' Club cards and charged $350,000 in travel and meal expenses related to criminal activites.[105] Of the total 1.5 million credit cards reported lost in the United States in 1966, an estimated 300,000 were stolen, leading to illegal charges estimated at between $20 million to $50 million.[106] These problems led President Richard Nixon in 1970 to sign the first law covering credit cards. It banned unsolicited distribution, limited consumer liability to $50, and made credit card theft a federal offense. The legislation was a boon to the early movers: applauded by banks that had already built a large credit card customer base, but opposed by those banks that had been slow to enter the credit card business.[107]

The second front on which credit card companies competed was in registering affiliated retailers that would accept payment on the new credit cards. As new cards began to proliferate, retailers balked at affiliating with a growing number of local, regional, and national banks. The solution came in the form of new interbank payment networks. The first of these, created by Bank of

[103] CHA, "La Carte de Crédit en Grande-Bretagne," June 30, 1966, Cetelem internal document, D90.

[104] Michel Schlosser and Gérard Tardy, *Les Cartes de Crédit* (Paris: Dunod, 1971).

[105] *New York Times*, November 11, 1967.

[106] RLDM, box 35, folder 4, E. J. Kersting, *Credit Cards: Thirty Days to Reality*, August 1967.

[107] IFREF, *Cartes et Crédit*, No. 1, April 1971, 1.

America in 1965, was the cooperative Bank of America Service Corporation. In 1966, a syndicate of credit card issuers in Chicago founded the competing Midwest Bank Card System. Within two years, it had 15 core banks and 819 affiliated banks.[108] The third and last major interbank network, the nonprofit Interbank Card Association, was formed in the Eastern United States in 1967. Initial members included Marine Midland, Mellon National, Pittsburgh National, and Valley National Banks. In 1968, these were joined by 120 banks in California that hoped to compete with Bank of America's network, including United California and Wells Fargo.[109] Other smaller payment networks also briefly surfaced. Three large banks in Connecticut formed the Connecticut Charge Plan in 1966. Banks in the Pullman banking group in Chicago created the Bankcharge Service network. In 1968, the Midwest network joined with the Interbank network. All local payment networks were quickly absorbed into either the Bank of America (Visa) or Interbank (Mastercard) networks. By 1969, the Bank of America network included 180 core banks, 2,900 affiliated banks, 23 million card holders, and 450,000 points of sale. Interbank had 500 core banks, 2,550 affiliated banks, 21 million card holders, and 450,000 points of sale.[110] The duopoly of American payment networks was cemented.

Creating these networks proved to be expensive. The dramatic growth and organizational innovation that characterized the credit card sector during the 1960s belied the sector's mediocre financial performance. By 1970, with both inflation and lending rates on the rise, many bankers looked back ruefully at their credit card experience. Only a few lenders were reporting profits, and bank credit card operations in general reported average losses of 1.8 percent.[111] Chase Manhattan alone lost an estimated $7 million because of its brief foray into credit cards with the CMCP card.[112] John Bunting, president of First Pennsylvania Banking and Trust Co., captured the dour mood of the sector at the time: "A lot of bankers I talk to are sorry they ever got into [credit cards] and want out before they lose their shirts."[113] These costs were not lost to outside observers. One French banking researcher who surveyed the U.S. credit card market in 1970 remarked: "The credit card appeared at a very bad time, in terms of the profitability and image of the banks."[114] It was an

[108] Michel Schlosser and Gérard Tardy, *Les Cartes de Crédit* (Paris: Dunod, 1971), 13.

[109] Michel Schlosser and Gérard Tardy, *Les Cartes de Crédit* (Paris: Dunod, 1971), 11–12.

[110] Michel Schlosser and Gérard Tardy, *Les Cartes de Crédit* (Paris: Dunod, 1971), 13.

[111] JC Penney Corporate Records (JCPCR), Degolyer Library, Southern Methodist University, Dallas, Texas. Credit Matters, July 1971, "The Role and Functioning of Consumer Credit," A Report by the Sub-Council on Credit and Related Terms of Sale of the National Business Council for Consumer Affairs, March 13, 1972, 37.

[112] Michel Schlosser and Gérard Tardy, *Les Cartes de Crédit* (Paris: Dunod, 1971), 65.

[113] "A Banker's Pipe Dream?" *Forbes*, June 15, 1971, 36.

[114] Paul S. Nadler, "Les Cartes de Crédit Deteriorent l'Image des Banques," *Centre d'Information et d'Étude du Crédit*, 10–1725, April 10, 1970, 2.

unpromising start for a sector that would eventually become a leading source of bank profits. But it was a start.

Conclusions

The early move by U.S. banks into consumer lending set the course for both the shape of the credit market and the regulatory decisions that followed. Because banks were both trusted and politically influential, their growing interest in the consumer credit sector meant that they consistently advocated policies and laws that would extend that market. This situation was very different from conditions in Europe and Japan, where banks remained silent as regulators placed restrictions on lending. The social legitimacy of banks made consumer borrowing seem to be not merely acceptable but virtuous. If banks were willing to offer a consumer credit, that access was itself an indicator of worth. Finally, because U.S. banks were already engaged in consumer lending when electronic payments systems and the card payment format emerged, they had an interest in tying the newly emerging card-based payment system to a credit facility. For banks in most other countries, and in particular in France, electronic payments were not initially linked to credit. In all of these ways, the move by banks into consumer lending set the foundations for banks to marry credit to the new card payment systems that would prove highly popular.

The rise of bank card lending was at least partly an accident. The social campaign to bring respectability and oversight to consumer finance companies, and to displace existing loan sharks, ultimately created the conditions for commercial banks to move into consumer lending. With support from the RSF and a growing number of progressive consumer finance firms, state after state adopted small-loan laws that allowed lenders to lend at up to 42 percent in exchange for transparency in pricing. The new laws made consumer lending respectable. They also forced consumer finance companies to advertise their actual interest rates, which, because of the costs of making small loans, proved to be high. When banks entered consumer lending in the 1930s, they were not bound by the strict transparency standards with which consumer finance companies had to comply. They could advertise interest rates far below those advertised by non-bank lenders, even if the effective rate was as high or higher. The watershed date came in 1943, when, in the midst of war, the ABA fought a pitched state-by-state struggle to defeat legislation that would impose transparency on banks. From 1939 to 1950, the bank share of non-auto consumer lending increased from 40 percent to more than 80 percent of the U.S. market.

The displacement of consumer finance companies by banks in the 1940s and 1950s also signaled a shift in the politics and purpose of postwar consumer credit. From its origins in social protection, credit was reimagined as a tool for amplifying household procurement and industrial production. Social credit became sales credit. With the change of purpose came a change in the political coalition that supported credit extension. Industrialists targeting new middle-class markets and anxious to quell worker radicalization came to common terms with the labor left, which was promoting credit as a means both to meet the new material aspirations of workers and finance early strike actions. What held this cross-class coalition together was a shared emphasis on scale and productivity. Through at least the 1950s, easy consumer credit seemed to drive a virtuous cycle in which new demand increased production scale, scale increased productivity, and productivity made real wage increases possible. This virtuous cycle sustained a productivity coalition that supported liberal credit terms through the 1950s and 1960s.

3

Banks against Credit

Consumer Finance in France

While American banks were rushing headlong into providing consumer credit, their counterparts in France bided their time. Crédit Lyonnais was the first bank to offer personal loans in France, beginning in 1959, thirty-five years after the first full-fledged personal loan department was created by a U.S. bank. In three successive waves – 1962, 1972, and then beginning in the mid-1980s – France's major banks tested the water of consumer lending.[1] On each occasion, they tried to compete with dedicated consumer finance companies by offering lower rates. On each occasion, they faced unexpectedly high costs associated with both nonpayments and administrative procedures, and were forced to pull back from the practice. What mattered most for the role of French banks in the evolution of consumer credit was something that did not happen: the failure of French banks to move earlier into personal and sales lending. Explaining such historical nonevents can be especially challenging for social scientists. This chapter relies on an explicit comparison with the experience of commercial banks in the United States to parse out causes.

One obstacle was the reputational cost of small lending. Unlike in the United States, the French small-loan sector was never fully rehabilitated in a way that made it feasible for commercial banks to enter the sector. Part of the problem was the link between credit and welfare. Early French welfare advocates envisioned a role for credit as a form of self help, just as they did in the United States. Indeed, self-help credit had deep roots in France, in the form of charitable pawn. France's monts-de-piété, a system of charitable pawn shops with origins in the middle ages, enjoyed a state-mandated monopoly on pawn lending. But

[1] Laure Lacan, Jeanne Lazarus, Ana Perrin-Heredia, and Sébastien Plot, "Vivre et faire vivre à crédit: Agents Économiques Ordinaires et Institutions Financières dans les Situations d'Endettement," *Sociétés contemporaines* 76, no. 4 (2009), 6; Crédit Lyonnais, *Un Siècle d'Économie Française: 1863–1963* (Montrouge: Draeger Frères, 1963), 191.

the business model and governance of charitable credit in France took a different tack than in the United States that failed to provide a broader mantle of legitimacy for bank-led consumer lending. Ironically, the principle of charitable credit came to be so fully accepted in France that it was embraced by the French state, which in the wake of World War II absorbed the functions of charitable pawn into France's emerging welfare state apparatus. Unlike charitable pawn in the United States, which became the springboard for a broad private-sector effort to provide self-help through credit on fair terms, the French version never led to a popular linking of private credit with welfare. Small lenders outside of the realm of charitable pawn remained publicly suspect.

A second challenge for France's banks had to do with the form of small lending that did emerge in France in the early decades of the twentieth century. In America, consumer finance companies such as the Morris Plan banks pioneered lending strategies that were then directly appropriated by commercial banks. The first widespread form of modern consumer lending to emerge in France was a form of door-to-door lending called coupon credit (*bons de crédit*). In these schemes, sales agents sold credit coupons to households, and those coupons were in turn redeemable with retailers for consumer products. Sales agents then repeatedly visited customer households to collect installments on the loan. The coupon-credit format posed a range of problems for banks. The approach was labor intensive, tied to local retailers, and incompatible with standard bank lending practices. Moreover, door-to-door lending was traditionally associated with questionable sales and collections practices – activities with which commercial banks did not wish to be associated.

Distinctive features of France's postwar development strategy also discouraged a move by banks into consumer lending. First, French banks in the postwar period were able to reap stable profits on industrial investments that, because they were supported by state industrial policies, entailed relatively little risk.[2] To the extent that France's industrial planners addressed issues of consumer credit, they mainly expressed concern. In particular, they worried that unbridled access to credit would increase consumer demand for a still-limited supply of goods. The resulting inflation would then hurt French exports, and increasing exports was a central goal of French planning. Second, the relatively small number of banks in France, and the role that government-owned financial institutions played in distributing capital among banks, meant that France's banks in the early postwar period did feel the need to compete for depositors in the way that banks had in the United States. This left France's large banks with an indirect role in consumer credit. They helped finance consumer finance

[2] Andrew Shonfield, *Modern Capitalism: The Changing Balance of Public and Private Power* (Oxford: Oxford University Press, 1965), 166–171; Peter Hall, *Governing the Economy: The Politics of State Intervention in Britain and France* (Oxford: Oxford University Press, 1983), 243.

companies through loans and bond purchases, but they did not engage directly in retail consumer lending.

The absence of banks in the French consumer credit sector ultimately had important economic and political ramifications. Economically, the inexperience of banks in making consumer loans meant that the universal card-payment system they ultimately developed, the Carte Bleue (later Carte Bancaire) was not linked in a systematic way to a revolving credit facility. The critical American-inspired link between universal card payment and consumer credit was not forged in the public mind. Politically, the absence of banks from consumer lending meant that the sector had little interest in public policy with respect to terms of credit. Governments on the left and right could restrict credit extension without having to worry about bank opposition. Socially, the absence of banks engaged in consumer lending denied consumer credit the legitimacy that association with the formal banking sector would have supplied. Banking was built on trust, and if banks certified the value of consumer lending by engaging in it, then consumer borrowing was *ipso facto* legitimate. Without bank participation, the legitimacy of consumer lending remained an open question – one that non-bank consumer finance companies ultimately addressed through close collaboration with France's financial regulators.

Social Credit and the Monts-de-Piété

In the United States, the recognition of consumer credit in the early 1910s as a form of scientific philanthropy served to legitimate consumer lending as a for-profit activity. In France, the link between consumer credit and public welfare had even deeper roots. France had a long history of charitable pawnshops that made loans to the poor. It was a leader in *crédit populaire*, including credit unions and loans from consumer cooperatives. In the wake of World War II, a range of worker and family associations organized lending programs to support the financial needs of their members. Many of these small-loan institutions became models for American consumer credit pioneers in the early twentieth century. But they never led to a legitimation of commercial consumer lending in France of the sort that occurred during the interwar period in the United States. What distinguished these French tools of social credit from their American successors was their direct link to the state. The French small-loan institutions were not a private-sector alternative to state supports. They were state-run alternatives to private financial arrangements that were perceived as inadequate or exploitative. As such, they never offered a route by which private consumer lending might be legitimated as an alternative to a public welfare state.

Oldest of the social lending institutions were the charitable pawnshops called monts-de-piété. The first charitable pawn shop was opened in France by the Franciscan monk and surgeon Théophraste Renaudot in 1637. With the death of Louis XIII in 1643, Renaudot lost his royal commission and closed shop.[3] Monts-de-piété were reopened in 1777 under Louis XVI's liberal finance minister, Jacques Necker, and continued to play a role in French poor relief through the nineteenth and twentieth centuries.[4] They became a model for nineteenth-century welfare reformers seeking to improve the situation of the poor. Any borrower with collateral to pledge as pawn could borrow. Annual interest rates averaged 9 percent, but ranged from 5 percent to 12 percent or even sometimes 15 percent, depending on the availability of capital. And because the monts-de-piété charged the same rate for all borrowers, the higher cost of making smaller loans was subsidized from profits on larger loans. A researcher in the 1880s estimated that 75 percent of all loans were made at a loss, funded through subsidies by the remaining 25 percent.[5] Excess profits then went to support local charities for the poor, especially charitable hospitals that offered free services to the indigent. These early monts-de-piété operated independently of the state, although they enjoyed a monopoly over pawn lending.

Despite their charitable orientation, the monts-de-piété faced the same challenges that plagued other small lenders. The high overhead associated with making small loans was a constant source of financial stress. In the 1830s, the cities of Metz, Nancy, and Avignon experimented with joining their monts-de-piété to savings banks (*caisses d'épargne*). Sharing staff helped them to reduce the costs, and because the monts-de-piété were frequently short of capital, the *caisses d'épargne* helped fill that gap.[6] These experiments were short-lived. After the revolution of 1848 threw them into financial distress, a new law of June 24, 1851, unified the monts-de-piété in France under the administrative control of mayors' offices and set common terms under which they operated. Among other limitations, the monts-de-piété had to be financially independent.[7] By the end of the nineteenth century, there were forty-two monts-de-piété operating in France. The Paris branch, together with its satellite offices, offered more loans than the rest of them combined.[8]

By the turn of the twentieth century, these nonprofit lenders began to face criticism as a tool for welfare policy. Observers noted that they did not serve the poorest customers, as they required that borrowers have property in order to secure their loans. Those who did have property for collateral were forced

[3] The first monts-de-piétés were formed in Italy, beginning in 1462, and were formally sanctioned by the Pope as a tool for improving welfare.

[4] Cécile Abdesselam, "Les Prix de la Crise," *Télérama*, January 7, 1998.

[5] Emily Green Balch, "Public Assistance of the Poor in France," *Publications of the American Economic Association* 8/4–5 (1893), 159.

[6] Ange Blaise, *Des Monts de Piété et des Banque de Prêt sur Gage* (Paris: Pagnerre, 1856), 267–8; Clovis Eyraud, "Caisses de Crédit Municipal et Monts-de-Piété," Doctoral Thesis, University of Paris Law Faculty, May 1935, 31–42.

[7] Clovis Eyraud, "Caisses de Crédit Municipal et Monts-de-Piété," Doctoral Thesis, University of Paris Law Faculty, May 1935, 22.

[8] Emily Green Balch, "Public Assistance of the Poor in France," *Publications of the American Economic Association* 8/4–5 (1893), 158.

to go without the furniture or clothing that they handed over as pawn. If borrowers could not afford to repay, the monts-de-piété sold their forfeit pawn, but did not return any excess profit.[9] Moreover, monts-de-piété did not have an independent source of funding, so they found themselves short of capital at precisely the times when they were most in need. A survey of the lending patterns of the monts-de-piété in Rouen suggests that the bulk of their loans were made during periods of relative prosperity.[10] During periods of economic hardship, the monts-de-piété were forced either to curtail lending or find alternative sources of capital. In the 1870s, in the wake of the Franco-Prussian war, for example, the monts-de-piété were borrowing at 4–5 percent and lending at 9 percent, which, after covering administrative costs, resulted in a net loss. A British government survey of the French monts-de-piété in the 1880s reported that the Paris branches were being subsidized out of the budget of the general hospital fund, rather than the other way around.[11] Others had to raise their interest rates to cover the high cost of borrowing. And because they were required to transfer excess earnings to charitable hospitals and other benefits for the poor, they were not permitted to build up capital to carry them through financial crises.

The periodic financial challenges of the monts-de-piété came to a head with the onset of World War I. As borrowing increased and repayments fell, the government moved to block the monts-de-piété from auctioning off unclaimed pawn. With dwindling revenues, their lending ground rapidly to a halt. With the end of the war, the monts-de-piété had no capital to restart. If they were to reopen, they would need to raise funds. Because the government ban on auctions had been the proximate cause of their failure, the decision was made to recapitalize the monts-de-piétés with public funds. For the first time, in 1918, they began to receive direct government support. The Paris mont-de-piété, France's largest, continued to accept public support until 1933. They were also allowed for the first time to issue their own debt securities. And, in a sign of the extent that lending to the poor was still viewed with deep skepticism by investors, they were allowed to change their names to the innocuous-sounding *caisses municipals de crédit* (municipal credit unions) in order to market their debt.[12]

The interwar period was a busy time for the new *caisses municipals*. They continued to accept most household goods as collateral, and demand remained high. The Crédit Municipal de Paris built a new eleven-story warehouse to

9 Alfonse Desjardins, *The Cooperative People's Bank* (New York: Russell Sage Foundation, 1914), 4–5.

10 Yannick Marec, "Au Carrefour de l'Économie et du Social: L'Histoire du Mont-de-Piété de Rouen (1778–1923)," *Le Movement Social* 116 (1981), 68.

11 "Report from the Select Committee of the House of Commons on Pawnbrokers," *The Quarterly Review* 155 (1883), 131; Rosa-Maria Gelpi and François Julien-Labruyère, *Histoire du Crédit à la Consommation* (Paris: Editions la Découverte, 1994), 165, 170.

12 Clovis Eyraud, "Caisses de Crédit Municipal et Monts-de-Piété," Doctoral Thesis, University of Paris Law Faculty, May 1935, 40–42.

store all of the goods it accepted. But they also progressively expanded their activities to provide other welfare-related credit products. Most began offering title loans. They also began offering advances on pension payments. Both practices opened their business to larger and more affluent borrowers. Their role was expanded again following World War II. In 1954, in the wake of a government investigation into the cost and abuses of the private small-lending sector, the *caisses municipals* were allowed to make unsecured loans to government employees and employees of nationalized companies.[13] Although their lending was quickly exceeded by other forms of consumer lending, the *caisses municipals* remained popular and enjoyed a surge in demand during the downturn of the 1970s.[14] And their link to the government welfare system helped reduce the stigma associated with borrowing.

Following World War II, a range of new unsecured social lending programs emerged that reinforced the link between credit and welfare. Many French families looked to lending programs offered by family or other associations to finance household equipment. In 1950 in Rouen, for example, the Departmental Committee on Rural Life formed a Feminine Commission to Ease Household Work, which sought to make household loans available to all members out of the agricultural social security fund (Caisse d'Allocations Familiales Agricoles).[15] Over the next two years, it was able to release 14 million francs to 411 families in the form of loans for household equipment. The terms were favorable, with an interest rate of 2 percent and repayment periods ranging from six months to a year. But, as with most of the social credit providers, the application process was cumbersome. Borrowers had to present documentation of employment, residence, and parenthood of at least two children. They were also required to purchase sufficient life insurance to cover the loan and to prepay a retailer a 20 percent down payment on the product. The entire approval process, overseen by the Feminine Commission, required a month.[16] And, like the salary loan experiments, neither was equipped to provide the volume of capital that French households appeared to need.

Another experiment, launched in 1954, was a form of salary credit for the private sector that was modeled on public-sector credit offered by the *caisses municipals*. The idea was advocated by Sylvain-Paul Bonnaure, who argued that salary credit should entirely replace commercial installment credit, which he advocated banning. Under Bonnaure's system, each social security dossier

[13] Claude Duport, *Le Crédit à la Consommation* (Paris: Conseil Economique et Social, 1982), 13.

[14] Houda Laroussi, *Le Prêt sur Gage au Crédit Municipal de Paris: Clientèle et Mondes Sociales* (Paris: Editions Karthala, 2012), 32.

[15] Adolphe Kaufman, "Le Crédit à la Consommation en France de 1945 à 1956," Doctoral Thesis, University of Paris Law Faculty, December 1956, 76–77.

[16] CHA, M. Jaillet, "Mesures Finacières Propres à Favoriser l'Équipement Ménager dans les Campagnes," report presented to the Congrès de la Confédération Nationale de la Famille Rurale à Bordeaux, May 11–12, 1952.

would include a "credit file" that would centralize control over lending – although actual loans would in fact be made by diverse financial institutions. Under this system, employees could borrow up to two months of salary to be repaid over twelve months, at an interest of 0.65 percent per month. Large manufacturers would be encouraged to create their own lending groups.[17] A variety of associations and employers experimented with this sort of salary credit. One of these was Maurice Martell, president of the Syndicat National du Crédit Social, which offered up to three months of salary in credit for employees of at least two years covering up to 75 percent of the value of goods. The interest rate was 5.6 percent per year, which included life insurance and one month of unemployment coverage.[18]

What was critical about all of the French experiments with social credit was the direct link to the state. American philanthropists who observed the limitations of charitable pawn as a response to worker needs turned toward alternative, private-sector strategies for providing low-cost loans to the working classes. Although new social lending programs that emerged in the 1970s were funded in part through government agencies, the main focus was on encouraging private lenders to serve poor and vulnerable populations. In France, it was the government that increasingly stepped in to support the social functions provided by the monts-de-piété and other forms of charitable lending. This state endorsement had an unexpected consequence. Although it helped stabilize and capitalize these lenders, it also reinforced the impression that legitimate consumer lending demanded intervention from the state. Purely private lending, without state sanction, remained suspect.

Coupon Credit and the Reign of Doorstep Lending

In the United States, the early small loans offered by consumer finance companies were not necessarily targeted at retail purchases. They were commonly used to pay taxes, cover medical expenses, or consolidate other loans. By contrast, early French small loans took the explicit form of sales credit. Most of these loans were sold as coupon credit, marketed door to door on the basis of reputation and without collateral. Coupon credit was not unique to France; similar doorstep coupon lenders emerged at the same time in Germany, Japan, and the United Kingdom.[19] They were unusual in France, however, in the extent to which they dominated the interwar consumer-lending market. Especially in the wake of the Great Depression, doorstep lenders were virtually the

[17] Gabriel Veraldi, "Une Solution au Problème du Pouvoir d'Achat," *La Vie Française*, October 3, 1958.

[18] *Combat*, November 24, 1959.

[19] Sean O'Connell, "The Business of Working-Class Credit: Subprime Markets in the United Kingdom since 1880," in Jan Logemann, ed., *The Development of Consumer Credit in Global Perspective: Business, Regulation, and Culture* (New York: Palgrave, 2012), 95–97.

only legitimate small lenders still operating. They set a pattern of lending that was both challenging and unattractive for commercial banks to emulate.

As elsewhere, small retailers in France had always offered informal credit to regular clients. In typical sales, goods were sold on credit, and accounts were cleared at the end of the week or month. During hard times, retailers commonly offered open-book credit, in which the terms of repayment were extended. Modern sales credit, in which a regular installment payment schedule was built into the loan, seems to have had its roots in the 1850s. The Paris retailer Les Enfants de la Chapelle offered installment sales credit beginning in 1852.[20] In 1866, Eduard Cohen formed the retail chain Aux Classes Laborieuses, targeting workers with sales credit. Another Paris store, Bon Génie, tried in the 1860s to offer a form of general sales credit that could be used by multiple retailers. The experiment failed.[21] And beginning in 1878, the retail chain Paris-France, owner of the popular Dames de France chain of women's clothing stores, extended working-class credit sales to the whole of France.[22] But the retail pioneer who offered an early glimpse of both the promise and challenges that consumer credit posed for retailers was the retail magnate Georges Dufayel. Dufayel's innovation was to give the working class access to the *grand magasin* shopping experience through the provision of retail credit. He also developed one of the most sophisticated credit distribution and collections systems that existed at the time.

Dufayel entered the lending business by managing the credit office for Jacques-François Crépin, who in 1856 had opened a furniture store called Le Palais de la Nouveauté in a working-class neighborhood off the rue Barbès in Paris's 18th Arrondissement. In 1865, Crépin began to offer credit in the form of credit coupons (*bons*) that could be purchased for a 20 percent down payment and used to purchase goods in affiliated stores.[23] Once a product was purchased, the buyer was billed weekly to repay the principal. These coupons could be used at the Palais and other retailers who agreed to accept them. The merchant who accepted the coupon then redeemed it with Crépin for 60 percent of its worth. In this arrangement, the retailer bore the cost of the credit, not the consumer, and fees were strikingly high.[24] Still, for stores that hoped

[20] Philippe Herail, "Cetelem: une Histoire des Valeurs, un Avenir," Cetelem Historical Archive, August 2002.

[21] Charles Couture, "Des Différentes Combinaisons de Ventes à Crédit dans Leurs Rapports avec la Petite Épargne," Doctoral Thesis, Paris, 1904, 80.

[22] Jean Romeuf, "Pour une Banque de Crédit à la Consommation," *l'Observation Économique* 65 (July 1953), 62–63; Fernand Bouquerel, *L'Étude des Marches au Service des Enterprises*, volume 2 (Paris: Presses Universitaires de France, 1964), 584.

[23] The first product sold on credit was a group of twenty photographs, to be paid in twenty weekly installments. Jacques-Bernard Voirin, "Les Aspects Financiers et Économiques du Crédit à la Consommation: Étude Comparative et Évolutive," Doctoral Thesis in Economics, March 1959, 40.

[24] The implied APR on such a loan would be around 200 percent. First, the down payment to purchase the coupon meant that the credit customer was borrowing only 80 percent of the final

to attract new working-class customers, the Crépin coupons seem to have been attractive.

Starting in 1869, Dufayel began promoting Crépin's coupon credit via a small army of door-to-door sales and collection agents. He hired 780 sales representatives, divided Paris into 178 sales areas, and sent teams to canvas in groups of 3 (to avoid fraud). These mobile sales agents took applications from new customers, enquired with their concierges about regular rent payment, and talked with their neighbors, employers, and fellow workers. They also collected weekly or biweekly payments from existing customers and chatted with neighborhood businesses to find out if their clients had any problems or might face difficulties paying. Data collected by the sales staff were processed, filed, and tracked in the bureaucracy of the Administration Crépin. Once accepted, the terms of credit were permissive. If the sales staff found out that a customer had fallen sick or lost his job, they would commonly suspend payment for up to six months or longer. Good clients were occasionally forgiven outright.[25]

When Crépin died in 1888, Dufayel took over. In 1892, he renamed the store the Grand Magasin Dufayel.[26] He invested heavily and installed novel electric lighting, gaudy art, and an indoor theater seating 3,000. He then opened branches in all of the major cities of France. As his retail chain grew, the coupon-credit business also flourished. By 1904, 700 stores were participating in the program, including La Samaritaine, where the introduction of credit doubled its sales in a single year.[27] At its peak, Dufayel had 2 million credit clients and maintained records on 3.5 million individual households across France. The records, including current and past address, age, marital status, profession, employer, and salary, were probably the largest and most complete set of consumer credit data assembled at the time. In addition to managing the coupon-credit business, Dufayel tapped into his database to create what may also have been the first large-scale targeted direct-advertising service.[28] He also organized some of the first "credit vacations," which took customers to his home town of Sainte-Adresse, near Le Havre on the English Channel.[29]

price. Second, loans were typically repaid over a six-month period. Third, because the customer was repaying the loan in steady increments, he or she was effectively borrowing only half of the 80 percent (i.e., the more the customer paid back, the less outstanding loan remained). Hence, on a loan of only 40 percent of the original price of the product, the retailer was being charged 40 percent. For a half-year loan, that implied an annual interest rate of 200 percent. Smaller loans could have down payments as high as 50 percent, increasing the effective APR even more.

[25] Marjorie Anne Beale, "Mort à Crédit: The Credit Department Store and the Parisian Lower Classes, 1856–1920," Harvard History Department undergraduate thesis, 1982, 14–16.

[26] Michael Steven Smith, "The Emergence of Modern Business Enterprise in France, 1800–1930." (Cambridge, MA: Harvard University Press, 2006), 508.

[27] Gerard Constant, "La Vente à Crédit," *Les Cahiers Français*, April 1965, 17–20.

[28] Marjorie Anne Beale, "Mort à Crédit: The Credit Department Store and the Parisian Lower Classes, 1856–1920," Harvard History Department undergraduate thesis, 1982, 19–29.

[29] Dufayel's tourism residences later became the base for Belgium's government during World War I. Michel Drancourt, *Une Force Inconnue: Le Crédit* (Paris: Hachette, 1961); Elizabeth Dryden, *Paris in Herrick Days* (Paris: Borgon-Ainé, 1915), 117.

Contemporary opinion of Dufayel's empire was decidedly mixed. Some applauded the spectacle. A reporter in 1896 wrote: "A visit to this palace of credit makes clear that the owner has neglected nothing in order to make this one of the most beautiful monuments of [Paris]."[30] Others scorned him for popularizing bad taste. Frantz Jourdain, the art nouveau architect who was designing the new store for La Samaritaine – and may therefore have felt professionally obliged to criticize the competition – derided Dufayel as a "petty money-lender who has poisoned an entire generation with the furniture we know today."[31] In his public image, Dufayel blurred the lines between the working class and France's elites. He emphasized his humble origins and was a close friend of France's socialist Prime Minister, Pierre Waldeck-Rousseau, whom he drove around in his car. But he also reveled in financial success, plastered his name across his stores, and built an ostentatious personal residence on the Champs Elysées.[32] However disconcerting this blurring of social hierarchy was for France's upper class, Dufayel's lasting mark was in demonstrating to a new generation of store managers that the combination of large-scale retailing and consumer credit could be highly profitable.

Success seems to have made Dufayel unbearable. In 1913, a group of his employees quit and founded an independent retail credit group, La Semeuse, dedicated to door-to-door coupon-credit sales. Like Dufayel, the new lender embraced working-class customers. The communist daily *L'Humanité* described the founders fondly as "syndicalists and revolutionaries," and the new organization went under the slogan: "Capital must work; workers must have [capital]."[33] Some of the sales force from the Administration Dufayel were lured away to work with them.[34] Critically, they also took over the La Samaritaine account. Dufayel attempted to block La Semeuse by pressuring La Samaritaine to sign a long-term credit arrangment with Dufayel. When it refused, Dufayel retaliated by launching a line of clothing, a first for Dufayel, that placed his company in direct competition with La Samaritaine.[35] La Samaritaine then acquired La Semeuse outright. With Dufayel's death in 1916, his empire quickly declined; La Semeuse prospered. By 1929, La Semeuse coupons were accepted by 300 different retailers.[36] Competitors also emerged: Le Progrès Commercial, a coupon-credit vendor

[30] La Nature: Revue des Sciences et de Leurs Applications aux Arts et à l'Industrie, 1896.

[31] Jourdain had been a source for Émile Zola's novel *Au Bonheur des Dames*. Marjorie Anne Beale, "Mort à Crédit: The Credit Department Store and the Parisian Lower Classes, 1856–1920," Harvard History Department undergraduate thesis, 1982, 22.

[32] Anaïs Albert, "Le Crédit à la Consommation des Classes Populaires à la Belle Époque: Invention, Innovation ou Reconfiguration?," *Annales: Histoire, Sciences Sociales* 67/4 (2012), 1055.

[33] "Il faut que le capital travaille; il faut que le travail le possede," *L'Humanité*, November 21, 1924, 2.

[34] Hubert Balaguy, *Le Crédit à la Consommation en France* (Paris: Presses Universitaires de Paris, 1996), 18.

[35] Michel Drancourt, *Une Force Inconnue: Le Crédit* (Paris: Hachette, 1961).

[36] Roger Nathan, "Le Financement de la Consommation," *Revue de l'Économie Politique*, March–April 1929, 249.

founded by the retailer La Bonne Ménagère, was accepted at 600 retail sites by 1930.[37]

Coupon lenders provided credit for many of France's second-tier retail chains through the first half of the twentieth century. These so-called credit houses included Les Classes Laborieuses, Le Tapis Rouge, La Place Clichy, Paris-France, Petit Saint Thomas, Bon-Génie, and Galeries Voltaire.[38] Some, such as Bon Génie and Classes Laborieuses, offered their own coupons. The most prolific of the credit houses outside of Paris was Paris-France, which by 1911 had opened 150 outlets across France's smaller cities.[39]

France's small retailers were reportedly "stupefied" at the new credit-sales strategy being adopted by larger retailers, and sought to offer credit of their own.[40] Many of those that did not subscribe to La Semeuse or similar services created new cooperative lending arrangements, called economic unions, on the basis of similar lending technology.[41] In the economic unions, small local retailers pooled their capital to provide coupon credit that could be used at any of their stores. Most emerged in working-class communities, especially in the Nord and Midi-Méditerranée regions. The first of the economic unions was the Crédit Lillois, formed by Lille retailers in 1885.[42] Other regions followed suit, including the Economic Union of Saint-Quentin in 1901 and the Economic Union of Amiens in 1903.[43] They provided 95 percent of their credit to workers; a third of their sales were for clothing.[44] Their numbers grew rapidly in response to the spread of large store chains across France: roughly 30 economic unions operated in 1906, 67 in 1907, and 130 in 1911.[45] In 1910, economic unions had enrolled an estimated 10,000 retailers that

37 *L'Humanité*, November 21, 1924, 2.

38 J. Milna, *Les Erreurs du Petit Commerce: Les Grands Magasins, Les Unions Économiques et les Maisons de Vente à Crédit* (Lyon: Tadeau, 1911), 3–4. Leora Auslander, *Taste and Power: Furnishing Modern France* (Berkeley: University of California Press, 1996), 340.

39 Paris-France went by locally adapted names, such as Paris-Lyon, Paris-Dijon, and Paris-Caen. J. Milna, *Les Erreurs du Petit Commerce: Les Grands Magasins, Les Unions Économiques et les Maisons de Vente à Crédit* (Lyon: Tadeau, 1911), 16.

40 Cujas Law Library (CLL) archives, "Discours Pronouncés par M. Robert Chaplain," Fédération des Unions Économiques et Société Similaires de France, Pamphlet, 1913, 2–3.

41 Meg Jacobs, *Pocketbook Politics: Economic Citizenship in Twentieth-Century America* (Princeton: Princeton University Press, 2005), 33.

42 Charles Couture, "Des Différentes Combinaisons de Ventes à Crédit dans Leurs Rapports avec la Petite Èpargne," Doctoral Thesis, Paris, 1904, 81.

43 Michel Drancourt, *Une Force Inconnue: Le Crédit* (Paris: Hachette, 1961).

44 CNC, 1427200301, box 318, Grande Bretagne, Crédit à la Consommation, 1950–1968, Philippe Dargenton, Inspecteur des Finance, Ambassade de France à Londre, "Note sur le Crédit à la Consommation en Grande-Bretagne," August 12, 1954, 2.

45 A. de Foville, "Premier Congrès des Unions Économiques et Sociétés Similaires de France," *Bulletin du Comité des Travaux Historique et Scientifique* (1907), 13; *Bulletin de la Fédération (Journal of the Fédération des Unions Économiques et Sociétés Similaires de France)*, No. 1 (December 1907), 16–19; J. Milna, *Les Erreurs du Petit Commerce: Les Grands Magasins, Les Unions Économiques et les Maisons de Vente à Crédit* (Lyon: Tadeau, 1911), 4.

accepted their coupons.[46] Financially, the economic unions were self-financing until World War I. In general, participating retailers contributed 6 percent of their credit-sales volume to the union for working capital, and participating retailers had to wait ninety days to be paid. During the war, banks began discounting the coupons, a practice that continued through the interwar period.[47] In 1906, the economic unions formed a national federation to support their interests. They successfully fought off a legislative effort to impose usury restrictions on economic unions in 1910, accusing legislators of attacking a "useful tool in the very difficult struggle waged by small retailers against the large stores."[48] The federation also organized a list of "disappeared" customers that allowed the unions to track nonpayers as they moved from city to city.[49]

Most economic unions sold credit on subscription, following the model of La Semeuse. Credit was offered and collected door to door, and late payments were not penalized.[50] The bulk of the cost of the system was paid by retailers rather than the customers. In a typical loan, a borrower would purchase a 100-franc coupon for 103 francs (coupon plus fee), with a 4-month repayment period. Retailers accepted the coupons for purchases, then took a 12–15 percent discount on payment from the economic union.[51] Between the fee and discount, and the relatively short period of the loan, annualized interest rates on economic union credit could be very high. Advocates of the economic unions emphasized their virtues. The director of the economic union in Tarbes described the institution as philanthropic: "Workers come to borrow from us . . . with a simple guarantee: their honesty."[52] And because the coupons could only be redeemed at participating retailers, users could not go into debt for "gambling or cabaret."[53] Critics accused retailers that accepted the coupons of raising their prices to offset the discount. Indeed, retail employees that did not add the price of the coupon into the price of a product commonly had their

[46] CLL, "Discours Prononcé par M. Robert Chaplain," Fédération des Unions Économiques et Sociétés Similaires de France, Pamphlet, 1913, 2–3; A. de Foville, "Premier Congrès des Unions Économiques et Sociétés Similaires de France," *Bulletin du Comité des Travaux Historique et Scientifique* (1907), 13.

[47] The Banque de France, which regularly discounted other debt paper, refused to purchase economic union "bons." Adolphe Kaufman, "Le Crédit à la Consommation en France de 1945 à 1956," Doctoral Thesis, University of Paris Law Faculty, December 1956, 21–22.

[48] CLL, Letter from F. Guyot, president, the Fédération des Unions Économiques et Sociétés Similaires de France, Pamphlet, March 18, 1910, 1–5.

[49] *Bulletin de la Fédération* (Journal of the Fédération des Unions Économiques et Sociétés Similaires de France), No. 1 (December 1907), 13–19.

[50] "Panorama du Crédit 1966," *L'Économie* 998, March 11, 1966.

[51] J. Milna, *Les Erreurs du Petit Commerce: Les Grands Magasins, Les Unions Économiques et les Maisons de Vente à Crédit* (Lyon: Tadeau, 1911), 4–16.

[52] A. Daubois, "Le Petit Commerce," *Bulletin de la Fédération* (Journal of the Fédération des Unions Économiques et Sociétés Similaires de France), No. 1 (December 1907), 5.

[53] A. Daubois, "Le Petit Commerce," *Bulletin de la Fédération* (Journal of the Fédération des Unions Économiques et Sociétés Similaires de France), No. 1 (December 1907), 5.

pay docked. To avoid such mistakes, employees were accused of raising prices on all customers.[54]

Credit and Reconstruction

The now-pervasive doorstep credit had relatively little impact on the top-tier Paris *grands magasins*. By the early 1950s, most were offering their own in-house credit. The credit they offered took a variety of forms. The Bazar de l'Hotel de Ville (BHV) offered a coupon-credit service that was managed by La Semeuse. Le Bon Marché and Trois Quartiers both offered a credit system like BHV, but used checks rather than coupons.[55] The department store Printemps had a similar system of credit checks, in addition to conventional monthly payment booklets.[56] The Galleries Lafayettes offered an installment credit plan for household goods.[57] Most of the *grands magasins* offered similar credit terms: all required a 25 percent down payment, plus between three and twelve additional monthly payments. But it was not heavily used. In 1953, store credit accounted for only 10 percent of sales at the *grands magasins*, and only 3 percent was longer-term installment credit.[58] Until the mid-1960s, these store lending plans were supported by a store's own funds and subsidized from general revenue.[59] Credit checks were rudimentary, if done at all, and credit was granted without any delay. As one worker at BHV said in 1966: "The French are honest and only purchase on credit during times of prosperity, preferring to hold back when they see symptoms of recessions."[60]

If credit sales were a modest part of the business of the top-tier *grands magasins*, they were central to the success of France's rapidly growing second-tier retail chains. For stores such as Nouvelles Galeries, Galeries Modernes, and Dames de France, credit sales in the early 1950s accounted for half of all sales. On the basis of the model of La Semeuse, their in-house credit tended to be marketed by door-to-door sales forces, with interest rates that were higher than the 1 percent per month offered by the *grands magasins*, but always below 25 percent per year.[61] Other midscale chain stores, ones such as La Belle Jardinière, continued to rely on La Semeuse coupons. By 1953, La Semeuse had 5 billion (old) francs in consumer sales loans outstanding,

[54] J. Milna, *Les Erreurs du Petit Commerce: Les Grands Magasins, Les Unions Économiques et les Maisons de Vente à Crédit* (Lyon: Tadeau, 1911), 18.

[55] Roger Nathan, "Le Financement de la Consommation," 252; *Le Monde*, December 15, 1966.

[56] "Le Developpement des Ventes à Crédit dans la Region du Nord," *Perspectives*, June 2, 1954, 6.

[57] *Le Monde*, December 15, 1966.

[58] Direction Générale des Prix et des Enquêtes Économiques, *Enquête* No. 5417, Note sur le Crédit à la Consommation, 1954, 8.

[59] "Panorama du Crédit 1966," *L'Économie* 998, March 11, 1966, 10.

[60] "Panorama du Crédit 1966," *L'Économie* 998, March 11, 1966, 10.

[61] Direction Générale des Prix et des Enquêtes Économiques, *Enquête* No. 5417, Note sur le Crédit à la Consommation, 1954, 8.

accounting for a third of sales credit by registered lenders, and was accepted at 1,300 stores.[62] Some of the large furniture sales chains did up to 75 percent of their business on credit in the 1950s. This high level of credit put pressure on small furniture stores, which typically offered their own credit programs, but made only 10 percent–20 percent of total sales on credit.[63] As credit by larger retail chains grew, independent stores increasingly embraced economic unions.

Occupation during World War II had been devastating for France's economic unions. Of the roughly 100 economic unions operating in 1939, only 20 survived through the war.[64] Those that remained were small and poorly capitalized. When the new Bank Law was passed in 1941, registering all financial institutions, economic unions were deemed too insignificant to be regulated. This unregulated status, which initially gave the economic unions broad latitude to operate, ultimately abetted their downfall. But not right away. With the end of the war, consumer demand rose, some of the loans made before the war were repaid, and many of the economic unions were able to restart.[65] As France's larger retail chains began to expand through the offer of credit, independent stores flocked to economic unions to offer credit of their own. By 1953, when the Banque de France conducted a survey of informal lending in France, it found 52 economic unions with 5,000 participating retailers, 150,000 clients, and 4 billion (old) francs in loans.[66] They accounted for 16 percent of total (formal and informal) consumer credit.[67] As demand grew in the early 1950s, the economic unions approached banks and manufacturers to supply more capital.[68]

In 1954, the Banque de France imposed a general restriction on consumer lending. Lenders had to meet minimal capital requirements, and comply with minimum down payment and maximum repayment periods for sales credit. The goal of these restrictions was to fight inflation in the economy, which the Banque de France saw in part being stoked by excess consumer demand. Critically, the national federation of economic unions negotiated an exemption for its

62 Marius Allègre, "Étude du Crédit à la Consommation," *Conseil Économique*, March 4, 1954, 267–279; Roger Nathan, "Le Financement de la Consommation," 249; CNC, 1427200301, box 111: Crédit à la Consommation et Vente au Crédit, Correspondence, from Jacques Herisse, Commissaire de Police to Monsieur le Directeur de la Police Économique, "Vente à Crédit de Trousseaux et de Linge de Maison," 1957.

63 "Le Developpement des Ventes à Crédit dans la Region du Nord," *Perspectives*, June 2, 1954, 6.

64 Sabine Effosse, "Unions Économiques de Commerçants," *Quaderni Storici* 137/2 (2011), 582.

65 René Creussol, "Le Developpement des Ventes à Crédit," *Économie et Politique* 22 (1956), 78–79.

66 Sabine Effosse, "Unions Économiques de Commerçants," *Quaderni Storici* 137/2 (2011), 582–583.

67 Marius Allègre, "Étude du Crédit à la Consommation," *Conseil Économique*, March 4, 1954, 267–279.

68 Adolphe Kaufman, "Le Crédit à la Consommation en France de 1945 à 1956, Doctoral Thesis, University of Paris Law Faculty, December 1956, 21–22.

members. This was due partly to the prior unregulated status of the economic unions under the Bank Law of 1941, and partly in deference to concerns over the fate of small retailers in France.[69] But the exemption came with a cost. The Banque de France stipulated that they could lend only to member retailers on the basis of coupons and, critically, could not go outside of their membership to raise capital.[70] This put an end to bank and manufacturer discounting of economic unions, and gradually starved them of capital. Their exempt status also attracted illegal high-rate lenders that masqueraded as economic unions in order to avoid regulation. These lenders, many offering loans for motorcycle purchases, tarnished the reputation of economic unions generally.

Coupon credit as a whole, including economic unions, La Semeuse, and its competitors, continued to prosper. In 1957, this door-to-door format still accounted for 21 billion (old) francs in loans, or about 12 percent of the total 169 billion francs of outstanding consumer credit that year.[71] If we exclude auto sales credit, which represented two-thirds of all consumer credit at the time, credit coupons such as those offered by La Semeuse and the economic unions accounted for a third of all credit sales.[72] But their time was quickly waning, as a new breed of bank- and manufacturer-sponsored sales finance companies began offering credit for consumer durables. These included general household equipment lenders such as Cetelem and Crédit Electricité et Gaz (CREG), plus a range of existing auto finance companies that began expanding their activities into financing household goods (see Chapter 5). Rather than selling door to door, these lenders worked directly with retailers. They allowed retailers to offer credit at the point of sale, without having to worry about raising capital or managing payments. This so-called indirect credit – marketed via retailers rather than directly to consumers – became the standard for consumer lending in France for the next thirty years.

Why did France's banks not step in to offer credit to France's small retailers as they had in the United States? Had they done so, the landscape of French consumer credit might have evolved differently. Banks would have had a stake in the consumer credit sector and how it was regulated. They could have lent some of their own public legitimacy to the new consumer credit market. And they would have been in a position to blend their credit products with the new payment-card technology that would appear in the 1960s. We have no records of how banks decided not to offer consumer credit, but three features of the sector almost certainly gave them pause. First, doorstep lenders relying on coupon credit were already serving the retail market, and their doorstep-selling

69 Bulletin du Conseil National du Patronat Français, June 1959.

70 Annexes au Huitième Rapport Annuel du Conseil National du Crédit (Paris: Imprimerie Nationale, 1956), 21–24.

71 "Le Crédit à la Consommation en France," *Agence Économique et Financière*, June 9, 1959; Conseil National du Crédit, *Rapport pour l'Année 1959*, 1960.

72 Jean Luc, "La Réglementation des Ventes à Tempérament et la Protection des Acheteurs," *Le Monde*, December 22, 1956.

model fit poorly with conventional banking. Second, doorstep lenders adopted practices that raised public suspicion about the legitimacy of consumer lending as an economic activity. They commonly collected from wives while their husbands were away at work. They also commonly resorted to wage garnishment in order to collect on unpaid loans. Employers, seeking to avoid the administrative hassle of debt collections, also commonly fired workers whose wages were garnished.[73] Finally, the unregulated status of economic unions was a magnet for lenders with questionable lending and collections practices. For large commercial banks already engaged in profitable industrial lending in support of France's reconstruction effort, consumer loans must have seemed a circus sideshow with little profit and a high potential cost to their reputations. They would lend money at arm's length, helping finance independent consumer finance companies, but did not try to compete with them.

The War of the Cards

France's banks could avert their gaze from consumer lending so long as the sector did not seem to infringe on their business. That changed with the rise of credit cards, which arrived in France as an American import. The first of them – Diners' Club and American Express – were travel and entertainment cards rather than genuine payment cards linked to credit. They charged no interest, and customers had to pay the entire bill at the end of the month. Diners' Club France, a wholly French-owned affiliate of the American Diners' Club World network, introduced the Diners' Club card in 1954. Like the consumer lending companies that were emerging at the same time, Diners' Club was financed by a consortium of smaller banks: Neuflize, Schlumberger, Mallet, and others. These banks were also among the first customers, offering the new card to their own employees. Within three years of launching in France, Diners' Club had 800 corporate accounts. Ten years later in 1967, it had 35,000 accounts, represented 85 percent of all payment cards (with or without a credit facility) in France, and was accepted at 10,000 points of sale. The card made money from annual customer fees, set initially at 60 francs per year, but also on fees assessed on retailers, equal to 8 percent of the sales price.[74] Retailers, who saw Diners' Club as primarily a travelers' card, were willing to accept the high fees because it offered to bring in new customers rather than make inroads into their existing customer base. In 1961, American Express followed Diners' Club into France.

France's large retailers responded by offering their own in-house cards that were tied to credit facilities. Some, like the credit card offered by the Galeries

[73] The law of June 1895 reinforced lender access to wage garnishment. France Direction Travail, *Saisie-Arrêt sur les Salariés* (Paris: Imprimerie Nationale, 1899), 19.

[74] Claude Villeneuve, "Yves Gautier, Directeur Général du Diners' [sic] Club," *France-Soir*, July 1, 1967.

Lafayette, were managed by separate finance companies. Others, like that offered by the mass retailer Prisunic at each of its 400 retail sites, were managed in-house. Nouvelles Galeries, for example, had by 1967 given out 20,000 client cards that permitted deferred payment.[75] The new surge in branded payment cards was not limited to retailers; car rental companies had also begun creating their own cards. By 1965, Hertz had 35,000 card members and Avis had 20,000.[76] The oil and gas company Elf distributed 30,000 payment cards to its customers. Some sectors came together to offer a unified payment card. The airline industry launched the Carte Verte, financed by Crédit Agricole, that allowed payment of airline tickets on an installment plan over a period up to twelve months. France's association of hotels and restaurants launched two travel and leisure cards, the Carte Blanche and Eurocard, that offered lower fees than did American Express or Diners' Club.

More worrisome to the banking sector than these retail cards, which generally were not accepted outside of the particular store that issued the card, was a new wave of homegrown general-purpose credit cards that threatened to permanently exclude France's large banks from the growing credit card business. The most important of these was the Carte d'Or, launched in 1967. Like Diners' Club, Carte d'Or was based on a U.S. model but owned and operated by a consortium of French banks (including the Union Industrielle and Financiére and the Banque Nationale de Paris) and one U.S. partner: Marine Midland Corporation. This American firm, which had launched its U.S. Gold Card in 1959, introduced the Carte d'Or in France in 1965.[77] By then, it already had 6 million Gold Cards in the United States that were accepted in 200,000 retail sites. The consortium created a new French company to manage the French card – the Society for Financing Household Expenses – and hired Henri Dhavernas, the former head of Diners' Club, as its president.[78] The idea of the card was that it could be used for smaller items, including children's clothing and school gear. Stores that accepted the card showed a sticker that read: "Crédit familial permanent." The card was financed through a 6 percent fee on retailers and interest payments on any unpaid balance. It was the first general-purpose revolving credit card in France.

While Marine Midlands was launching the Carte d'Or, France's dedicated consumer finance companies were experimenting with similar products. In 1965, Cetelem began offering a card-based revolving credit account called

[75] This was not a true revolving credit account because the terms of repayment were set for each sale. Jean Arnaud, "La Carte Bleue: Dialogue ou Épreuve de Force," *Les Echos*, October 13, 1967.

[76] Lydie Nicaise, "Les Cartes de Crédit Dévorent l'Argent," *Témoignage Chrétien*, November 16, 1967.

[77] The Marine Midland Company formed the Interbank Card Association, bringing together 500 U.S. banks with their own cards. ICA would eventually become MasterCard.

[78] *Le Monde*, February 28, 1968.

Crédit en Poche (pocket credit). Cetelem's competitor, Sofinco, launched a similar product called the Carte d'Argent.[79] For France's big banks, which had been observing the rapid spread of credit cards in the United States, these new revolving credit cards offered by consumer finance companies seemed poised to take over banks' traditional role in managing payments. To stop them, banks needed to find an attractive alternative, and to do so quickly.

Carte Bleue

In 1965, the Association of French Bankers (AFB) began sending members to the United States to evaluate their system of credit cards. These visits to the United States evoked a strong conclusion among bankers. Publicly, they argued that French consumers would never accept credit cards as they were used in the United States.[80] Privately, they understood that credit cards were the future, and that they would have to act decisively if they were not to lose control over France's private payments network. Initially, the AFB approached the Banque de France with a proposal for an interbank payment system that would combine payment with credit. The Banque de France accepted the idea of a payment card but blocked the credit component of the project on concerns over inflation.[81] The new card system, called Carte Bleue, would be a dedicated card-based payment network managed collaboratively by commercial banks. Bernard Süe, the head of the new Carte Bleue system, later explained: "To the extent that the credit card is intended to replace the check, it is an instrument that falls specifically into the domain of the banks. Banks must take the lead in order not to be surpassed as they were in the United States."[82] Critically, however, Carte Bleue would be a debit card, with no associated credit facility.

With support from France's National Credit Council, the big banks set about creating a new and efficient payment system for the country. Five of France's big bank groups – Crédit Lyonnais, Société Générale, Banque Nationale de Paris, Crédit Industriel et Commercial (CIC), and Crédit Commercial de France – collaborated to roll out Carte Bleue.[83] Like Diners' Club and American Express, Carte Bleue was initially funded through annual fees (20 francs per year) paid by card holders, plus a percentage of the sales price of goods paid by retailers. Retailer fees included 2 percent of purchases made via Carte Bleue, plus a 1 franc charge per transaction and rental fees for the point-of-sale

79 *Le Figaro*, June 14, 1968.

80 Serge Sainloup, "Après la Bataille, la Coopération," *La Vie Française*, May 23–29, 1983, 32–34.

81 Bernard Desjardins, Michel Lescure, Roger Rougaret, Alain Plessis, and André Straus, *Le Crédit Lyonnais, 1863–1986* (Geneva: Droz, 2003), 87.

82 Quoted in Michel Schlosser and Gérard Tardy, *Les Cartes de Crédit* (Paris: Dunod, 1971), 55.

83 *Le Monde*, November 7, 1967.

equipment. For a bill of 100 francs, the total charge would be 3 percent, well below the 8 percent being charged at the time by Diners' Club and American Express.[84] In exchange, retailers received guaranteed payment within forty-eight hours of submitting their receipts. As with similar payment cards in the United States, customers paid a single bill for all of their charged purchases at the end of the month.[85] Customers could charge up to 500 francs per day on the card.

Whereas Diners' Club and American Express were specifically prestige cards, the Carte Bleue was touted as the "democratization" of the credit card. But this description perhaps overstated the case. Initially, banks offered the new card only to clients holding more than 5,000–6,000 francs in savings in their bank account. Insofar as charges were financed until the end of the month, the Carte Bleue provided credit. Most participating banks also offered new overdraft facilities in conjunction with the new card. The CIC bank, for example, created an automatic line of credit for Carte Bleue holders called *crédimatic.* The interest rate was favorable, ranging from 9.5 percent to 12 percent. But because these programs took the form of overdraft protection, the high savings requirement for card holders meant that they almost always had sufficient ready savings to make their monthly payment.[86]

Without interest income to offset its high cost, the Carte Bleue was an expensive program. For the first twenty years of its existence, participating banks lost billions of francs financing it. The high cost of the program included the installation of 10,000 ATMs, as well as the embrace of expensive microprocessor technology for the Carte Bleue cards. Bankers justified their continued support for the system on the grounds that it represented a savings over the comparatively higher cost of the conventional check payment system.[87] In 1976, they estimated the full cost of a check, including the tellers to process it, at between 1.5 francs and 5 francs. In that year, 1.3 billion checks were written in France, representing still 80 percent of all payments.[88] Even a modest reduction in the use of paper checks could make the high cost of the Carte Bleue system worthwhile.

To the broader public, the Carte Bleue system was justified as a project to forestall an invasion by American credit cards. Bernard Süe, the general secretary for the Carte Bleue, proclaimed: "We do not want to be colonized by American cards."[89] Although this appeal to economic nationalism fit well with the anti-Americanism being promoted by President de Gaulle at the time, it did not reflect the focus of French bankers. Rather, the greatest challenges to

[84] *Le Monde*, October 11, 1967.
[85] *L'Express*, March 27, 1967.
[86] *Le Monde*, September 17, 1968.
[87] Henri d'Armagnac, "Les Cartes de Crédit," *Les Échos*, May 11, 1978.
[88] *Le Monde*, May 23, 1978.
[89] Catherine Nay, "La Carte Bleue Contre la Paperasse," *L'Express*, October 16, 1967.

the Carte Bleue system came from within: from other French banks and French retailers.

Even before its launch, retail opposition to the Carte Bleue was strong. Nearly all of France's retailers, including the large department stores, the smaller family-run stores, as well as most hotels and restaurants, complained that the fees for processing payments through Carte Bleue created an extra cost that they had not had to bear before. Carte Bleue responded that its payment system was both inexpensive and secure. With fees of 2 percent of sales, it would be, it argued, the most efficient payment system in the world. One study commissioned in preparation for the launch of the Carte Bleue found that the cost to retailers of dealing with traditional customer payments and collections was 12 percent of sales. Retailers objected that consumers, rather than retailers, should be made to pay for the service. Bernard Süe responded: "The client already pays his fee; we cannot ask him for more. In the United States, fees range from 3% to 10%. Department stores, for example, pay 8% of their sales to use the Diners' Club." Indeed, Süe was happy to show critics a letter from the president of Diners' Club accusing Carte Bleue of "dumping" because of its low fees. France's department stores pointed out that Diners' Club was mainly used by foreigners, and thus constituted new business for them, whereas Carte Bleue would cut into their existing customer base without increasing purchases. They also had their own payment cards that they worried, correctly, Carte Bleue would undermine. Initially, France's *grands magasins* simply refused to accept payment by Carte Bleue.

Small retailers and restauranteurs in particular were upset by the new payment system. Because of the 1-franc fee added to each transaction, small purchases were especially costly under the Carte Bleue system. For purchases such as shoes or clothing, effective charges could be as high as 5 percent–6 percent of the cost of a purchase.[90] Associations representing small business fought against the Carte Bleue plan. Jean Paquette, president of the Conseil National du Commerce, the trade association that included small retailers, explained his objection: "The government asks us to stabilize prices, but they struggle to decrease our profits. The client should pay the banks for the payment services they provide."[91] The head of the CFPME, an association of small business interests, argued that a payment card without a credit facility would impose fees without increasing consumer purchases: "The real goal is to increase the base of clients for the banks." The general assembly of the CFPME voted unanimously against the Carte Bleue system.[92] Both the Paris Chamber of Commerce and Industry and the National Federation of the Hotel Industry also came out against the Carte Bleue.[93] The hotel sector had been trying for several

[90] Jean Arnaud, "La Carte Bleue: Dialogue ou Épreuve de Force," *Les Échos*, October 13, 1967.
[91] Catherine Nay, "La Carte Bleue Contre la Paperasse," *L'Express*, October 16, 1967.
[92] Jean-Claude Klotchkoff, "Les PME Attaquent la 'Carte Bleue'," *Paris-Presse*, October 28, 1967.
[93] *Le Monde*, November 17, 1967.

years in France to promote its own payment card, and it saw the Carte Bleue as a threat to that plan.[94] Although Carte Bleue did eventually prevail, struggles over retailer fees continued. As late as 1985, small shopkeepers in Midi-Pyrénées boycotted the Carte Bleue to protest the 2.5 percent they were being charged per payment. France's competition authority eventually found in their favor, and Carte Bleue was forced to accept a lower charge.[95]

The greatest competitor to the Carte Bleue was a rival card-based payment system called Intercarte.[96] Launched by competing banks (Banques Populaires and later Crédit Mutuel) in 1968, the Intercarte was in many ways more attractive for consumers and retailers. The Intercarte was a check card, of the kind that was being widely adopted at the time by banks in Germany. The card provided a complete guarantee for payments made with specialized Eurochèques of up to 500 francs. The retailer compared the signature on the card with that on the check, then wrote the number of the card on the back of the check. Payment was free for the retailer. A larger purchase could even be made with several Eurochèques, each written for up to 500 francs. For cardholders, the Intercarte charged no annual fee and allowed holders to withdraw money from any bank teller or automatic teller of the Crédit Mutuel or Banques Populaires. Checks could also be written in any of eight European currencies, and holders could use the card to access funds in any of thirty-seven countries.[97]

The launch of Eurochèque precipitated a protracted and hard-fought struggle with Carte Bleue. In 1976, the banks that participated in Carte Bleue began imposing a 10-franc fee per check for retailers who also accepted Eurochèques. As intended, many retailers opted simply to refuse to cash Eurochèques. Intercarte founders Crédit Mutuel and Banques Populaires protested before the Professional Association of Banks (APB), and the Carte Bleues banks finally agreed to stop the practice. By 1981, France had 1.4 million Cartes Bleues in circulation, and 500,000 Eurochèque cards (the new name of the Intercarte).[98] In 1984, Carte Bleue and Eurochèque merged to become the Carte Bancaire. Consolidated as the market leader, Carte Bancaire made broad strides to extend credit card use in France. A decade later, in 1994, French wallets and purses held 22 million Cartes Bancaires.[99] The next-largest payment card in distribution

[94] Jean-Claude Klotchkoff, "La Carte Bleue 'Fait' Chaque Jour 5.000 Adhérents," *Paris-Presse*, November 10, 1967.

[95] Jeanne Villeneuve, "Cartes de Paiement: Le Petit Commerce Fait Plier les Banques," *Libération*, September 30, 1985, 17.

[96] In 1976 the name was changed to Eurochèque.

[97] Jean-Marc de Preneuf, "La Bataille d'Eurochèque," *La Croix*, April 22, 1976.

[98] *Les Échos*, March 23, 1981.

[99] Tamara Thorgevsky, "Le Grand Saut est pour 1985," *Le Matin*, May 28, 1984; Yves Guihannec, "Ce que Vous Coûte Vraiment le Crédit," *L'Express*, November 28, 1985, 43; *Figaro-Économie*, May 14, 1990; *Figaro-Économie*, January 24, 1994.

was the Carte Aurore, a competing credit card that included a revolving credit facility that was offered by Cetelem. It had only 6 million users.[100]

From Personal Loans to Revolving Credit

The introduction of Carte Bleue in France coincided with a broad effort by banks to provide banking services directly to consumers. The trigger was a liberalization of branch banking in 1967 under the financial reforms of finance minister Michel Debré. In a *cours aux guichets*, banks hired new staff and opened new branch offices throughout France.[101] Banks that had traditionally relied heavily on business clients moved to attract household depositors. The share of French adults with bank accounts rose from 35 percent before the reforms to more than 90 percent by the 1980s.[102] Writing in 1970, Pascal Lebée, head of CIC Bank, explained: "It is a profound change.... The goal today is to have as many deposits from individuals as from companies, whereas before the proportions were roughly 25% and 75%."[103]

As had occurred in the United States, these banks began to offer personal loans as a way to attract new depositors, beginning in earnest in 1971 and 1972.[104] The activity was not entirely new for them; France's established commercial banks had occasionally offered such personal loans. But these were almost always provided as a special service to valued customers, and not a mass product.[105] In fact, France's banks had from the early 1960s faced pressure from consumer groups and trade unions to enter the small-loan sector. These groups argued that competition from banks would force down interest rates charged by consumer finance companies.[106] They therefore welcomed the launch of personal loans by France's commercial banks. The experience was ultimately disappointing. Repayment rates were low. To add insult to injury, the finance ministry in 1973 allowed consumer finance companies for the first time to make unsecured personal loans. This intensified competition and virtually drove banks out of the personal lending business. The experience made France's major commercial banks wary of offering small loans. They would not reenter the market for nearly a decade.

100 CHA, credit card data, 1994.

101 Christian de Boissieu, "Recent Developments in the French Financial System: An Overview," in Christian de Boissieu, ed., *Banking in France* (New York: Routledge, 1990), 2.

102 Jonathan Story, *The Political Economy of Financial Integration in Europe: The Battle of the Systems* (Cambridge, MA: MIT Press, 1997), 192; Michael Loriaux, *France after Hegemeny: International Change and Financial Reform* (Ithaca: Cornell University Press, 1991), 175.

103 Jean-Claude Klotchkoff, "Il y a Déjà Plus de 400.000 Cartes Bleues... " *Paris Press*, January 28, 1970.

104 *Les Échos*, December 19, 1974.

105 André Malterre, "Problème du Crédit à la Consommation," *Journal Officiel* 20, August 11, 1961, 761–776.

106 *Le Monde*, January 2, 1965.

When they did, it was in the context of financial deregulation in the early 1980s. Expansionary fiscal and monetary policy under Socialist President François Mitterrand's first term brought France to the financial brink. Under threat of reprisal from international investors, Mitterrand embraced a grand policy U-turn. Formerly nationalized companies were reprivatized. Government spending programs were reduced and monetary policy reigned in to hold down inflation. France's banking system, which had been at the heart of its state capitalism approach to economic development, began to be liberalized. Between 1984 and 1987, the entire French financial sector was dramatically liberalized. Among the changes were an abandoning of sectoral credit limits, set administratively under *encadrement de crédit*, and a shift in authority over banks from the finance ministry to the competition ministry.

For both banks and finance companies, liberalization changed their approach to consumer lending. For consumer finance companies, liberalization opened the market for revolving credit accounts of the kind that American consumers had long enjoyed. For banks, liberalization initiated a period of rapid expansion into the personal loan business, followed by another round of failure and retrenchment. Ironically, it was the failure of many personal loans that led France's commercial banks finally to experiment with revolving credit accounts.

In the past, France's state-led industrial policy had relied on banks to finance its projects, and banks became dependent on these investments for their profits. Liberalization changed this. Firms in France began to seek non-bank sources of capital. They increasingly began to look to the stock market, factoring, and self-financing through retained earnings.[107] Bank corporate lending fell from 159 billion francs in 1982 to 109 billion in 1983, corresponding to a steep rise in interest rates. However, even as interest rates began to fall off, corporate borrowing continued to decline. By 1986, outstanding corporate loans had fallen to 75 billion francs. As banks sought other sources of revenue, consumer lending became a focus of intense interest.[108] One observer noted: "Banks live from lending. Once they realized that companies had less and less need for them, they turned to households with increasing ease as credit was liberalized."[109] To break into the market, France's large banks allocated large blocks of funds to extending their consumer lending businesses. Crédit Agricole alone invested 20 billion francs in consumer credit in 1986 and 1987.[110] Through this push, they were able dramatically to increase their share of consumer lending

[107] Richard Deeg and Mary O'Sullivan, "The Financialization of Europe," paper presented at the Annual Meeting of the American Political Science Association, Philadelphia, 2006.

[108] Jean-Pierre Robin, "Crédit à la Consommation, les Français s'Americanisent," *La Vie Française*, June 21, 1987.

[109] Françoise Fressoz and Philippe Boulet-Gercourt, "Les Français Flambent à Crédit," *Libération*, August 13, 1987.

[110] Florence Paricard, "Consommation: Le Taux de Crédit Doit Baisser," *La Vie Française*, March 30, 1986.

market. Between 1984 and 1987, banks' share of total consumer lending grew from 18 percent to 25 percent.[111]

They accomplished this in three ways. First, they offered lower rates than the consumer finance companies. Whereas the latter were charging in the range of 15 percent to 18.25 percent during the mid-1980s, banks began offering rates from 12 percent to 16 percent.[112] They justified these lower rates on the basis of their lower cost of capital, but also on their detailed knowledge of their clients, many of whom were long-term depositors. Second, they began aggressively expanding their credit agreements with retailers. In 1986, for example, BNP allied for the first time with a retail chain (Euromarché) to provide a co-branded Carte Bleue.[113] Third, France's big banks started providing their best customers with access to revolving credit accounts. Traditionally, banks lent in the form of personal loans with fixed repayment schedules. Now, they began pitching revolving credit as a luxury product for their most reliable customers.[114]

The banks' plan failed for two main reasons. First, they had not made the necessary investments in skills or equipment that was required for success in consumer lending. As Jean-Christophe Goarin, head of the consumer finance company Groupe Paiement Pass, explained: "The handicap for banks is that they have too many products. We have only a few, but we present them well and they are well adapted to the needs of our clients."[115] Second, whereas consumer finance companies had embraced the idea of tracking past repayment as a predictor of future repayment, banks were still relying on their relationships with their depositors to hold down non-payments. They assumed that because they had known their clients for years, the risk associated with repayment would be low. Instead, they found that they faced higher default rates than did consumer finance companies. The high rate of defaults was aggravated by their effort to expand their customer base rapidly, which led some banks to offer loans indiscriminately. Pierre Marleix, head of the trade union-affiliated consumer group Association Force Oeuvrière Consommateur (AFOC), explained that banks "were increasingly unconcerned about finding reliable borrowers; they simply wanted to increase their loan volume in order to be big."[116]

By the early 1990s, most banks were moving to close smaller and delinquent accounts. It was clear that they would not be leading players in French consumer lending, at least not directly. Those that continued to lend focused their

[111] Françoise Fressoz and Philippe Boulet-Gercourt, "Les Français Flambent à Crédit," *Libération*, August 13, 1987.

[112] Françoise Fressoz and Philippe Boulet-Gercourt, "Les Français Flambent à Crédit," *Libération*, August 13, 1987.

[113] Florance Pricard, "La Carte Bleue Fait Crédit," *La Vie Française*, October 12–18, 1987.

[114] Crédit Agricole, for example, formed a consumer finance affiliate called Unibanque to offer revolving credit.

[115] Catherine Rigollet, "Le Bazar des Produits Financiers," *L'Express*, March 6, 1987.

[116] Françoise Fressoz and Philippe Boulet-Gercourt, "Les Français Flambent à Crédit," *Libération*, August 13, 1987.

lending on their most affluent customers.[117] Banks such as Crédit Agricole that had created their own consumer finance affiliates closed them.[118] What they did instead was start acquiring existing consumer finance companies. BNP Paribas bought Cetelem; Crédit Agricole bought Sofinco; Crédit Lyonnais bought "Citifinancement" from Citicorp France.[119] The combination of fewer competitors and high demand for ownership was good for the dedicated consumer finance companies. In 1992 alone, Cetelem stock rose 60 percent in value.[120]

Ironically, the failure of personal lending by banks did finally lead many of them to introduce new mass-market revolving credit accounts, but the reasons were mainly accidental. Faced with a surge of non-payments, banks discovered that they could avoid write-offs by converting distressed installment loans into revolving accounts that had longer repayment periods and flexible repayment schedules. Indeed research at the time found that only 1.1 percent of revolving accounts ended up in legal recovery, compared to 3.2 percent for traditional installment-style personal loans. Driven first by luxury and then by necessity, revolving loans as a share of total bank consumer loans grew from 8.5 percent in 1986 to 17 percent in 1990.[121]

The persistent failure of France's commercial banks to develop in-house consumer lending had broad regulatory implications. From the immediate postwar period until the move by banks to make consumer loans in the late 1980s, the banks mainly stood aside as the consumer loans were regulated. Most importantly, they never rallied in a sustained way behind the cause of consumer credit extension. Nor did they lend their own legitimacy to the small-loan market. A brief exception came during the period when banks made an effort to move into consumer lending, in the mid- and late 1980s. At that moment, with skin in the game, they became advocates of a more liberal approach to usury. They blocked a universal positive credit-rating database out of concern that finance companies would poach their customers. And they fought a liberal bankruptcy reform that would have given consumers access to automatic discharge. But this period of bank support was short-lived. As the large commercial banks began to step back from consumer lending in the early 1990s, a regulatory backlash also began.

117 Philippe Reclus, "Les Grands Réseaux s'Alignent sur le Taux à 9%," *La Tribune Desfossés*, September 7, 1993.

118 *Le Figaro*, May 30, 1991.

119 Renaud de la Baume, "Les Banques Peinent sur le Marché du Crédit à la Consommation," *La Tribune de L'Expansion*, March 26, 1992.

120 Roland Laskine, "Au Mieux de sa Forme," *La Vie Française*, January 9–15, 1993.

121 Roger Leron, Rapport sur l'Application de la Loi No 89–1010 du 31 Décembre 1989 Rélative à la Prévention et au Réglement des Difficultés Liées au Sûrendettement des Particuliers et des Familles, 1990, Annex II.

4

American Retailers and Credit Innovation

From the turn of the century until the 1970s, American retailers that sold on credit did so mainly as a customer convenience. Offering extended payment terms allowed them to attract and retain customers. During most of this period, few lenders earned any profits on their customer credit accounts. Most treated lending as a sales promotion, similar to advertising costs, and cross-subsidized the lending departments out of sales profits. The emphasis on customer convenience pushed early retailers toward innovations that were initially costly but also tailored to improve the shopping experience. The first was the credit card itself; the second was the revolving charge account. Both would eventually be adopted by bank lenders, but had their roots in retail.

Ultimately, the way in which American retailers managed their credit programs helped change public perceptions of credit. Because retailers focused on the customer experience, they developed collections techniques that were highly accommodating to consumer borrowers. They rarely harassed late borrowers. They also rarely pursued so-called hard collections, meaning repossession, because their goal was to attract customers. Instead, they discovered the value of timely, friendly reminders for keeping repayment rates high. In order to maintain amicable relations with borrower-customers, they were also rigorous about evaluating the creditworthiness of credit applicants. Together, these policies taught American households that store credit was hard to get, but once one was approved, convenient and forgiving. It also led them to one of the most important insights of modern lending: keeping customers happy and treating them with respect, along with careful management of accounts and collections, could dramatically reduce the apparent riskiness of consumer credit.

The Allure of the Credit Sale

Retail credit had deep roots in the nineteenth century, but it began to be popularized for the general public in the 1920s and 1930s in the form of two distinct products offered by different kinds of stores. Charge accounts were offered initially by high-end department stores to allow customers to pay for all of their purchases at the end of each month with no interest charge. Charge accounts were offered as both a convenience and a retainer for the most valued, and thus most affluent, customers. Retailers catering to working-class customers offered a different arrangement: installment credit, which allowed customers to pay for products in regular intervals over a longer time frame. Installment credit was intended for customers who did not have sufficient savings to purchase products outright.

This clear segregation of customers by credit type did not survive the Great Depression. With the economic downturn, charge-account customers began requiring more time to pay for their goods, and were given extended repayment terms. Conversely, working-class customers were increasingly given access to thirty-day charge accounts, allowing them to delay payment until the end of the month when they received their monthly salaries. In a survey of merchants in 1938, store owners estimated that 65 percent of their customers used charge accounts not for convenience but because they did not have enough cash to pay for what they charged.[1] Quite apart from the convenience of store credit, credit buyers also spent 25 percent more than cash buyers.[2] The popularity of retail credit, in either form, meant that it spread quickly through the sector. As large retailers began offering installment credit, small retailers found they had to follow suit in order to be able to compete, although their smaller scale and higher cost of providing credit eventually hurt many small shops.[3] In 1950, 140,000 retailers were registered with the Federal Reserve as offering credit.[4]

It was in this period of rapid retail credit extension that the idea of the modern credit card had its roots. The physical form of the modern credit card came from the retail Charga-Plates of the 1910s. Retailers still managed their own credit accounts, but these stamped metal plates allowed retailers to identify approved clients and to print the holder's name and address using a range of newly patented machines employing rollers and ink to transfer the raised information to a sales or credit slip. What was distinctive about the Charga-Plate system was that a customer only needed to carry one card. For each store at which the customer had a charge account, the Charga-Plate was notched at an exact spot that corresponded to that particular retailer. Rectangular notches on the top of the card indicated different store chains; rounded notches on the bottom corresponded to different cities. In an early variant on the general-purpose payment card, the Charga-Plate allowed each store to do its own

1 Arthur H. Hert, "Charge Accounts of Retail Merchants," *Annals of the American Academy of Political and Social Science* 196 (1938), 112.

2 *JC Penney Credit: 40th Anniversary Booklet*, 1998.

3 Meg Jacobs, *Pocketbook Politics: Economic Citizenship in Twentieth-Century America* (Princeton: Princeton University Press, 2005), 33.

4 *Statistiques et Études Financières* 21 (1954), 62.

accounting and billing, but left the customer with only one card in her or his wallet. The system was not entirely reliable. It quickly became clear to retailers who did not participate in the Charga-Plate plan that customers whose plates had many notches were more likely to be creditworthy. More than one retailer was caught using bootleg Charga-Plate imprinters without tangs to engage the notches, allowing them to accept any Charga-Plate card.

By 1935, 22 percent of all retail sales were made on charge cards. But none of these early "credit cards" offered credit for more than thirty days. They were in fact simply private payment cards. Extended credit was managed separately, typically through installment sale contracts that set regular payments lasting anywhere from six months to three years. In 1935, 11 percent of non-auto retail sales were made on such installment plans.[5] Many of these early card-payment systems disappeared in World War II with the tightening of government credit restrictions and the move to gas rationing, although most of the larger retail chains retained their Charga-Plate payment systems.[6]

In the late 1930s, retailers brought together the credit card format with another American invention: the revolving credit account. Unlike earlier installment or personal loans, revolving credit was not tied to a specific purchase or expenditure. Rather than applying for a new loan with each new need, revolving credit approved customers for any amount of credit up to a preset ceiling. Revolving credit had become so familiar to borrowers by the 1990s that it is difficult to capture the novelty and uncertainty that surrounded this new financial instrument when it was first introduced by a few American retailers in the late 1930s, then copied by American banks in the 1950s. The first revolving account was offered in 1938 by Bambergers, a retailing subsidiary of Macy's in Newark, New Jersey. At the time, retailers commonly offered fixed-repayment installment plans for specific products, as well as shorter-term "controlled accounts" with ninety-day repayment periods designed to help charge-account customers space out their repayments. Bambergers's idea was to set a global ceiling on credit extended to each of its customers, and then set their monthly repayment at one-sixth of that limit. Customers who bought less than a sixth of their total credit allotment would be expected to repay the full amount at the first billing. For larger purchases, it looked like an installment plan. For small purchases, the new scheme was equivalent to a traditional store charge account. M. L. Mans, head of credit at the retailer John Carrol Company in Newark, Ohio, made a further refinement. He had the idea of setting each customer's monthly repayment as a share of the customer's outstanding balance, rather than as a share of her or his total credit ceiling. This meant that even small purchases made on credit would be repaid over the full period of the loan. Managing this new system was more burdensome for the retailer, as the interest charged did

[5] Milan V. Ayres, "The Economic Function of the Sales Finance Company," *Journal of the American Statistical Association* 33/201 (1938), 69.

[6] Michel Schlosser and Gérard Tardy, *Les Cartes de Crédit* (Paris: Dunod, 1971).

not cover the considerable administrative costs. But it was especially attractive to consumers because it smoothed out monthly repayments over time.[7]

As with many of the early credit innovations, the idea of revolving credit spread rapidly. In 1939, Bloomingdale's introduced a revolving credit program as a supplement to its standard thirty-day charge account. The new extended-repayment account allowed stores to offer their credit services to customers who might not necessarily be able to pay off their account at the end of each month. Customers who applied and were rejected for a charge account could be offered the revolving credit account instead; charge-account customers who were found to be slow to pay might also be transferred to a revolving credit account.[8] In the mid-1950s, "dime" and variety stores catering to working-class customers began offering "budget" or "extended" credit plans that emulated the revolving credit plans of the large department stores. J. J. Newberry Co. introduced the Newberry Credit Plan that included plastic Charga-Plates similar to the metal cards that had been offered by the big department stores since the 1930s. Sears Roebuck launched its revolving charge account plan in February 1953. By the time JC Penney began experimenting with revolving credit accounts in 1957, it was already coming late to this activity. In 1959, an estimated 88 percent of department stores offered revolving credit accounts.[9]

Revolving credit accounts had a number of attractive features. First, they enabled stores to have more control over how much credit they gave to an individual. Rather than granting several installment loans to the same customer for each purchase, the revolving account set a global credit limit, typically equal to one month's pay. Second, it allowed stores to sell smaller items on credit. A customer buying a piece of furniture on credit could also put additional miscellaneous merchandise on credit – something that would not be possible with an installment loan. Third, they were appreciated by customers, and this built goodwill.[10] Department stores that offered both charge and revolving accounts were surprised to find their charge-account customers opting voluntarily for the revolving credit plans that had originally been intended for less-reliable customers. William Whyte later described this trend, in which products intended for the poor were adopted by the wealthy, as a "reversal of the usual trickle-down effect" that characterized most consumer products.[11]

[7] J. L. Hudson, the first large chain store to copy this revolving credit scheme from the John Carrol Co., is usually credited with inventing revolving credit. JCPCR, Recollections by Wallis B. Hocker, retired credit manager, 1989, responses to clarifying questions, 6–7.

[8] Winston C. Fournier, "Retailers Hike Sales with Revolving Credit," *Wall Street Journal*, June 22, 1956.

[9] Estimated by the Credit Management Division of the National Retail Merchant Association (NRMA). Lelia Easson, "New Developments in Consumer Credit," *Journal of Home Economics* (December 1959), 847.

[10] Arthur H. Hert, "Charge Accounts of Retail Merchants," *Annals of the American Academy of Political and Social Science* 196 (1938), 118.

[11] William H. Whyte, *The Organization Man* (Philadelphia: University of Pennsylvania Press, 2002), 328.

The rise of revolving credit accompanied a decline in the status of the charge account.[12] Some observers predicted, correctly, that revolving accounts would displace the traditional charge accounts. By the mid-1950s, one retail lender acknowledged that "the 30-day charge account as we've known it for years is definitely on the way out."[13]

Another attractive feature of the new revolving plans for retailers was that they brought in revenue. Unlike the thirty-day charge accounts, which earned no interest, most of the new revolving plans charged between 1 percent and 1.5 percent per month on the outstanding balance. Whether or not these revolving accounts covered their own administrative costs depended largely on scale and interest rate. Sears, the largest retail lender, claimed already in 1954 that the 1.5 percent monthly rate (18 percent annually) it charged on its revolving plan covered its expenses "under normal circumstances."[14] JC Penney's credit plan, the second-largest retail plan in the country, became profitable for the first time only in 1974 despite being founded in 1958. Stores such as J. J. Newberry's and Filenes, which were regional rather than national and charged only 1 percent per month, never managed to cover the cost of their credit programs from interest income.

For retailers, the lack of profitability was not a major deterrent, because credit had always been a cost center. What made revolving credit accounts attractive for them was simply that the alternative forms of consumer credit were even more costly. Charge accounts earned nothing, and installment accounts during the 1950s typically charged around 12 percent annually. Compared to this, the 13–20 percent annualized interest on the outstanding balance of revolving accounts was attractive. Surprisingly, these accounts also experienced favorable repayment rates. Although customers granted revolving accounts often could not qualify for the thirty-day charge account, retailers found that repayment rates for the two kinds of accounts were roughly the same. Allied Stores reported the same low nonpayment rate, 0.4 percent of credit sales, on both kinds of accounts in 1952.[15] As one retailer effused: "If you want to know whether we like the [revolving] plan, just ask us if we like money."[16]

For all their advantages, the new revolving accounts also posed new management challenges. First, they required a large amount of capital to finance. The longer repayment periods allowed by revolving accounts meant that sales on revolving credit accounted for a disproportionate share of store accounts

[12] Arthur H. Hert, "Charge Accounts of Retail Merchants," *Annals of the American Academy of Political and Social Science* 196 (1938), 111.

[13] Winston C. Fournier, "Retailers Hike Sales with Revolving Credit," *Wall Street Journal*, June 22, 1956.

[14] Winston C. Fournier, "Retailers Hike Sales with Revolving Credit," *Wall Street Journal*, June 22, 1956.

[15] Allied Stores Corporation, *1952 Annual Report*, 1953, 12.

[16] William H. Whyte, *The Organization Man* (Philadelphia: University of Pennsylvania Press, 2002), 327.

receivables. A study by the National Retail Merchants Association found that whereas charge accounts in 1959 accounted for 70 percent of all credit sales and 39 percent of receivables, revolving accounts that accounted for only 21 percent of sales made up nearly the same share (35 percent) of receivables.[17] And, unlike traditional installment loans offered by retailers, revolving credit accounts could not easily be resold to banks or finance companies. Retailers either had to collaborate closely with sales finance companies to finance these programs or create their own consumer finance subsidiaries to raise and manage the necessary funds.

A second challenge concerned customers who exceeded their credit limit. Initially, the plans called for customers to immediately pay back any amount that exceeded their credit limit. But retailers worried that this could cause them to lose customers. One response was to increase interest rates as the volume of credit increased. In 1956, the retailer Famous-Barr began offering a revolving plan with no ceiling, but with interest rates ranging up to 20 percent as the outstanding balance increased. This so-called chart plan, which was also quickly adopted by Federated Department Stores, is probably the first systematic application of the principle of applying higher interest rates to riskier borrowers.[18]

Collections raised its own distinct set of challenges. Retailers needed to appear customer friendly while keeping customers paying and the credit plan profitable. The secret, they found, was careful attention to communications with customers. The Ruedebusch System, developed in the early 1910s by the Wisconsin retailer Charles Ruedebusch Company, provided the founding example of the "new collections" approach. The core of the system was a new method of more rigorous accounts bookkeeping and a set of form letters that were sent to clients at different stages of late payment under different circumstances. Ruedebusch explained: "Our former crude methods always caused considerable irritation on both sides and kept a lot of persons away from our store, while we now make all our charge accounts – even uncollectible ones – bring us in extra trade."[19] Applying the Ruedebusch system to revolving accounts was administratively challenging. Because the balance on the account changed from month to month, bills had to be redrawn at the end of each month. And because overdue accounts were blocked from further purchase, only prompt repayment allowed continued purchasing. As one collections expert advised: "Immediate awareness of delinquency is extremely important, since the longer a delinquent account is unattended, the harder it becomes to collect.... A delinquent account is a stagnant

17 Estimated by the Credit Management Division of the National Retail Merchant Association (NRMA). Lelia Easson, "New Developments in Consumer Credit," *Journal of Home Economics* (December 1959), 847.

18 Fournier.

19 Edward Hall Gardner, *New Collections Methods: A Systematic Treatment of the Place of Collections in Marketing* (New York: Ronald Press, 1919), 397–398; Edward Hall Gardner and Frank A. Fall, *Effective Collection Methods* (New York: Ronald Press Company, 1932).

account."[20] The secret for successful retailers was to combine administratively rigorous bookkeeping, customer-friendly reminders, and gracious forbearance in cases of special hardship. Wallis Hocker, JC Penney's credit manager in the 1960s, recalled the company's care to avoid collection pressures that might lead customers to hardships such as divorce or job loss. "To give full consideration to the customers' problems while protecting the company assets was a continuing challenge."[21] Retailers that found the right balance could attract and retain customers, increase sales, and, by the mid-1970s, even make some profit on interest income.

Sources of Finance

Early retailers without sufficient capital to finance their installment credit plans on their own typically resold their credit contracts to independent sales finance companies. By the end of the 1930s, they were financing 60 percent of all retail credit sales. This was the heyday of the American sales finance company. By the early 1950s, everything had changed. Partly the change was brought on by commercial banks, which began purchasing bundles of retail loan contracts (a practice called "discounting") as a means of financing retail credit.[22] But it was also the result of retailers who opted to bring their retail credit financing operations in-house.

There were several reasons for retailers to take back the financing function in their sales. First, because sales companies typically discounted at a higher rate than the interest charged to customers – which was often zero – retailers found themselves making ever larger payments to sales finance companies. Even if they could not break even on their credit accounts, larger retailers felt that they could at least reduce the cost of the service by providing it in-house. More importantly, retailers worried about the quality of the service provided by independent sales finance companies. They tended, for example, to use more aggressive, less-customer-friendly collections techniques. These techniques were effective for collections, but they were damaging for retailers, whose primary goal in offering credit was to attract and retain customers.[23] Perhaps most consequentially, retailers felt that they were missing a valuable opportunity to build a lasting relationship with customers. Charge-account customers, which were typically self-financed by the retailers, were already the target of early direct mail campaigns. Retailers saw the regular billing cycle of

[20] Harold B. Smith, *Effective Collection Methods and Control* (New York: National Retail Merchants Association, 1962), 25.

[21] JCPCR, Recollections by Wallis B. Hocker, retired credit manager, 1989, responses to clarifying questions, 2.

[22] Bank share of auto lending rose more modestly, from 30 percent of total credit offered in 1939 to 40 percent in 1952. UFB, "Notes sur le Financement des Ventes à Crédit aux États-Unis," December 1952, Cetelem Historical Archives, 5.

[23] David Caplovitz, *The Poor Pay More* (New York: Free Press, 1967), 22.

the installment business as another means to reach out directly to a large and growing group of customers with a proven willingness to buy.[24]

As the funding requirements of consumer borrowing grew, the large national retailers formed subsidiaries to finance their own receivables. These included the Macy Credit Corp., City Stores Credit Corp., Montgomery Ward Credit Corp., Sears Roebuck Acceptance Corp., W. T. Grant Credit Corp., and Gamble-Aldens Credit Corp.[25] Unlike independent finance corporations, these subsidiaries played no role in managing the loans. They also earned no interest income from the loans. They earned revenue only from service fees paid by the retailer. Initially, the purpose of these captive retail finance companies was to make it easier to raise funds from banks that tended to be hesitant to fund retail receivables directly. But the new approach to funding had other advantages. By cutting out the third-party finance companies, retailers were able to become much more creative about their consumer credit programs. This proved essential for financing revolving credit accounts, which finance companies would not discount. But it also allowed creative forms of credit targeted to specific consumer needs. In the late 1950s, for example, Neiman Marcus was offering five different credit plans. These included its signature Pivot Account, which combined the functions of a charge account and installment credit; a twelve-month installment Table Top Plan for china, glassware, and silver; and a Summer Plan for purchasing winter furs that allowed buyers to begin making payments during the summer, pick up the fur in the fall, and continue paying off the fur through the spring.[26]

Inventing Profitable Lending: The Penney Card

In the spring of 1958, the Board of Directors of America's largest cash-and-carry retail chain, JC Penney, gathered in New York City to discuss the possibility of selling goods on credit. Credit sales would mark a major change in the company's historic practice, and a stinging rebuttal of its founder's philosophy. James Cash Penney was, as his name intimated, deeply averse to offering credit. When he opened his first retail store, the Golden Rule, in 1902 in Kemmerer, Wyoming, critics and investors argued that he could not succeed selling only on a cash basis. A typical mining town, Kemmerer had 14 saloons, 2 brothels, and a population of 1,000. Most of the miners were perpetually in debt to the coal company store.[27] But the cash-only Golden Rule proved to be a hit. Customers appreciated the lower prices Penney charged and the high quality of his goods relative to those offered in the company store. For the next sixty

24 Arthur H. Hert, "Charge Accounts of Retail Merchants," *Annals of the American Academy of Political and Social Science* 196 (1938), 112.

25 John F. Stack, "Giant Retailers Banking on Wholly-Owned Credit Firms," *Women's Wear Daily*, November 21, 1966.

26 Stanley Marcus Collection (SMC), Degolyer Library, Southern Methodist University, Dallas, TX, box 104, folder 12, Credit Department, Brochure for Charga-Plate.

27 JCPCR, Press/News Releases, July–Dec 1958, News Release, September 5, 1957.

years, as competing retail chains moved to lure customers by offers of sales credit, the JC Penney chain stuck with its cash-and-carry model. By the 1958 meeting, JC Penney was out of step with the rest of American retailing.

For James Cash Penney, opposition to credit sales was more than a business niche. It was, at its heart, a deeply personal conviction. JC Penney CEO William "Mil" Batten, who oversaw the company's move to credit, recalled that paying in cash was for Mr. Penney "almost a religion."[28] Cash emphasized the high social costs of credit both for borrowers and non-borrowers. On the one hand, he worried about stress for families that took on debt. JC Penney advertisements from the early 1950s read: "Here the policy is to *Pay Cash*, and consequently the First of each month, and every day after it, can be faced without fear of unpaid bills and installment charges.... 'Charge it' is one of the most wasteful expressions in the English language."[29] On the other hand, he saw credit as unfair to those who abstained. He noted that credit would raise the cost of goods for those who did not borrow, as retailers at the time regularly cross-subsidized credit sales from non-credit sales. In a 1948 speech, Penney warned: "Today, millions of people are paying other people's bills. But they don't know it. Industrious, honest folk always have to pay the bills of those who are unable or unwilling to pay. And that is just what you are doing when you do business on the time or credit basis."[30]

However, for new store chains competing in the fragmented American market that emerged at the end of World War II, the logic of offering retail credit was virtually irresistible. As the JC Penney corporate board convened in New York, Mil Batten made the pitch for offering credit. It attracted new customers. It helped to retain and increase the purchase volume of existing customers. It allowed retailers to move up-market both into higher-quality products and into larger consumer durables that fit in the expanded floor space of the new suburban stores. Indeed, some chain retailers had come to see consumer credit as their primary function, and merchandise as a secondary activity.[31] Although not pushing this far, Batten saw credit as a means to ensure that American families would stick with JC Penney as the retailer followed those families into the country's booming suburbs. As each board member expressed his support for Batten's proposal, James Cash Penney, now retired but retaining a seat on the board, listened. Then he spoke:

> I have heard... these arguments many times before. They did not persuade me in the past. They do not persuade me now. I agree that if we go into credit we will increase our sales and our profits. In my mind, that is not the issue. The issue is a moral one. We all know that there will be times when business is very hard to get. Profits will

[28] JCPCR, Oral History Interview with William Batten, Session 1, Document #1071L, July 16, 1987, Interviews 1–2, 2–7.

[29] JCPCR, Press/News Releases, July–Dec 1958, JC Penney ad copy.

[30] Nearly all retailers at the time cross-subsidized their credit sales from non-credit sales. *Penney News*, January 1948.

[31] "Cash and Caution," *Forbes Finance Monthly Magazine*, March 1, 1958.

be under pressure, and management during those times will try very hard to get sales and profits. With credit you will have a tool by which it's going to be possible to oversell the customer and help get them into financial difficulties. I know you won't do that intentionally. It will only happen because you are trying to maintain sales and profits. It will be a by-product of that effort. And I think that is wrong. It is wrong for the Company to contribute to people getting into financial difficulty. Of course, it is easy for me to say what I have said, because I do not have responsibility for the company.... You believe that this is the right thing to do, and you believe it very deeply. You have no choice. You must do it.[32]

A vote was taken, and Mr. Penney was the only board member to dissent.

Fourteen years later, the year after James Cash Penney died, his prophecy was fulfilled. Facing a downturn in demand, JC Penney moved credit sales into its own department and began a major advertising campaign to sign up new customers for the JC Penney Card. Its campaign, which pioneered mass mailing techniques that would later become commonplace for marketing credit, was successful beyond their expectations. By 1987, another fourteen years later, JC Penney's credit division had become the second-largest provider of consumer credit in America, and the largest source of profits for JC Penney.

Penney was not alone among the early generation of JC Penney pioneers who felt that the move to credit betrayed a basic principle. In 1964, Penney was invited to Los Angeles for a meeting of retired store managers convened by Roy Johnson. Johnson had worked for the company in Seattle, where he had been the manager of its largest store. At that meeting, the retirees railed against the company's decision to accept credit and asked Penney to approach the board in order to have Mil Batten fired. Mr. Penney responded by touring the country to visit local store managers. What he found was a generational shift, with the newer store managers showing greater enthusiasm for the credit plans. For them, credit had become inseparable from the broader logic of retailing. Writing to a store manager in Albuquerque in 1966, Penney, then ninety-one years old, confided, "It was a very difficult matter for me to consent to go on a credit basis."[33]

JC Penney's relatively late move to offer consumer credit offers insights into the economic, technological, and organizational challenges that consumer credit posed for large retailers. JC Penney initially launched two different credit plans. One was a "title retention" installment plan for durable goods. The second was a store card, the Penney Charge Card, which combined charge card and revolving account functions. Either the Penney Charge Card balance could be paid off at the end of the month at no cost, or any unpaid balance could be repaid in monthly tranches subject to an interest rate of 1.5 percent per month

[32] JCPCR, Oral History Interview with William Batten, session 1, document #1071L, July 16, 1987, Interviews 1–2, 2/10–2/13.

[33] JCPCR, Mr. Penney on Credit, Letter to Martin Vancil, June 22, 1966.

(18 percent annually).[34] In introducing these programs, JC Penney began cautiously. In 1957, it ran a pilot lending program in twenty-four stores. The goal of the study concerned one of Mr. Penney's basic objections, plural to providing credit: "We had to create a Penney charge plan that would protect Penney cash customers from paying any kind of penalty."[35] In the first four months it received 80,000 applications and approved 68,000 for credit accounts. By the end of 1957, credit represented 22 percent of sales at the test stores, and repayment rates were favorable. In the following year, JC Penney extended the experiment to 169 stores. When the results from that study were deemed favorable, Mil Batten announced that credit would be offered in all of its stores by 1963.[36] When the credit rollout was complete, in 1962, Penney had put 4 million charge cards into circulation. By 1963, credit accounted for a quarter of total sales.

In certain ways, JC Penney benefited from its late move to credit. Partly this was fortuitous. During the early and mid-1950s, the company had remained primarily in soft goods (mainly clothing) as other chain retailers had moved into more expensive household equipment sold on credit. In 1955, the market for household refrigerators and stoves slumped, hurting many retailers. But sales of soft goods remained strong, and JC Penney continued to expand. JC Penney also enjoyed late-mover advantages in technology. By the time it introduced its credit program, computer systems were just coming online that made it possible to automate many of the administrative functions. In 1962, JC Penney purchased IBM's new 1401 computer systems for each of its four regional consumer credit offices. Computerization allowed JC Penney to centralize credit decisions. For any sale over $5, the sales person had to call into her or his regional credit center for approval.[37] Central credit approval by regional credit centers gave the company greater control over credit risk. It also made it possible for JC Penney to offer the first retail card that could be used in any of its stores nationwide.[38] By introducing centralized credit approvals from the outset, JC Penney avoided the organizational struggles other stores faced when they tried to wrest credit-granting authority away from individual store managers. By 1967, JC Penney had 12 million charge account customers and $1 billion in credit sales accounting for 38 percent of total turnover. The regional credit

[34] Penney only applied interest charges to the balance that remained after any payments had been deducted. This meant that the first month of credit was free, even if it was going to be paid back over time.

[35] JCPCR, Credit – 1959 Spring Convention, Section on Credit, "Your 1959 Spring Convention 'Report to the Partners,'" Condensed for presentation to all Penney Management Associates by the Store Manager, 5.

[36] JCPCR, President's Report on Credit, May 1960, "The President's Report," Remarks of William M. Batten, President, JC Penney Company, at the Annual Shareholders' Meeting, May 26, 1960.

[37] JCPCR, Credit – "How to Write a Sale," 1960.

[38] JCPCR, Updates on Credit – W. M. Batten Speeches, 1962–1964, 6.

centers, now eleven in number, again became early customers for IBM's new 360 mainframes.[39]

Even as its credit division grew, JC Penney was careful to emphasize that its credit operation was intended solely to promote the sales goals of the company. As Mil Batten, the company's CEO, told the annual shareholders' meeting in 1962, "Though we have one of the largest, most efficient and highly-mechanized credit operations in the country, we continue in our firm belief that the profit potential of our credit system lies in the selling of *merchandise* . . . not in service charge income."[40] Through the 1960s, its credit policies reflected this sales priority. Late-payment fees were kept low. Reminder letters sent to customers were cordial. Accounts more than six months late were simply canceled. Even in its installment plans, for which JC Penney retained title to products during the repayment period, repossession was never attempted. The Penney Card was marketed passively and to existing customers. Sales clerks were instructed to ask every customer at the check-out point: "May I have your charge card?" They were then urged to explain the non-credit benefits: the safety of not carrying cash; the advantage of being able to buy products on temporary sale even if the customer did not have enough cash; nationwide acceptance; and the value of the end-of-month statement to track expenses.[41] In 1964, JC Penney created a wholly owned financing subsidiary to raise funds to purchase credit contracts. But the management of credit extension and collections was all retained within the JC Penney retail operation.[42] Wallis Hocker, a JC Penney credit manager during this early period of the credit plan, described its goals: "The credit executive . . . should provide the means of increasing and maintaining profitable merchandise sales, of controlling bad debt and of enhancing customer relations."[43]

Despite these efforts to make credit subservient to the interests of merchandizing, the potential for making consumer credit a profit center was hard to ignore. In 1971, under pressure from lagging sales growth, JC Penney management decided to reduce the monthly required payment schedule for its revolving credit plan. The move was not dramatic. Whereas borrowers in the past were required to pay 10 percent of their maximum balance monthly, Penney in 1971 decided to reduce this slightly. On a balance ranging between $150 and $200, for example, the consumer would now have to make a minimum payment of $10 rather than $15. For Penney, the change offered a range of benefits at no measurable cost. Lower minimum monthly payments extended customer repayment periods, enabling them to carry higher balances. It also lowered

39 Annual Report, 1967, JC Penney Credit Corporation.

40 JCPCR, Updates on Credit – W. M. Batten Speeches, 1962–1964, Remarks of William M. Batten, president, JC Penney Company, at the Annual Shareholders' Meeting, May 15, 1962, 3–4.

41 JCPCR, Credit Selling Charge Accounts, 1967, 3, 7.

42 The financing company earned a simple fee paid by JC Penney, and unrelated to the performance of the consumer lending operations. Annual Report, 1965, JC Penney Credit Corporation.

43 JCPCR, Recollections by Wallis B. Hocker, retired credit manager, 1989, 1.

the rate of missed payments, as customers faced lower monthly obligations. Both effects increased interest income from credit accounts. Internal company communications prior to the decision made clear that their primary goal was to "produce an increase in finance charge." Only as a secondary consideration did they note a "side benefit" of potential increased sales.[44]

JC Penney also changed the way it assessed interest on revolving accounts. By the 1960s, many of its competitors, and in particular Sears, had adopted the so-called prior balance method of calculating interest on its revolving accounts. In this scheme, which ultimately became the standard for the industry, accounts for which the entire balance was not paid at the end of the month were charged interest on the entire balance of the first month. JC Penney initially objected to the prior balance approach on the grounds that it was unfair to consumers. It instead used an "adjusted balance" approach in which only the balance remaining after the first 30 days was subject to interest charge.[45] In 1972, it shifted to the prior balance method.[46] The impact of these changes on interest income was positive and dramatic.[47] For the first time since it had begun offering credit, the credit division in 1972 raised nearly enough interest income to cover its operating costs.

Convinced that the credit division could become a profit center rather than a cost center, and in the face of a lagging economy because of the 1973 OPEC oil embargo, JC Penney management decided to launch its first company-wide credit promotion campaign. Penney had never made a concerted effort to promote its credit program beyond its own customers. Although some mention of the Penney Charge Card had been included in advertisements sponsored by individual stores, such efforts were purely ad hoc. The new centralized credit campaign would be run by the credit division and have its own dedicated funding. New initiatives included a chain-wide schedule of "credit days" on which customers using the Penny Charge Card received 10 percent off on all sales.[48] They also experimented with phone, door-to-door, and direct-mail campaigns to promote their credit plan. They found that direct mail had a far lower yield (application and approval rate) than either door-to-door or phone solicitation, but that it was so much cheaper that it offered the lowest-cost means to acquire new customers.[49] The new credit campaign seems to have been effective. Active Penny Charge Card customers grew from 9.3 million in

[44] JCPCR, Credit Matters, July 1971, Credit Intra-Company Correspondence, from R. J. Brown, Credit Department, "Terms Extension," October 6, 1971; also, E. Petti to W. G. Hocker, Intra-Company Correspondence, "Re: The impact of Reducing the Minimum Payment Schedule," February 24, 1971.

[45] "The Credit Crunch," *Penney News*, April–May 1971, section II.

[46] JCPCR, Recollections by Wallis B. Hocker, retired credit manager, 1989, 9.

[47] Lewis Mandell, *The Credit Card Industry: A History* (Boston: Twayne, 1990), 72.

[48] JCPCR, Credit: Credit Growth Campaign, 1973, "Credit Promotion Recommendations and Concepts," 1973, 6.

[49] JCPCR, Credit: Credit Growth Campaign, 1973, Note from L. A. Latour to F. J. Depkovich, "Credit Promotions – New Store Openings," December 23, 1970.

1973 to 15.4 million in 1982.[50] Credit sales grew from $2.2 billion (39 percent of sales) in 1973 to $5.2 billion (47 percent of sales) in 1982. With greater scale and more interest income, JC Penney's credit operation became profitable for the first time in 1975. It fell back into losses in 1979 and 1980, when high inflation ate into interest revenue. Starting in 1981, however, credit became a large and growing profit center for JC Penney. No longer simply a means to sell merchandise, the consumer credit division had become a source of profitability in its own right.

JC Penney's attitude toward credit changed. In order to put a price on the services it provided to the retail side of the business, the credit division charged an internal fee for credit transactions that was equal to the rate (1–2 percent) charged by third-party credit cards (primarily Master Charge and Visa).[51] As the company newsletter explained: "Credit has become such an important part of today's retailing equation that we can no longer afford to subsidize it."[52] The credit division was also given greater autonomy in how it managed credit approvals and collections. New statistically grounded behavioral collections techniques adopted in 1983 were designed to optimize repayment rather than customer satisfaction or retention for the retail stores.[53] Finally, in 1986, the company took the decision to raise annual interest rates for the first time, from 18 percent to 21 percent.[54] Ralph Spurgin, the head of the credit division, explained the reasoning in his presentation to the JC Penney Management Council: "In the past, consumers have generally not been rate-sensitive. Our surveys have consistently shown that they are more concerned about annual card fees than finance charge rates."[55] With credit now an important source of profitability for the company, it made sense to provide credit at the highest price it could without scaring away customers. Less than thirty years after Mr. Penney had voiced his warning about the siren call of credit, his worst vision for the future had come to pass.

Credit and Technology

From the start of its credit program, JC Penney's management made substantial investments to improve operations and lower costs. Beginning in the early 1960s, Penney management began working closely with both IBM and

[50] JCPCR, JCP Credit – 10-Year Strategic Plan, 1983–1993, Part 1, JC Penney Credit Division, Strategic Plan, April 1983, A-7.

[51] JCPCR, JCP Credit – 10-Year Strategic Plan, 1983–1993, Part 1, JC Penney Credit Division, Stategic Plan, April 1983.

[52] "Credit Card Rates: Fact vs. Fiction," *JC Penney Today* 51/1 (1986), 4.

[53] JCPCR, JCP Credit – 10-Year Strategic Plan, 1983–1993, Part 1, JC Penney Credit Division, Stategic Plan, April 1983.

[54] JCPCR, JCP Credit – 10-Year Strategic Plan, 1983–1993, Part 2, B-3.

[55] JCPCR, Credit: Credit Rates, 1986–1987, *Ralph Spurgin, Presentation: JC Penney Finance Charge Rates*, Management Council, January 27, 1986, 11.

National Cash Register (NCR) to develop a point-of-sale machine that would allow them to process Penney credit cards at any of their stores. IBM spent $20 million studying the idea, then backed out. As Penney CEO Mil Batten recalled the conversation, IBM replied: "These specifications are really a small computer. We don't think there's ever going to be any kind of market for small computers."[56] In 1968, JC Penney purchased the NCR 280, the first point-of-sale equipment that allowed stores to track inventory, though not process credit sales. That project waited until 1974, when it leased 7,000 sales credit communications terminals and eleven System 4000 computers from TRW. By 1975, JC Penney had created a nationwide Interconnect System that enabled instant credit authorization from any of the stores. Other lenders were making similar investments. In 1970, the Interbank (MasterCard) credit network introduced the Omniswitch system, based on three IBM 360 machines. In 1973, the BankAmericard (Visa) network introduced a similar system, called Base I, which provided twenty-four-hour credit-approval services. Its average response time was eight seconds.[57]

The combination of telecommunications and computing provided the platform for more sophisticated accounts processing. In 1977, JC Penney began to deploy new statistical risk-evaluation systems at each of its twenty-two regional credit offices. Managers estimated that these systems would increase credit application approval rates by 18 percent.[58] Automated IBM remittance processing equipment was installed in 1978.[59]

Each of these investments helped streamline credit processing. Interestingly, they did not reduce the cost of making loans. In fact, account administration rose as a share of funds lent – from 4.7 percent to 5.1 percent – over the decade from 1973 to 1982. The cost of financing also rose over this period, from 4.8 percent to 5.5 percent of funds lent. Provisions for bad debt did decline, from 2.8 percent to 2.6 percent, but not enough to offset higher administrative and financing costs. Instead, virtually all of the profitability for 1981 and 1982 came from the increase in the effective interest rate. Between 1973 and 1982, interest income measured as a share of total outstanding loans rose from 11.5 percent to 15.3 percent. This rise in interest income had two sources. First, as a result of state-level usury reform, JC Penney was able to increase its lending rate to a uniform 18 percent virtually across the country. Second, a growing number of Penney Credit Card holders who had previously used their cards only as charge cards, and therefore paid no interest, began carrying a balance. These changes drove a burst in new revenue.

[56] JCPCR, Oral History Interview with William Batten, session 1, document #1071L, July 16, 1987, 7–29.

[57] Lewis Mandell, *The Credit Card Industry: A History* (Boston: Twayne, 1990), 62.

[58] "Report to Credit Management," *JC Penney Management Report* 4/8 (September 1977).

[59] JCPCR, Credit: Credit Growth Campaign, 1975, Steve Kernkraut, "Update: Net Cost of Credit," Internal document, Credit Department, September 28, 1975, 1, 8.

Credit was not a salve for all retailers. W. T. Grant was a dime-store-format mass discounter founded in 1906 in Lynn, Massachusetts. Through the 1950s, it grew to be the second-largest variety store chain after JC Penney, with more than a thousand outlets countrywide by 1960. In 1975, it also became the second-largest bankruptcy filing in the United States.[60] The primary cause of its failure was the mismanagement of consumer credit. Like nearly every other major retailer in the United States, W. T. Grant began offering credit soon after World War II. It introduced coupon-book installment credit in 1946. In the late 1950s, W. T. Grant followed other retailers into the consumer durables market, at the same time updating its credit system. In 1961, it began offering a new thirty-day revolving credit card. It initially resold its installment contracts to banks, then, in 1966, formed a captive finance company called the W. T. Grant Credit Corporation to finance its revolving accounts.[61] It sold refrigerators and washing machines under its own store brand, Bradford, and relied heavily on credit to promote sales. Credit sales rose from only 8 percent of total sales in 1956 to 17 percent in 1963 and 25 percent by 1969. But the early success hid underlying problems.

W. T. Grant confronted two challenges that were typical of early revolving-credit programs. The first was that W. T. Grant did not centralize credit approvals. Individual managers were given strong incentives to sell on credit, but bad debts were never charged back to local stores, giving local managers little incentive to evaluate customer creditworthiness. Only 5 percent of all credit applicants were ever screened with a credit bureau.[62] As one contemporary remarked: "About the only requirement was for the customer to sign his name."[63] Second, W. T. Grant's decentralized system of credit entailed high administrative costs. In 1961, the cost of administering its credit program amounted to 12 percent of credit sales, compared to only 4 percent for industry leaders Sears and JC Penney.[64] In 1975, as the store was about to collapse, the company move to streamline credit administration and centralize credit approvals, but by that time it was too late.[65] The painful collapse of the W. T. Grant empire, and the high price that investors paid for a disorderly unwinding, became the main impetus for the 1978 reform act. The same act also liberalized household access to automatic discharge in personal bankruptcy.

60 "Grant Goes Under," *Time*, October 13, 1975.

61 *New York Times*, January 11, 1966.

62 Tennant Tranchin, "The W. T. Grant Bankruptcy," Senior Honors Thesis, Harvard College, April 1977, 109.

63 William Weitzel and Ellen Jonsson, "Reversing the Downward Spiral: Lessons from W. T. Grant and Sears Roebuck," *The Executive* 5/3 (1991), 15.

64 Tennant Tranchin, "The W. T. Grant Bankruptcy," Senior Honors Thesis, Harvard College, April 1977, 136–137.

65 In 1974, a consortium of 143 banks extended Grant $600 million secured against its consumer credit receivables. They moved to accept Master Charge and BankAmerica cards and slowed credit extension on their own credit program. *Wall Street Journal*, October 3, 1975.

The Rise of Universal Cards

Perhaps ironically, newfound profitability spelled the end for branded retail credit. The same forces that made retail lending profitable also raised the profile of bank-sponsored credit cards. In 1984, universal bank credit cards exceeded all other classes of bank lending in terms of profitability.[66] Initially, these cards were embraced only by retailers that were too small to have their own brand of card. By the mid-1980s, however, virtually all retailers had begun accepting universal bankcards.

Large retail chains that had their own card programs initially rejected universal bankcards, for three reasons. For national chains such as JC Penney and Sears, the 3–5 percent service fee charged by banks was higher than what it cost them to manage their own credit systems. Moreover, because the goal of retail credit was to promote sales of products, they saw the more aggressive collections used by banks as counterproductive. JC Penney's internal newspaper reported: "With our own credit system, we are able to control not only the kind of plans we offer, but also the criteria used for extending credit and the procedures for handling inquiries and adjustments." Finally, large retail chains used their monthly billing to distribute promotional material to its customers. These mailings served as a "periodic reminder of the relationship that exists between Penney's and the customer."[67] Accepting universal bank cards risked losing contact with reliable customers. These objections were a major obstacle to the proliferation of universal bank cards. Contemporary observers attributed the failure of Chase Manhattan's CMCP card primarily to the unwillingness of the big New York retailers to accept it alongside their own branded cards.[68]

Two factors eventually won retailers, large and small, over to universal bankcards. First, local and regional store chains found they did not have the scale or expertise to administer their credit plans at a lower cost than the fees charged by banks, especially as those fees began to decline. Second, a number of U.S. states began in the late 1960s and early 1970s to lower their statutory usury caps on retail credit from 18 percent to 12 percent or even 10 percent. Because bank cards were able to recover some of the cost of lending through customer and retailer fees, banks were hurt relatively less than retail lenders by these rate-cap reductions.[69] By 1971, many stores that had formerly managed their own credit programs, including big chains such as Murphy's, Kroger, and Kmart, had closed their own credit services and were relying on bank cards.[70] As the number of customers with bank cards grew, even the largest retailers eventually accepted them. In 1971, JC Penney's vice president for

66 Lewis Mandell, *The Credit Card Industry: A History* (Boston: Twayne, 1990), 78.

67 *Penney News*, April–May 1971, Section II, "The Credit Crunch," 6.

68 Michel Schlosser and Gérard Tardy, *Les Cartes de Crédit* (Paris: Dunod, 1971), 9.

69 JCPCR, Robert W. Johnson and Edgar A. Pessemier, Report on Long-Term Strategy for Retail Credit, 1971, 7.

70 JCPCR, Credit Matters, July 1971, Intra-Company Correspondence, from W. P. Campbell to K. Alexson, "Re: Bank Credit Cards," October 1, 1971.

finance mused, "I don't know of any individuals who would want to substitute a single master credit system for their various retail charge accounts – as has sometimes been proposed for the coming 'cashless society.'"[71] Nonetheless, JC Penney accepted MasterCard in 1979 and Visa in 1980. In 1980, banks were providing half of all retail credit in the United States.[72]

By the mid-1980s, the high profitability of remaining retail credit cards made them targets for consumer finance companies that hoped to break back into the credit card business. Smaller retailers that wanted to retain branded affinity cards typically contracted out the service to consumer finance companies such as HBSC and GE Capital. Larger retailers with profitable in-house credit programs attempted to break into the universal credit card market. In 1985, JC Penney attempted to expand its in-house credit card for general use by acquiring the First National Bank of Harrington, Delaware. It renamed it the JC Penney National Bank and moved its credit operation to the bank.[73] In 1986, Sears used its successful retail credit system to launch the general-purpose Discover Card, on which it offered fees and a 1 percent refund. With the addition of insurance and real estate services, financial services accounted for the lion's share of Sears's earnings between 1986 and 1991.[74]

Ultimately, these retail-based cards were sold to outsiders. The Discover network was acquired in 1997 by Morgan Stanley. The JC Penney Bank was acquired in 1999 by GE Capital. As the last major retail credit cards were acquired by consumer finance companies, the shifting status of sales and credit was complete. From credit as a tool to merchandize products, the sale of products had become a means to market credit.

71 JCPCR, Credit: Developments in Retail Credit – Speech, 1971, Kenneth S. Axelson, VP finance and administration at JC Penney, "Developments in Retail Credit: A Report to the NRMA Board of Directors," June 9, 1971, 7.

72 "Rapport du Groupe de Travail sur la Réforme du Crédit à la Consommation," Ministère de l'Économie, March 1979, Annex X.

73 JCPCR, JC Penney Credit: *40th Anniversary Booklet*, 1998.

74 Ronald D. Michman and Alan J. Greco, *Retailing Triumphs and Blunders: Victims of Competition in the New Age of Marketing Management* (Westport, CT: Greenwood Publishing, 1995), 39.

5

Selling France on Credit

Consumer lending in postwar France was dominated by sales credit. These loans were offered not primarily by the retailers themselves, as in the United States, but by independent consumer finance companies that emerged from collaborations between banks and consumer goods manufacturers. The earliest were in the auto sector. Furniture and kitchen-equipment manufacturers quickly followed their lead. By the mid-1950s, a set of general-purpose sales credit companies had emerged that provided the bulk of consumer credit in France for an entire generation. Even large retailers that wanted to offer specialized credit products partnered with the big sales finance companies to provide it. This pattern of lending persisted through the postwar period. It shaped the way French lenders responded to computer and telecommunications technologies, new models of consumer lending, and financial deregulation in the 1980s.

Consumer loans in the early postwar period were expensive to originate and manage. Successful lenders combined interest income with subsidies from retailers or manufacturers whose products they helped finance. Even with this extra source of income, the lenders faced a constant struggle to find profits in a challenging sector with narrow profit margins. Those that succeeded invested heavily in automation and continuously refined their strategies for controlling nonpayments. They also paid careful attention to their public image.

France's dedicated consumer finance companies were especially vulnerable to a social and political critique of their business. They were not directly associated with reputable retailers or commercial banks. They were also under the scrutiny of financial regulators, who set the terms on which consumer credit could be lent. The National Credit Council (CNC) in particular regulated the volume of outstanding credit on a lender-by-lender basis. Under this system, called *encadrement de crédit*, successful lenders operated in ways that the CNC condoned. These two features of French sales credit – independence from retailers and administrative limits on credit volume – meant that lenders emphasized different categories of loans than did their American counterparts. They favored installment loans (fixed term with regular repayments), which were relatively inexpensive to administer, and avoided revolving credit, which was more expensive, less profitable, and challenging to manage within administratively set limits on credit volume.

This chapter traces the opportunities and constraints faced by France's independent consumer-finance companies through the experience of Cetelem, which in the 1980s became Europe's largest consumer-lending company. What distinguished Cetelem from its American counterparts was neither technology nor lending know-how, but instead the dual imperatives of defending the legitimacy of its business and maintaining profitability in the challenging consumer-lending sector. Contrary to our common perceptions of American and French industry priorities, France's successful consumer lenders were focused more intently on profitability than were their American counterparts. At the same time, Cetelem needed to manage public perceptions of its actions and reputation. In this vulnerable context – seeking profits but facing potential public recrimination – Cetelem came to see government regulators as partners in the effort to construct a narrative that portrayed the consumer lending sector as socially valuable. For a country that harbored deep cultural ambivalence toward credit, working amicably with regulators was one means to secure the legitimacy of the emerging consumer credit sector.

Reinventing Sales Credit

French retail credit prior to World War II was dominated by coupon credit created by and for retailers. Beginning shortly after World War I, however, a new set of manufacturer-sponsored sales finance companies emerged. These ultimately displaced the coupon lenders. Most prominent were automobile companies that established captive finance companies in the 1920s and 1930s to finance the brands they sold. Citroën's Sovac, the largest of these, began life in 1919 as Crédit Mobilier Industriel. Other auto lenders included Din (Peugeot), Diac (Renault), and Cavia (Simca). In the postwar period, most of these auto-based lenders branched out to provide general installment-sales credit. Other French manufacturers quickly moved to emulate them. The most common approach was for producers to form affiliated finance companies to purchase retail sales contracts. One of the earliest and most prominent of these was Crédit Électronique et Gazier (CREG), formed by a group of French electrical equipment providers organized by Thomson-Houston. CREG had 3 billion francs in outstanding consumer loans by 1939.[1] CREG was required to make industrial loans in the immediate postwar period. In 1953, it was allowed to return to consumer household-equipment

[1] In 1955 francs, adjusting for devaluation and the move to the "new franc."

lending, and by 1960, it was providing credit to 7,000 retailers across France.[2]

Other manufacturers followed the CREG model. Philips brought together a group of radio manufacturers to launch the consumer finance company Radio Fiduciare in 1932. Five of France's largest television manufacturers (the now-obscure LMT, Ribet-Desjardins, Schneider, Radio-Alva, and Ducastel) grouped together to form the sales finance company GETERA. Another large French radio and television manufacturer, Bendix, launched its own credit program that was tailored to family needs: those with one child received six-month installment loans; those with two children received nine-month installment loans; those with three were given twelve months to repay. It was also the first consumer lender in France to bundle life insurance for the borrower, at no extra cost.[3] One industry-affiliated sales finance company, the Société Caumutelec, offered loans to purchase new electrical equipment that could be repaid through the utility bill.[4] In 1951, the National Furniture Federation joined with the bank l'Union des Mines-La Hénin to form the consumer lender Sofinco.[5]

Most of these industry-sponsored lenders provided credit by purchasing loan contracts from the retailer "with recourse," meaning that their retail clients were responsible for assessing the client's creditworthiness and undertaking collections in case of nonpayment. All of these lenders charged about 1 percent per month. Most, such as CREG, discounted their loans by some percentage in order to cover the full costs of lending. This subsidy from retailers allowed them to make profits while charging the consumer a relatively low interest rate. Most required a 20 percent down payment, limited lending to 15–20 percent of a household's income, and had repayment periods of up to a year.[6] Manufacturers that sold directly to clients could not rely on retailers to ensure payment, but they found other means to assess the risk of prospective borrowers. Frigidaire, for example, retained a staff of traveling salesmen to market its products door to door. These staff visited potential customers' houses in the guise of giving advice, but with the additional goal of assessing creditworthiness.[7]

Formally, none of the consumer lenders were banks, as none took deposits in order to raise capital. Rather, all borrowed money either directly from banks or through the issue of debt. Unlike in the United States, where banks by the early 1950s were deeply engaged in consumer lending, French banks were involved only indirectly in the consumer lending sector. This created the possibility for

[2] Union Fédérale de la Consommation, *Bulletin Mensuel d'Information* 29 (1955).

[3] Andrée Braive, "Formules Actuelles de Crédit," *Réforme*, November 14, 1953, 5.

[4] "Le Developpement des Ventes à Crédit dans la Region du Nord," *Perspectives*, June 2, 1954, 6.

[5] "Panorama du Crédit 1966," *L'Économie* 998, March 11, 1966.

[6] Union Fédérale de la Consommation, *Bulletin Mensuel d'Information* 29 (1955).

[7] Hubert Fournolles, "Spéculation et Crédit à la Consommation," *France-Observateur* 227, September 16, 1954.

large, general-purpose consumer lenders to dominate the market. The largest and most innovative of these was Cetelem.

Cetelem and the Case for Consumer Credit

In 1952, the banking group Union Française de Banques (UFB) proposed the idea of establishing a general-purpose consumer lending company, Crédit Électro-Ménagere (Cetelem). It would eventually become the largest consumer lending company in France and across Europe. But first UFB had to assuage financial regulators who worried that consumer lending by Cetelem could hurt France's ambitious industrialization project. A series of hearings in 1953 raised concerns about the likely impact of unregulated consumer credit. Critics within the Banque de France worried that unregulated consumer loans would divert limited capital away from needed industrial investments. They also worried that consumer credit could drive domestic inflation that would hurt exports. In order to be registered as a new lender, UFB's founder Jacques de Fouchier had to address these concerns.

He did so by linking its proposed credit products to savings. Partly, the link was symbolic. Cetelem's logo, a house with a slot in the roof that looked like a coin bank, made the point that credit was a form of savings. It emphasized that the purchase of household equipment was itself a form of investment, equivalent to savings. More concretely, Cetelem initially offered a delayed credit product that it called "savings credit" alongside its conventional installment-loan plan. The savings credit required that customers make several deposits *before* they made a purchase on credit. Savings credit allowed Cetelem to reduce the amount of capital it needed, thus reducing the cost of the loan. Cetelem's standard "pink" credit (so-called for the color of the application form) carried an interest rate of 7–11 percent; the "green" savings credit charged only 3–5 percent.[8] The offer of savings credit was central to Fouchier's case before the Banque de France, and he proposed that savings credit would make up one-third of Cetelem's portfolio. UFB even proposed that the Banque de France might vary the period of delay in response to macroeconomic conditions.[9] But Fouchier's estimate proved wildly optimistic. Once Cetelem was licensed to make loans, the delayed lending program was quickly eliminated for lack of demand.

Fouchier's other strategy for building support for Cetelem was to line up investors in the household-equipment (white goods) sector. They first approached the household manufacturers' association, the General Syndicate for Electrical Construction, which agreed to recommend Cetelem to its members as "one of the best firms to provide credit."[10] UFB then worked to form

[8] CHA, Crédit à l'Équipement Électro-Ménager, Des Possibilités Nouvelles pour le Financement de vos Ventes à Crédit, 1955 (internal publication to explain Cetelem to resellers).

[9] CHA, "Interview with M. de Foucher," April 26, 1985.

[10] Jean-Jacques Petin, "Problèmes Théoriques et Pratiques du Crédit à la Consommation," Dissertation, Institut d'Études Politiques, Grenoble, 1968.

partnerships directly with France's large white-goods manufacturers, including Frigidaire, Arthur Martin, Electrolux, and Bendix, in an effort to get them to commit to recommend Cetelem to their own distributors.[11] This group of manufacturers indicated that they were "in principle agreed on the interest of this project."[12] Manufacturers that sold door to door and were therefore already familiar with consumer in-house credit quickly embraced the Cetelem idea and agreed to require their retailers to offer it. Arthur Martin and Frigidaire, who were at that time already providing their customers with credit, saw the UFB project as a better alternative. By the launch of Cetelem, in 1953, most of the large white-goods manufacturers in France had been convinced to contribute to the initial 400 million francs of capital with which it started.

TV and radio manufacturers expressed greater concern about the new lender. Philips, which already relied heavily on its own lender, Radio Fiduciaire, to finance sales, warned that the new lender would not have enough capital to finance the borrowing needs of its customers. It was projecting that a third of its sales in 1953 would be on credit. Phillips proposed instead that Cetelem join with Radio Fiduciaire to offer credit.[13] When the UFB declined, Radio Fiduciaire and another industry lender, Getera, asked regulators to block Cetelem from making loans for television and radio sales.[14] Initially the regulators agreed. But the lower interest charged by Cetelem quickly led regulators to expand the scope of its lending.[15]

Not all white goods producers who contributed to Cetelem were initially enthusiastic about offering sales credit. Many felt either that consumer credit would not be accepted by the French people or that it would draw in the least-desirable customers. The head of one producer observed: "I know the market, the French are opposed to credit, and those who do use it will not repay."[16] Even manufacturers that were enthusiastic about offering Cetelem credit found that its retail distributors tended to resist providing it. Frigidaire distributors who agreed to offer Cetelem credit initially refused to place the Cetelem logo in their windows for fear that it would attract the wrong kind of customer.[17] In making its case to manufacturers to adopt its credit program, Cetelem argued

[11] CHA, *Nous Avons 40 Ans*, April 1993, 39.

[12] CHA, "Note sur la Vente à Crédit du Matériel Électro-Ménager," JPS/ML, November 12, 1952.

[13] CHA, Correspondence – Philips to Cetelem, June 26, 1953.

[14] CHA, Correspondence, September–October 1953, various letters.

[15] In the summer of 1953, Cetelem had gained limited access to TV lending. They were allowed to provide credit for retailers who sold TVs and other appliances, but not for dedicated TV retailers. And their loans were limited to a lower limit of 70,000 francs (to keep them out of the radio market) and, for TVs, to an upper limit of 200,000 francs. The upper limit on TV credit was intended to increase the down payment for luxury televisions above the standard 25 percent. CHA, "Note Relative à la Position du Cetelem a l'Égard des Ventes à Crédit Portant sur des Appareils de Télévision," internal document, Boris Mera, July 15, 1953.

[16] Cited in: Jean Chicoye, "Le Cetelem," *Le Lien*, January 1984.

[17] Jean-Jacques Petin, "Problèmes Théoriques et Pratiques du Crédit à la Consommation," Dissertation, Institut d'Études Politiques, Grenoble, 1968.

that consumer credit would not just increase demand but increase demand for higher-priced, higher-quality products. Writing in 1959 to Frigidaire, Cetelem explained: "A buyer who has had to save for a certain time in order to procure an object [by] paying cash will be less inclined to pay a high price for... high-end equipment than the one who pays on credit, for [whom] the financial sacrifices come after the purchase."[18]

To make the link between quality and credit explicit, Cetelem launched its *opération confiance* (operation confidence) campaign. At its center was a program to ensure that both the products it sold and the retailers who sold them were grounded in quality.[19] First, Cetelem announced that it would finance only products that met professional standards of quality.[20] For refrigerators, that meant meeting the Norme française – Fédération nationale des activités frigorifiques (NF-FNAF) quality standard, and for gas-powered equipment, the Norme française – Association technique de l'industrie du gaz (NF-ATG) standard. When Cetelem moved to provide credit for television sales, the lack of a commonly accepted quality standard led Cetelem to create its own list of accepted manufacturers.[21] And when it moved to finance used cars, in 1961, it negotiated to have manufacturers certify the used cars prior to sale. Part of *opération confiance* focused on Cetelem's relationship with retailers. In its promotional materials, Cetelem emphasized its selectiveness in picking retailers that sold quality products. A slogan to endorse its growing list of affiliated retailers read: "Cetelem has confidence in them; it's the best recommendation."

The emphasis on quality was important for Cetelem's own approach to risk management. Surveys of consumers that had stopped payment found that the reason was often linked to a failure of the equipment they had bought on credit.[22] Jean Crusaz, the head of the vacuum manufacturers' Tornado-France, warned Cetelem that customers saw the credit as a payment for a working product, and if the product failed, customers would stop repaying.[23] Emphasizing quality products therefore contributed to keeping down nonpayments. But it was also part of a public campaign to portray consumer credit as supporting French industrialization. In the initial years of Cetelem's lending program, only French companies could receive the necessary quality certificates. This avoided any perception that Cetelem credit was promoting sales of foreign products.[24]

18 CHA, "Pourquoi Vendre à Crédit?," document prepared for presentation at Frigidaire (c. 1959).

19 CHA, UFB, "Note Relative à la Vente à Crédit des Biens d'Équipement Électro-Ménager," January 3, 1953.

20 Marius Allègre, "Étude du Crédit à la Consommation," *Conseil Économique*, March 4, 1954, 267–279.

21 CHA, "Note Relative à la Position du Cetelem a l'Égard des Ventes à Crédit Portant sur des Appareils de Télévision," internal document, prepared by Boris Mera, July 15, 1953.

22 René Sedillot, "Le Crédit à la Consommation," *La Vie Française*, February 5, 1954.

23 CHA, Correspondence, J. Crausaz, director-general of Tornado-France, to M. de Fouchier, February 25, 1953.

24 CHA, Crédit à l'Équipement Électro-Ménager, Des Possibilités Nouvelles pour le Financement de Vos Ventes à Crédit, 1955 (internal publication to explain Cetelem to resellers).

Risk Management

From the outset, Cetelem focused on keeping nonpayment rates low. The reasons were partly to manage the costs of lending, but more importantly to combat the public perception of consumer lending as a risky activity that lured consumers to behave irresponsibly. Cetelem's strategy was to reduce the need to enforce collections by carefully selecting borrowers. Key to its success was the use of retailers to manage relations with borrowers. Initially, all Cetelem loans were made indirectly via retailer affiliates. These stores pre-evaluated customers and collected credit information – address, employer, and salary – for review and approval by Cetelem. Once a loan was made, the retailer was paid immediately. Cetelem then collected monthly payments from the customer over the course of a typical one-year loan. This meant that Cetelem never had a direct contact with the customers to which it lent money. To manage their repayment risk, they focused on selecting reliable retail affiliates.

The early history of consumer lending was littered with failed indirect lending schemes of this sort. One of the biggest of these failures had been the result of a foray by France's insurance companies into consumer lending in the interwar period. Looking for an outlet for their considerable cash holdings, a collection of insurance companies formed the consumer lender Paris-Négoce in the 1920s to provide financing for household furniture retailers. The loans were secured on the furniture and offered indirectly by furniture stores. Everything seemed to be going well until the financial crisis of 1932–1933, when many of the loans went bad. Paris-Négoce quickly became the owner of one of France's largest furniture collections. (It was stored through World War II and auctioned off in the early postwar years.) This painful and expensive experience led France's insurers in the postwar period to stay away from consumer lending. But their experience held two lessons for Cetelem.

First, it had become clear that retailers offering Paris-Négoce sales credit had been defrauding the lender. This took the form of loans to patently unsuited customers, as well as outright fabrication of sales contracts. For sales credit to work, lenders needed to know and trust their distributors, and those distributors had to share some of the risk of customer default. The second lesson was that securing credit on consumer durables was not necessarily an effective means of reducing collections risk. Once customers had lost their furniture or refrigerator, they would no longer pay, and the bank would be left with the considerable costs of storing and auctioning repossessed merchandise. These two lessons shaped Cetelem's approach to lending.

To reduce the risk of being exploited by retailers, Cetelem's strategy for managing default risk combined careful selection and monitoring of affiliated retailers; risk sharing that placed some of the burden of nonpayment on the retailers themselves; an independent, centralized credit-approvals process; and a friendly, convenience-oriented stance toward end borrowers. The idea was to emphasize the selection of retail affiliates and then give them wide latitude to judge the creditworthiness of the end customer.

Store evaluation and selection was the front line of defense against borrower defaults. Cetelem's strategy for locating affiliate retailers was to send inspectors to visit prospective clients. Thanks to detailed archives that were kept from these early years, we know a lot about the life of these retail inspectors. Initially, in 1953, there were four inspectors and a fleet of two cars. It was a modest operation: the cars were a Renault 4CV and a Citroën 11CV. Their routes kept them out of the office, and away from home, for most of the week. On Mondays they prepared their list of visits. Tuesdays through Fridays were spent visiting potential retail clients. They returned to the office on Saturday to file all of the documents. Inspectors covered 50,000 km, and most of France's territory, in each of the first two years. The inspection visits were an effective marketing tool. Retailers reported being impressed that Cetelem took the effort to visit them in their stores. Cetelem offered clear pricing that allowed them to compare Cetelem prices with whatever credit service they were currently using. Typically, Cetelem was 25–50 percent less expensive. And, with a relative dearth of quality lenders operating in France, Cetelem could afford to be picky. In its first seven years of operation, Cetelem approved only 7,000 of the 16,000 retail applicants it visited.[25]

Each visit generated a detailed report on the state of the store, impressions of the manager, and a recommendation about whether Cetelem should pursue credit sales there. These reports give a sense of the subjective evaluations that went into approving affiliates. One report reads: "Excellent impression, orderly and methodical. He is considering door-to-door sales, but is worried about the risks. . . . Attached to CREG by force of habit."[26] CREG, a competing credit service, charged its customers higher rates but required less paperwork from the retailer. Another visit, to Caffiaux et Debatte, a hardware store and distributor of Thomson electrical products, reported that it had also used CREG since 1957. But the inspector noted that repayment rates were low and the store engaged in extensive door-to-door collections of late payments. Cetelem opted not to work with them.[27] In some cases, the sales strategies were more aggressive. Inspectors might threaten to blacklist retailers if they did not agree to work with Cetelem. Visiting one Frigidaire distributor in 1959, the inspector noted that the company had dropped Cetelem the previous year when it had refused to provide credit to cover store inventory. It had instead approached a competing lender, Sovac, which was willing to offer a generous "floor plan."[28] The Cetelem representative told the owner that it would no longer be able to do business with Cetelem if it did not become more "serious."

[25] Michel Drancourt, *Une Force Inconnue: Le Crédit* (Paris: Hachette, 1961), 99–100.

[26] CHA, Compte Rendu d'Inspection, June 9, 1959.

[27] CHA, Inspection, Caffiaux et Debatte (hardware store), a Thomson distributor, June 9, 1959.

[28] Sovac had its roots in auto lending, and providing floor plans was a core competitive function of that business.

The owner suddenly became amenable, agreed to have his sales staff promote Cetelem credit, and offered to send them to a meeting at Cetelem.[29]

Not all retailers were enthusiastic about offering their customers credit. Retailers worried that a posted offer of credit would attract bad clientele, and that this could, in turn, hurt the image of the store. Some stores agreed to offer Cetelem credit but refused to post the cardboard (and later tin) Cetelem announcement in their storefront window. In some respects, shopkeepers' concerns about their image worked to the advantage of their customers. Because both seller and buyer were worried about reputation, both were discreet about the credit application process. These sorts of concerns about the perception of offering credit tended to be regional. In the industrial north, consumer credit was widely distributed and socially accepted. In much of the south, especially the more heavily agricultural areas, credit was still viewed with skepticism.

Even retailers who were accustomed to selling on credit were often skeptical of the relatively low rates offered by Cetelem, a new and unknown lender. This sort of skepticism was understandable in a sector that had a deep history of fraud and charlatanism. To win over these retailers, store managers and sales staff were invited to visit the Cetelem headquarters in Paris, where most were reportedly awed by Cetelem's extensive use of mechanographic equipment to automate loan processing. Files entered on punch cards were managed by IBM's impressive sorting equipment. As one former Cetelem staff later explained, it "gave us an image of a serious marquee financial establishment and not a small lender with exorbitant rates."[30]

The careful vetting of retail affiliates was reinforced by formalized arrangements for credit approval and risk sharing. First, although Cetelem relied heavily on retailers to use their judgment in prescreening customers and collecting accurate customer information, all applications were also sent to Cetelem for final approval. Retailers were required to ask applicants for a pay stub and a rental contract or title. This information allowed Cetelem to confirm employment, speak with employers or landlords, and ensure that borrowers met Cetelem's own internal guidelines. For example, loans were typically limited to 10 percent of the borrower's annual income. Although Cetelem initially operated without any formalized credit-scoring system, it adjusted its approval criteria and rates in order to manage the overall risk of its loan portfolio.[31] All loan applications were either approved or rejected within five days.[32]

Second, affiliated retailers agreed to a system of risk sharing that placed a share of the burden in cases of nonpayment on the seller. For the normal

29 CHA, Inspection, Sovem, Paris, a seller of Frigidaire, June 22, 1959.

30 CHA, "Entretiens du 28.09.83 avec MM. d'Arragon et du Penhoat," Cetelem Archives, September 28, 1983.

31 CHA, "Note Relative au Crédit à l'Équipement Électroménager," internal memo, April 1953, 3.

32 CHA, promotional material for launch of Cetelem, "Note d'Information Concernant le CETELEM," September 1953, 2.

installment loan agreement, the retailer left a security deposit with Cetelem equal to 7 percent of all outstanding credit. Of this, 5 percent went to the account of the seller and 2 percent went into a collective guarantee fund. In cases of nonpayment, the retailer was responsible for 50 percent of the unpaid loan amount, up to a total of 20 percent of the total sales price of the product.[33] Retailers with especially good loan-repayment performance were allowed to deposit lower security deposits (as low as 4 percent).

By 1961, Cetelem had 20 inspectors who covered 800,000 km each year visiting retailers across France.[34] In addition to inspecting premises and discussing strategies for ensuring customer repayment, they also offered the retailers other services. For distributors operating in the same area that sold the same brands of products, Cetelem organized joint advertisements in which they would all have individual promotions that also announced their common provision of Cetelem credit. Cetelem also worked closely with retailers to refine their sales techniques for offering credit. One instructional brochure, entitled "Some Things to Sell Easily: Try These Immediately without Restraint or Apprehension," directed sales staff to use the time that customers spent evaluating and comparing household equipment to find out basic information about them that would be needed for their credit application. This information included marriage status, number of children, profession, and name of employer. The brochure laid out the practical benefit of engaging the customer: "When the time comes to fill out the credit application, you can already fill [in] most of the information, since you have subtly enquired after these and you already know the answers."[35]

The sales promotional material proposed that retailers focus on features of Cetelem credit that they felt were most attractive for consumers. First, it allowed customers to buy more. Using the advertising slogan: "1 franc Cetelem = 5 francs Français," Cetelem suggested that retailers point out to customers that they could afford more and better buying on credit than they could in cash.[36] Two other selling points they emphasized were price and discretion. In promotion materials prepared by Cetelem for the auto distributor Jacob & Cognet in Brest, Cetelem boasted that it was "the cheapest credit in Europe." But it also emphasized that it was discreet. As it proudly announced: "No more door-step collections; no more bills or indiscretion!"[37]

33 CHA, "Conditions de Financement par le CETELEM des Ventes à Crédit d'Appareils Électro-Ménagers," April 1953; CHA "Note Relative au Crédit à l'Équipement Électromènager," internal memo, April 1953, 4; Jean-Jacques Petin, "Problèmes Théoriques et Pratiques du Crédit à la Consommation," Dissertation, Institut d'Études Politiques, Grenoble, 1968.

34 Michel Drancourt, *Une Force Inconnue: Le Crédit* (Paris: Hachette, 1961), 99–100.

35 CHA, *Choses pour Mieux Vendre* (Paris: CHA, c. 1955).

36 Initially, Cetelem required a 20 percent down payment for a product bought on credit, so for 100 francs a customer could buy 500 francs' worth on credit. CHA, Document 1958/d202, *Quelques Trucs pour Vendre Fluide – à Essayer Immédiatement sans Contrainte ni Complexe*, Cetelem, 1958.

37 Promotional material for launch of Cetelem, "Note d'Information Concernant le CETELEM," September 1953, 2.

France's Low-Cost Lender

Like many of the early consumer lenders, Cetelem was founded in part on the populist ideal of promoting access to modern products at a reasonable price. Its emphasis on dealing fairly with customers was undoubtedly partly instrumental. It was seeking to register a new consumer lender at a time when the government was intent on allocating credit to industrial investment. And, thanks to questionable practices of traditional door-to-door lenders, including a new group of fraudulent economic unions, the consumer-lending sector retained a vaguely unsavory reputation. Cetelem worked hard to combat that image. But there also seems to have been a genuine aspiration among the founders of the new company to pursue demonstrably fair relations with borrowers. As one of the early correspondents described their goal, "Without losing sight of the common interests in assuring a regular repayment of funds lent out, Cetelem will institute a climate of 'fair-play'[38] with buyers as well as with sellers, imposing more rigorous treatment upon those who do not respect the rules of the game."[39]

Careful attention to the selection of and relations with their retail affiliates gave Cetelem latitude to establish strong relationships with the end customers on the basis of a high level of trust. Four decisions were taken early on by Cetelem that paved the way for this high-trust strategy. Among the most important but also most radical for the time was a repayment strategy that relied on customers to make their own monthly payments. When a loan was issued, each customer received a book with monthly payment slips that they were to include with their payment. Printed in bold letters on the book was the statement: "Your credit is your capital. Preserve it by making your payments promptly."[40] Payments could be made through the mail, at an affiliated bank, or later through Cetelem's own branch offices. No reminders were sent to clients except in case of late payment.

This voluntary payment system was strikingly different from the way in which loans had traditionally been settled. Because banks and lenders were suspicious of consumers' intentions to repay, they had traditionally required that any borrower sign a bank withdrawal form (*traite*) for each of the monthly repayments he or she was required to make. Not only was the *traite* system cumbersome and expensive, it also required a letter be sent every month to the borrower's home, a process that Cetelem saw as indiscreet. By relying on customers to make their own payments, Cetelem avoided sending mail to customers' homes. When it did need to send correspondence, as for example in case of late payment, Cetelem used blank envelopes so that the letters could not be identified as coming from a lender. The other problem with the *traite* system was that many credit customers also did not have bank accounts. For

38 This term was written in English in the original document.

39 CHA, JPK, internal communication, April 28, 1953 (Cetelem archives).

40 Union Fédérale de la Consommation, *Bulletin Mensuel d'Information* 29 (1955), 47.

most working-class households, buying on credit required an initial trip to the bank to create a bank account before taking out a loan. Even once they had an account, customers commonly forgot to deposit sufficient funds, so that lender withdrawals were frequently rejected.[41] Cetelem's system avoided these problems. In 1962, 90 percent of its borrowers still did not have bank accounts.[42] In internal correspondence, Cetelem managers expressed surprise at the success of the voluntary payment system. After five years in operation, one official noted that "some are such good monthly payers that they continue to send a check after the debt is repaid, requiring Cetelem to send back the excess."[43]

Three other innovations helped Cetelem to develop long-term relations with its customers.[44] When customers were late making payments, Cetelem responded rapidly but courteously. Reasoning that most customers were not intentionally avoiding payment, it sent reminders inviting them in a friendly way to "regularize their situation." If the delay continued, the response became more rigorous. But collections staff were instructed to operate on the assumption that the customer was not at fault. In fact, an internal audit found that many cases of nonpayment were because of checks that had been submitted without an account number and misfiled. Cetelem also provided automatic life insurance to its borrowers at no extra cost. This helped them avoid complicated and costly collections efforts, and gave borrowers "a feeling of security as to the settling of their affairs in case of death."[45] Finally, customers who had successfully and regularly repaid their loans were sent a "good-payer" card that they could present to any retailer offering Cetelem credit, and later to Cetelem itself. This early "credit card" guaranteed that their application for Cetelem credit would be approved. By 1959, 38 percent of Cetelem's loans were made to repeat customers who had received the good-payer card at the end of their previous loan.[46]

The final piece of Cetelem's focus on fairness was an effort to offer the "most reasonable prices possible."[47] For most of the 1950s and 1960s, it

41 CNC, 1427200301, box 283, Comité National du Crédit, Comité du Crédit à Court Terme, December 1953–June 1961, Meeting of the Comité du Crédit à Court Terme, January 5, 1954, 93.

42 CNC, 1427200301, box 111: Crédit à la Consommation et Vente au Crédit, Pierre Lips, "A Propos des Tarifs Pratiqués dans la Vente à Crédit des Biens de Consommation Durables," Association pour le Crédit au P.M.E., Communiqué no. 58, December 1962.

43 CHA, "Pourquoi Vendre à Crédit?" (document prepared for presentation at Frigidaire), c. 1959.

44 Gérard de Chaunac-Lanzac, *La Vie m'a Fait Crédit* (Paris: Gérard de Chaunac-Lanzac, 2001), 234.

45 CHA, JPK, internal communication, April 28, 1953.

46 CHA, "Pourquoi Vendre à Crédit?" (document prepared for presentation at Frigidaire), c. 1959.

47 CHA, internal memo, "Note Relative au Crédit à l'Équipement Électromènager," April 1953, 3–4.

seems to have achieved that goal. In a 1957 survey, Cetelem was found to offer lower credit terms for household equipment (16 percent APR) than most of its competitors, who regularly charged in the range of 26 percent. It was also more competitive than banks, which were making personal loans at 18 percent to 22 percent.[48] When Cetelem first entered the auto loan market, in 1959, its rates were 25 percent below those offered by existing lenders. It charged 9 percent, compared to 11 percent or 12 percent offered by competitors. It also fought hard to eliminate dealer fees on auto credit sales, which pushed up interest charges. Most auto lenders at the time rewarded dealers with a finder fee, then added that fee to the cost paid by borrowers. Cetelem did not. "Our position [against dealer fees] emerges from the principle that the purchaser should pay the minimum possible and that any redistribution to intermediaries leads directly to a rise in price in interest paid by the buyer."[49]

To keep rates low, Cetelem focused aggressively on restraining costs. In 1960, the costs of a loan were primarily interest costs (35 percent) and administrative costs (38 percent), with the remainder going to taxes (20 percent), and a fund for nonpayments (6 percent).[50] A separate estimate found that 36 percent of Cetelem revenue went to administrative fees.[51] Because nonpayment rates were already very low, administration was the main area in which Cetelem could hope to reduce costs. Part of its strategy was to invest heavily in mechanization of the routine administrative functions. Even before the adoption of genuine computer technology in 1962, Cetelem recorded its loan records mechanically: first on punch cards (each application required 4–5 cards), then, from 1957, on magnetic tapes.[52] The file-processing facility in the headquarters was described as a "veritable mechanographic factory."[53] In 1962, Cetelem adopted the first functional business computer, the IBM 1401. By April 1963, all of its 350,000 files were transferred to the IBM system.[54] This move allowed Cetelem to reduce its staff from 830 in 1962 to 550 by 1969.[55] As one former manager explained: "This [computer] revolution was critical: it became easier to analyze risk and results, and [to generate]

48 BdF CNC, 1427200301, box 111: Crédit à la Consommation et Vente au Crédit, Correspondence, la Direction du Contentieux, June 1957.

49 CHA "Les Problèmes Commerciaux du Cetelem: Bilan de l'Année 1962," 1963, 18.

50 Jean Chicoye, "Les achats à crédit," *Revue de l'action populaire* 140 (July–August 1960), 794. France has a deep tradition of requiring stamps, typically sold by tabacs, in order to validate commercial transactions.

51 BdF CNC, 1427200301, box 283, Comité National du Crédit, Comité du Crédit à Court Terme, December 1953–June 1961, Meeting of the Comité du Crédit á Court Terme, June 19, 1961, 33.

52 Cetelem, *Nous Avons 40 Ans*, April 1993.

53 Michel Drancourt, *Une Force Inconnue: Le Crédit* (Paris: Hachette, 1961), 100.

54 These included outstanding loans as well as past account records.

55 Gérard de Chaunac-Lanzac, *La Vie m'a Fait Crédit* (Paris: Gérard de Chaunac-Lanzac, 2001), 234.

statistics. The use of punch cards was largely eliminated."[56] From 1963 to 1967, Cetelem doubled the number of files processed per employee – the key indicator employed by Cetelem to assess its operational efficiency – from 450 to 900.[57] The early embrace of technology became a hallmark of Cetelem's strategy. In the late 1970s, it deployed a new dedicated telecommunications network, TRANSPAC, to coordinate credit approvals among its 370 regional offices. In the early 1980s, the network was extended to all of its retail clients. And, in 1993, Cetelem set about creating the paperless office.[58]

But the embrace of new technologies was only half of Cetelem's effort to streamline its operations. Inspired by time-motion studies being conducted in factories, Cetelem from the start learned to rationalize workflow. It broke down the administrative personnel by function, and benchmarked each of these functions. By 1967, the entire loan administration process was separated into eight functions, grouped under marketing, credit, and collections. Employees in these areas were all given clearly defined job descriptions, and the flow of work was monitored and optimized. Always, however, cost cutting came second to loan repayment. The administrative functions that represented the greatest costs were those that were seen as most important for keeping down nonpayments. These included ongoing relations with retailers, applicant evaluations, and collections.

Cetelem was also quick to incorporate new credit strategies into its organization. One such innovation, brought back by Jean-Claude Gautier from a research trip to the United States and Japan, was the so-called new collections.[59] The idea of new collections was that a nonpaying customer should not automatically be treated as if he or she was acting in bad faith.[60] Cetelem created a new special branch, called Special Recovery Service, headed by Marcel Ciment, whom it hired away from a Canadian finance company. Ciment further softened its approach to customers, and focused on timely and frequent reminders about unpaid loans. The results for Cetelem were dramatic: the number of cases that made it to the "contentious" collections stage fell by two-thirds.

The importance of administration in the overall cost of making consumer loans posed a problem of public perception in how Cetelem priced its loans. The problem, shared by all consumer lenders in the early postwar period, was that administrative costs were the same regardless of the size of the loan. For larger loans of longer duration, the fixed administrative costs represented a relatively small charge as a percentage. For small, short-term loans, they could be considerable. Cetelem's approach to pricing – one that was later adopted

[56] Cetelem, *Nous Avons 40 Ans*, April 1993, 22.
[57] CHA, *Résultats de l'Évaluation de Cetelem et les Hypothèses de Travail qui en Ressortent*, May 21, 1969, Annex XI.
[58] *Libération*, March 20, 1993.
[59] Cetelem, *Nous Avons 40 Ans*, April 1993, 42.
[60] Cetelem, *Nous Avons 40 Ans*, April 1993, 35.

by French policymakers in setting interest rate caps – was to charge a fixed filing fee for all loans, plus an interest rate. Initially, loans for immediate delivery faced a filing fee of 1,000 francs and a per-month payment fee of 100 francs. These costs were then added to a modest interest charge, expressed as a premium above the cost of the original loan. A four-month loan had a 2.5 percent premium (equal to a 10 percent APR); a one-year loan had a 6.5 percent premium. This combined system of fees and repayment premiums could generate annual percentage rates that ranged from 15 percent to 64 percent, depending on the size of the loan. Loans made on the delayed-delivery "savings credit" plan had much lower rates, but small, short-term loans still faced APRs up to 40 percent.

The higher rates applied to small loans created the perception of unfairness, because lower-income customers typically took out smaller loans. Although the difference in rates reflected real differences in cost, public perception of unfairness ultimately pushed Cetelem to move toward a more "balanced" pricing scheme. It began to offer lower prices for smaller- and longer-term loans, on which it now accepted a loss, which it cross-subsidized from less-costly larger loans. This practice was codified for the entire consumer-lending sector in 1966, when France enacted a usury law that imposed a single consumer lending rate cap set at 50 percent above the average commercial bond rate. Only in 1989, when the usury law was revised, did it incorporate different interest-rate caps for different sizes of consumer loans.

Despite its best efforts at keeping down cost and expanding its lending activities into new product ranges, Cetelem could not escape the reality that consumer lending in the 1950s and 1960s was a low-margin/low-profit business. Compared to the other areas of business lending in which its parent company Groupe Bancaire (formerly UFB) was engaged, Cetelem showed poor profitability. Outside of a two-year period of unusually high returns in 1959–1960, Cetelem consistently showed the lowest profit of Groupe Bancaire's various lending groups (see Figure 5.1). Unlike its consumer-lending counterparts in the United States, Groupe Bancaire had no interest in cross-subsidizing Cetelem from its other lines of business. Because it was on its own, France's leading consumer finance company was more sensitive to the profitability of its loan portfolio than were its American counterparts. This cost sensitivity was one factor that kept Cetelem from moving more rapidly to embrace revolving credit as a core lending format.

The Move to Direct Lending

In August 1959, Cetelem began experimenting with direct-to-consumer loans. Making direct loans required fundamentally new approaches to risk management and customer relations, but Cetelem had good business reasons for branching into new markets. First, its mainstay business in financing white goods was becoming erratic by the late 1950s. Some of the problems were

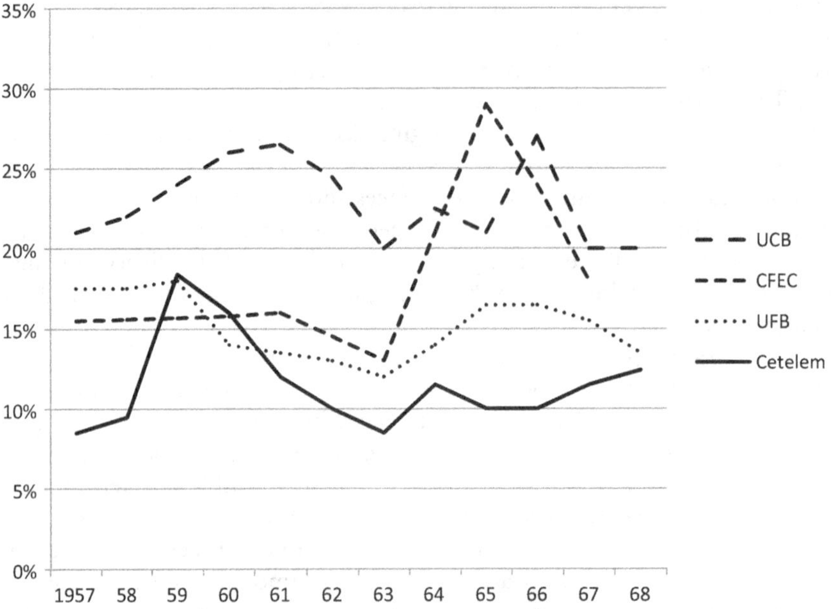

FIGURE 5.1. Profitability of Groupe Bancaire Units, 1957–1968[61]

man-made. When the government increased minimum down payment terms to 40 percent in the summer of 1958, as part of an effort to fight inflation, demand for refrigerators, which were still seen mainly as a luxury good, fell by 70 percent. Other core lines of business also declined: vacuums by 40 percent and washing machines by 24 percent.[62] Sales were also subject to natural forces. In 1962, France faced what came to be known as the refrigerator crisis. An especially cold year reduced demand for new refrigerators at the same time that manufacturers had opted to increase production. Sales and prices fell steeply;[63] lenders and manufacturers both suffered.

Apart from these fluctuations in Cetelem's core business lines, it also faced problems of declining profitability on its indirect loans. The direct-to-consumer lending experience of American and German consumer finance companies suggested that direct lending could be a source of new profitability.[64] One internal Cetelem study from the mid-1960s that broke out product categories in terms of their profit margins showed that Cetelem's indirect sales financing business was doing poorly. Kitchen equipment, which accounted for a third of

[61] CHA, *Résultats de l'Évaluation de Cetelem et les Hypothèses de Travail qui en Ressortent*, May 21, 1969, Annex VII.

[62] *La Vie Française*, August 1, 1958.

[63] CHA, "Les Problèmes Commerciaux du Cetelem: Bilan de l'Année 1962," 1963.

[64] CHA, "Les Problèmes Commerciaux du Cetelem: Bilan de l'Année 1962," 1963, 20.

outstanding loans, had gross margins of 0.4 percent. TVs, another traditional product, had gross margins of only 2 percent. Taken together, kitchen equipment and TVs accounted for half of Cetelem's outstanding loans but only one-sixth of profits. New categories of loans, including new and used cars (5.2 percent and 5.6 percent) and furniture (4 percent), were far more profitable.[65] Expanding in these areas also meant extending further into direct lending.

Both the automobile and furniture sectors had traditionally been ones in which finance companies competed for retailer contracts by offering dealer commissions. Cetelem reasoned that it could undercut the incumbents in these sectors if it offered low-interest-rate loans directly to consumers, effectively cutting out the retail middleman. This meant moving into direct lending. The first of these products, launched in 1959, was for auto loans. These were relatively safe, because Cetelem held the car title as collateral until the loan was paid off. For furniture sales, launched in 1960, Cetelem's early credit took the form of personal loans that were not secured against the furniture.[66] In fact, there was no guarantee that customers would use the loans for what they claimed. A survey in 1961 found that half of its non-auto direct loans already went to furniture, 14 percent to heating equipment, 11 percent to white goods, and 3 percent to radios.[67] Direct loans grew by 68 percent in 1961 and a further 108 percent in 1962.[68]

Once it became clear that unsecured personal lending could be done profitably, it became an attractive alternative to indirect installment lending, especially during periods when the government was tightening down payment and loan duration terms on sales credit. This sort of regulatory evasion led to a surge of direct personal lending in the early 1970s, as the government tightened credit terms in response to inflationary pressures driven by higher oil prices. At a time when installment loans were limited to a twenty-one-month repayment ceiling, personal loans were commonly repaid over 2–3 years. From a consumer credit market dominated by installment lending in 1969, personal lending exceeded sales credit by 1972. This shift did not go unnoticed; France's commercial banks jumped in to offer personal loans that competed with Cetelem's direct-lending program.

The move to direct lending required a different approach to managing loan risks. One of the basic differences was that direct loans, because they were not tied to the sale of a specific product, were unsecured. There could be no recourse

[65] Margins do not take into account default rates, but Cetelem finds that these are roughly equal across loan types. CHA, *Résultats de l'Évaluation de Cetelem et les Hypothèses de Travail qui en Ressortent*, May 21, 1969, Annex IX A.

[66] To make such personal loans, from which consumer finance companies were formally prohibited, Cetelem acted as an agent for the Groupe Bancaire, under whose name the loans were made.

[67] CHA, Note d'Information, December 1, 1961.

[68] CHA, "Une Voie Nouvelle pour Cofica?" *À Découvert*, no. 18, 1975; CHA, "Les Problèmes Commerciaux du Cetelem: Bilan de l'Année 1962," 1963.

to repossession in case of default. But Cetelem had in fact rarely resorted to repossession even for its secured loans. When it had, the value of the product had often not been enough to cover the unpaid principal. "Our collections services have almost never relied on the residual value of the good.... One might say that we have, in most cases, offered personal credit without knowing it."[69] In fact, Cetelem learned that collections rates on unsecured personal loans were very good.[70]

Two other features of direct lending forced real changes in its operations. First, Cetelem had traditionally employed retailer guarantee accounts to cover the costs of nonpayment and provide new capital.[71] As Jean Chicoye acknowledged in an internal memo written in 1962: "There is a contradiction between the principle of the seller guarantee, which was the basis for Cetelem's business, and the idea of direct credit."[72] Cetelem would now have to start making its own provisions for potential losses and raise additional funds to finance expansion. These greater capital needs eventually led to Cetelem's issuing of public shares in 1966.

Second, and perhaps more importantly, Cetelem could not rely on retailers to screen prospective clients for creditworthiness. With indirect lending, risk assessments had focused more heavily on retailers than on end borrowers. Cetelem was able to base much of its in-house approvals of credit applications on the historical repayment record of clients directed to them by specific affiliated retailers. Because turning down applications from retailers could hurt their business, those retailers that had shown strong records of client repayment were given broad leeway in credit-application approvals. With the retailer taken out of the transaction, Cetelem had to find new ways to evaluate borrower risk. Many of the early direct loans were offered to clients that Cetelem had special reasons to believe would repay. The largest share went to previous retail clients who had received a good-payer card at the end of their loan. In other cases, associations signed agreements with Cetelem to provide direct loans to their members that would be secured by the association itself. The first of these was signed with the union of state functionaries (Association générale des fonctionnaires).

For applicants who did not have this sort of precertification, credit evaluations required that Cetelem interact with customers, either over the phone or, ideally, in person. To facilitate direct interactions, Cetelem began opening offices for walk-in customers seeking to apply for loans directly. In 1960, regional offices in Marseilles and Lille that had been established in 1954 as a base for interacting with retail affiliates were opened to the general public. By

69 CHA, "Les Problèmes Commerciaux du Cetelem: Bilan de l'Année 1962," 1963, 22–23.

70 CHA, Note d'Information, December 1, 1961.

71 Jean-Jacques Petin, "Problèmes Théoriques et Pratiques du Crédit à la Consommation," Dissertation, Institut d'Études Politiques, Grenoble, 1968, 157.

72 CHA, Jean Chicoye, "Crédit Direct," internal note, F20, 1962.

1964, Cetelem had opened sixteen offices around the country, including a first retail office in Paris. These offices received 11,300 visitors, 80 percent seeking direct loans. In 1965, it opened further offices in Lyons, Pas-de-Calais, and Nord, as well as new offices in Nancy and Nantes.[73] By 1968, Cetelem had opened thirty-three offices across France. Unlike bank branches, the Cetelem offices were casual and comfortable, nicely decorated, and typically had play areas for children. Most were located in shopping areas, rather than in financial districts. The idea was to make the experience more like entering a retail store than entering a bank. The strategy seemed to work. A survey of good-payer card holders found that they perceived Cetelem differently from banks. As one analyst noted: "Compared to a bank, if it has a little less standing, it is perceived as more human, closer to the client."[74]

Until Cetelem adopted formal credit-scoring technology, in 1974, it staffed its visitor centers with agents trained to evaluate the creditworthiness of the clients they interviewed. Agents requested information about employment, residency, any other obligations, and the purpose of the loan. Internal guidelines for evaluating creditworthiness warned agents to be "extremely careful" when clients did not have any particular purpose in mind. In the case of applications taken by telephone, agents were instructed to listen for background noises, and to find reasons to return a call to the applicant at the number they gave so they could be sure of their identity.[75] Once all of the data were recorded and confirmed, the files were then passed to specialized "creditmen" (they used the American term) whose job it was to evaluate the overall repayment risk of each customer and make a final decision about offering loans. From the early 1960s, all applicants were also checked against a nonpayer blacklist (distributed on microfilm) shared among Cetelem and its largest competitors.[76]

As direct lending grew and became more profitable, it changed the way Cetelem looked at its customers. Indirect lending via retailers remained relatively unprofitable, but it became a channel for Cetelem to attract and evaluate potential customers for its more profitable direct-lending products. By 1968, its retail network had grown to 24,400 affiliates.[77] The idea was to use loans initiated by these retailers to select good re-payers, and then to build a long-term lending relationship that would last beyond their first transaction. An analyst explained: "The passage from retailer credit to direct credit is a particularly

[73] Jean-Jacques Petin, "Problèmes Théoriques et Pratiques du Crédit à la Consommation," Dissertation, Institut d'Études Politiques, Grenoble, 1968, 161–62.

[74] CHA, P. Raynaud, "Recherche d'Axes de Communication pour la Promotion du Crédit Direct," Paris: Synecteam, April 1972.

[75] CHA, D01/AH, "Clients Traités par Téléphone," 1973.

[76] Gérard de Chaunac-Lanzac, *La Vie m'a Fait Crédit* (Paris: Gérard de Chaunac-Lanzac, 2001).

[77] Jean-Jacques Petin, "Problèmes Théoriques et Pratiques du Crédit à la Consommation," Dissertation, Institut d'Études Politiques, Grenoble, 1968, 156.

important moment... not yet a marriage, but... more of an engagement."[78] This model of lending carried Cetelem through until 1985, when it embraced revolving credit as the core of its business.

The High Cost of Revolving Credit

Revolving credit did not emerge as a widely used form of credit in France until 1985, when Cetelem launched its popular Carte Aurore. This represented a delay of almost a generation over the widespread distribution of revolving credit, linked to credit cards, in the United States. The adoption lag was not because of a lack of innovation or technology. The first revolving-credit facility offered in France, Cetelem's *crédit en poche* ("pocket credit") was launched in 1965 and, like many of Cetelem's early innovations, followed a study trip to inspect contemporary practice in the U.S. consumer-lending market.[79] Starting in 1962, Cetelem had begun offering its best retail customers something akin to revolving credit. These were books of co-branded "purchasing checks" that it could offer to qualifying clients. Checks could be written for any amount, with repayments made on a fixed monthly schedule to Cetelem. In a typical arrangement, checks were offered to a client that had already bought products in cash for at least 150 francs. That customer was then also offered a checkbook (*chéquier*) for 700 francs to be repaid in 15 months at 43 francs per month.[80] As the purchasing checks became more popular, Cetelem shifted the payment function to a card and set a permanent credit ceiling. Thus was born its new pocket-credit product.

Initially, pocket credit was issued only indirectly. Cetelem's best retailers could offer pocket credit to their best clients. In 1966, Cetelem began offering a separate co-branded revolving-credit product specifically for Galeries Lafayette's clients. Trois Suisses, a catalog sales company, partnered with Cetelem to provide its customers a similar revolving-credit card in 1967. French retailers marketed the new pocket credit as a premium customer service, with greater status than a conventional charge account. They offered their revolving-account customers other perks, including special parking, dedicated check-out lines, and other specialty services. But the high status attached to the card also complicated relations between retailers and Cetelem. Whereas retailers saw the card as a means to ensure customer loyalty, Cetelem remained obsessed with profitable lending and timely collections. These goals were not always aligned. As Cetelem president Jean Chicoye explained: "At the time the legal relations were not clear, so these partnerships relied on mutual

78 CHA, P. Raynaud, "Recherche d'Axes de Communication pour la Promotion du Crédit Direct," Paris: Synecteam, April 1972, (27–3–10), 7.

79 Cetelem, *Nous Avons 40 Ans*, April 1993, 42.

80 *Multiplions Ensembles* (sales brochure), Cetelem Historical Archives, 1962.

confidence as the only cement."[81] Cetelem ultimately spun off independent joint ventures with Galeries Lafayettes and Trois Suisses in order to strike the correct balance between sales and collections. Conveniently, the joint ventures would also not be counted in Cetelem's own credit allocation under *encadrement*.

The new pocket credit was a clear improvement on the system of purchasing checks. Once a customer had a pocket-credit account, he or she could continue to purchase up to a preset ceiling. As the account balance was paid down, the consumer automatically had access to new credit.[82] For retailers, this arrangement allowed them to build long-term relationships with credit customers. And it removed the uncomfortable discussion of interest payments from each credit transaction. As one credit industry publication noted: "The flexibility ('*supplesse*') of revolving credit... allows [the seller] not to raise questions of interest rates with a good conscience."[83] Credit sales transactions became indistinguishable to the casual observer from cash or charge sales. In 1968, pocket credit was moved from the indirect distribution network to the direct sales division, where it was offered both over the phone and through Cetelem's growing network of branch offices.[84] Its competitors quickly followed suit. Sofinco launched the Carte d'Argent with a revolving facility in late 1968. In the same year, Sovac partnered with American Marine Midlands to offer the Carte d'Or, also with a revolving credit facility.[85]

Despite a promising start, Cetelem never showed the enthusiasm for revolving credit that its American counterparts demonstrated. One obstacle was that Cetelem, unlike American bankers and retailers, needed to make a profit on its lending products. Although pocket credit was more profitable than most of Cetelem's indirect credit products (sales credit provided via retailers), it was the least profitable of the company's emerging line of direct-to-consumer products.[86] This was due mainly to high administrative costs. Cetelem's secured and personal loans had fixed repayment periods and customers were relied upon to remember and pay each period. Revolving accounts had variable balances and therefore required monthly billing. Initially, only a small share of the approved pocket-credit accounts were actually used by customers, and many of these only for small purchases. Both trends increased the administrative cost of the program.

Apart from their high costs and low margins, the revolving plans also made it difficult for Cetelem to manage its credit portfolio under *encadrement*.

81 Cetelem, *Nous Avons 40 Ans*, April 1993, 39.

82 Claude Pasany, "La Carte d'Or: Un Nouvel Atout," *Témoignage Chrétien*, March 21, 1968.

83 WSA, *Image du crédit*, August 1987, 34.

84 *À Découvert*, no. 10, September 1973.

85 *Le Figaro*, June 14, 1968.

86 CHA, *Résultats de l'Évaluation de Cetelem et les Hypothèses de Travail qui en Ressortent*, May 21, 1969, Annex IX A.

In 1969, faced with an economy-wide downturn, Cetelem President Pierre Boucher called for a reduction in the company's overall level of lending and an increase in the credit standards for new loans. He also called for a halt to all revolving accounts, calling them "marginal."[87] But outstanding balances on existing pocket-credit accounts continued to grow, as customers with unused accounts tapped into the available line of credit. The share of active accounts rose from 28 percent in 1968 to 56 percent in 1972.[88] This inability to manage the outstanding balance on revolving accounts posed problems for Cetelem's relations with the National Credit Council, making it especially difficult for lenders to comply with hard credit-volume limits.[89]

All of this changed with financial liberalization in the early 1980s. In 1985, Cetelem launched its new Aurore card.[90] For Cetelem, the Aurore card was a way to counter the aggressive move by banks into personal lending. It offered it as a co-branded card that allowed it to reinforce its ties with retailers. It also already understood the technology, which it had showcased twenty years earlier with its pocket credit. Demand was apparently strong. By the end of 1987, the Aurore card already had 600,000 members.[91] Other consumer-finance companies quickly launched competing revolving products. They included the Accord card by Auchan, the Plus card by Cofinoga, and the Pass card by S2P. Crédit Commercial de France created an innovative revolving account with rates tied directly to the interbank lending rate.[92] Amid all of the new entrants, the Aurore card dominated the field. By 1995, ten years after its launch, Cetelem's Aurore card was used by 5 million French, and 1 million other Europeans.[93] By 2000, there were 13 million Cartes Aurore in use, with 250,000 points of sale.[94] Interest rates on these loans ranged from 12.4 percent to 16.1 percent.[95] Taking the cue from these new cards, France's banks responded by launching Carte Bleue payment cards tied to revolving credit accounts. Examples included the Alterna card offered by Société Générale and the Provisio card offered by BNP. By 2000, 26 percent of all non-mortgage household borrowing was in

87 CHA, P. Boucher, "La Nouvelle Politique de Sélection des Crédits Directs," 1969, Annexe I.

88 CHA, *À Découvert*, no. 10, September 1973.

89 Under the norms of the *encadrement de crédit*, at least half of consumer finance lending by any lender had to be for installment credit. Bruno Moschetto and André Plagnol, *Crédit à la Consommation* (Paris: Presses Universitaires de Paris, 1985), 97.

90 The word *aurore* means "dawn," but also sounds like *or-or* or "gold-gold." Catherine Rigollet, "Le Bazar des Produits Financiers," *L'Express*, March 6, 1987.

91 Jean-Philippe Vidal, "L'Explosion du Crédit à la Consommation," *Tribune de l'Économie*, October 27, 1987.

92 Florence Paricard, "Consommation: le Taux de Crédit Doit Baisser," *La Vie Française*, March 30, 1986.

93 *Figaro-Économie*, June 19, 1995.

94 CHA, Philippe Herail, "Cetelem: Une Histoire des Valeurs, un Avenir," August 2002.

95 *Le Figaro*, March 9, 1987.

TABLE 5.1. *Cost Components of Cetelem Loans, 1960–1992*

	1960[1]	1973[2]	1986[3]	1992[4]
Consumer lending rate	18.7%	19.2%	18.8%	17.6%
Breakdown of costs:				
Administration	7.0%	7.0%	5.1%	3.8%
Interest	6.0%	9.4%	10.3%	8.8%
Risk	0.7%	0.8%	1.0%	1.9%
Tax	4.5%	1.0%	1.2%	1.0%
Profit	0.8%	1.0%	1.2%	2.1%

[1] "Des Tarifs pratiqués dans la vente à crédit des biens de consommation durables," *Revue du Centre d'Information et d'Étude du Crédit*, no. 3 (October 1962); Michel Renault, "La Vente à Crédit s'acclimate en France," *Le Monde*, November 29, 1962.
[2] CHA, "La finance et la trésorerie," *à Découvert*, no. 9, June 1973, 6.
[3] CHA, Pascal Bonnet, "Tenir nos taux," *Nous*, no. 2, June–July 1987, 10–11.
[4] CHA, *Nous avons 40 ans*, April 1993, 25.
Source: Cetelem Historical Archives, data compiled by author.

the form of revolving credit. For consumer-finance companies, revolving loans accounted for 37 percent of all loans.[96]

Technology and the Cost of Credit

Financial data from Cetelem's historical archives give us a sense of how the costs of lending changed over the postwar period in France. Table 5.1 breaks down the total interest charged on a loan into its cost components. Administration and interest payments dominated costs, while provisions for non-payment were relatively small. The significant increase in the cost of capital from 1960 to 1986 was almost entirely offset by lower administration costs and a reduction in government taxes.

Despite changing patterns of consumer credit, the cost of credit offered by Cetelem did not change significantly over the postwar period. Effective consumer lending rates, taking into account all fees, were about the same in France in the 1960s and 1990s. Real interest rates varied with inflation. High inflation in the 1970s, for example, meant that real interest rates for consumers during this period were correspondingly low. Table 5.2 shows the nominal and corresponding real interest rates being paid by Cetelem consumers from 1960 to 1992. Although the average nominal consumer borrowing rate at Cetelem fell somewhat, from 19.2 percent in 1973 to 17.6 percent in 1992, an

[96] François Henrot, "Les Instruments du Financement à Crédit de la Consommation en France," in André de Lattre, ed., *La Consommation et son Financement en France et dans le Monde* (Paris: Berger-Levrault, 1994), 56–57.

TABLE 5.2. *Cetelem Nominal and Real Lending Rates, 1960–1992*

	1960	1973	1986	1992
Consumer lending rate (nominal)	18.7%	19.2%	18.8%	17.6%
Inflation (GDP deflator)	3.0%	9.0%	5.0%	2.0%
Consumer lending rate (real)	15.7%	10.2%	13.8%	15.6%

Source: Cetelem Historical Archives, World Development Indicators.

even more rapid fall in inflation meant that real rates actually increased quite dramatically: from 10.2 percent in 1973 to 15.6 percent in 1992. For the consuming public, borrowing in 1973 was considerably cheaper than borrowing in 1992.

The single most important factor in rising profitability was the reduction in administrative costs. From 1973 to 1992, the costs of administering loans were cut in half; computerization was a core reason for this change. As Cetelem's President Pierre Boucher acknowledged: "Computers . . . constitute the hard core of our strategy."[97] In December 1962, Cetelem installed two cutting-edge IBM 1401 machines. In 1973 it replaced them with an IBM 370/145, which was forty times more powerful than the two 1401 machines combined. In 1984, it upgraded to an IBM 3081, again, the latest computer technology; the computers allowed it to take advantage of telecommunications. In 1974, Cetelem installed an internal data network called TRANSPAC that connected all of the roughly 200 Cetelem offices and agencies. In 1980, it began making real-time approvals over the network, and by 1981 all approvals were made over TRANSPAC. In 1983, loan approval times were brought below one minute. By 1984, 3,000 affiliated retailers were connected directly to the Cetelem network via France's early public teletex network, Minitel.

By the 1980s, France's lenders were also thinking differently about their industry. The high inflation period of the late 1970s to early 1980s, in particular, had proved formative. Through the steep fluctuations in interest rates that the inflationary shock caused, lenders learned that consumer demand for credit was relatively insensitive to price. Not only did consumers not seem to care about nominal interest rates, they were also seemingly indifferent to real interest rates. The first lesson came from the rise in inflation in the late 1970s. After bouts of significant inflation during the 1970s, inflation in France briefly touched 20 percent in mid-1981. In order to maintain reasonable real interest rates, consumer finance companies pushed their consumer loan rates to almost 30 percent (see Figure 5.2). At first, they did not know how borrowers would respond. It had long been assumed that 25 percent represented a psychological ceiling for borrowers. However, as this barrier was passed, the head of the

[97] CHA, DO1, Correspondence from Pierre Boucher, director-general, October 4, 1982.

FIGURE 5.2. Nominal and Real Consumer-Lending Rates in France, 1979–1986[98]

Association of French Finance Establishments concluded that "30% per year could be adopted without significant consequences."[99] As the crisis deepened, loan applications actually increased.

The second lesson came with the decline in inflation in the early 1980s. It was during this period that lenders found consumers were also insensitive to real interest rates (i.e., nominal interest minus inflation). As inflation fell, lenders lowered their interest rates more slowly. Recurring bouts of inflation in the 1970s had taught them to be cautious. The result was a growing wedge between consumer interest charges and inflation. Between 1983 and 1986, as average real interest rates for consumer credit in France rose from 10 percent to 15 percent, demand for credit nonetheless continued to rise. By 1986, lenders who had observed this phenomenon drew the obvious conclusion. The head of one consumer finance company explained: "Consumers pay almost no attention to the absolute level of the rate. They are interested mainly in the monthly payment.... No study has ever shown the least correlation between a rise in the cost of credit and a reduction in consumption."[100] For Cetelem, the insight was decisive for the company's strategy. In 1986, CEO Pierre Boucher sent a note to the entire company announcing that "interest rate is not a decisive element in households' decisions to take a short-term loan."[101] From that point

98 Philippe Manière, "Les Constructeurs Auto 'Bradent' Leurs Prêts," *Quotidien de Paris*, April 30, 1986.
99 *Le Matin*, June 29, 1981.
100 *Le Matin*, June 29, 1981.
101 CHA, Pierre Boucher, internal memo, 1996.

on, Cetelem would no longer try to be the lowest-cost lender. It would instead focus on product features that consumers did seem to value and allow interest charges to rise.

Conclusions

For French lenders in the immediate postwar period, the challenge was to make consumer credit socially acceptable. And they had to do so in the absence of two groups that had proved critical in the United States: commercial banks that had embraced consumer lending in the interwar period and social activists who were pushing credit as a solution to social problems. In France, consumer credit found its legitimacy through the close interaction of government regulators and their interaction with the group of dedicated consumer finance companies that would come to dominate the sector.

For Cetelem, building close relations proved exceptionally beneficial. Upon taking office in 1981, President François Mitterrand nationalized France's largest financial institutions. During his campaign, Mitterrand had called for the nationalization of all financial institutions with capital exceeding 3 billion francs. On the day nationalizations were made, January 1, 1981, it was revealed that the threshold for nationalization would be lowered to 1 billion francs. Although no hard evidence exists, it appears that Cetelem was given advanced warning about the change. In the last days of December 1980, Cetelem was approached by Darty, one of its larger retail affiliates, with a request for a large inventory loan. Cetelem did occasionally provide this sort of floor plan for its better customers, but in this case it demurred. Darty responded by moving all of its sales credit business to Cetelem's biggest rival, Sofinco, which agree to finance the floor plan. Sofinco had been formed in 1951 by Suez-le-Hénin, before Cetelem, and had long dominated the French market for furniture sales credit. By 1979, the rival firms were virtually the same size. Both had a little less than 1 billion francs in capital. The large inventory loan to Darty turned out to be just enough to push either firm over the 1 billion franc threshold.[102] When Cetelem stepped back, Sofinco took the bait. With 1.05 billion francs in capital, it was nationalized the following week.[103] From that moment, Cetelem became France's largest consumer lender.

Cetelem also sought to build legitimacy with the general public. It placed itself in retail areas, designed friendly and accessible offices, and pursued amicable relations with customers. This helped distinguish it from banks, which many of its customers saw as stuffy and intimidating. It placed a strong emphasis on efficient operations and low administrative costs, and competed, until

[102] Authur interview with Arnaud Danloux-Dumesnil, Cetelem, June 23, 2008.
[103] Gérard de Chaunac-Lanzac, *La Vie m'a Fait Crédit* (Paris: Chaunac-Lanzac, 2001), 244.

the early 1980s, by offering the lowest interest rates. It treated customers with respect, offered loans with minimum paperwork and delay, provided discretion for borrowers, and embraced a respectful approach to collections. All of these practices contributed to an image of Cetelem credit not as a status symbol, but as a useful tool for responsible workers.

6

Credit and Reconstruction

World War II marked a change in how French and American policymakers conceived of consumer credit. Prior to the war, credit was debated in terms of its impact on workers and welfare. In the wake of the war, credit narratives were recast to emphasize the link between consumer lending and industrial production and economic growth. Yet how credit and growth were related was a matter of significant disagreement. Basic questions about consumer credit – including its effect on prices, household savings rates, and ultimately economic growth – became the focus of national policy debate. In the absence of definitive empirical evidence, national narratives diverged. In America, a coalition of organized labor and government policymakers came together around the idea of credit as a spur to growth. In France, a similar coalition of labor and policymakers came to the opposite conclusion. This chapter traces the role of lenders, organized labor, and central banks in framing these two alternative narratives about postwar consumer credit.

Consumer credit posed a particular conundrum for industrial policy. On the one hand, economic leaders saw the postwar demand for new products as the engine for manufacturing growth. With new housing driving a need for new household technologies, consumer credit could help to satisfy that demand. There was also an efficiency logic to credit. By speeding such purchases, credit could allow manufacturers to increase scale, and this would in turn lower costs for everyone. On the other hand, policymakers in both the United States and France worried that consumer credit would absorb capital that was needed by industry, thereby crowding out industrial investment.[1]

[1] Pierre Locardel, "L'Extension du Crédit à la Consommation Sera Reservé à Certains Articles Utilitaires," *Le Figaro*, April 14, 1953.

They also worried that liberal credit terms, and the heightened demand it generated, could aggravate the challenge of managing inflation. Both countries experimented with selective restrictions on consumer loans in order to fight inflation. In the United States, between 1950 and 1952, the Federal Reserve acting under Regulation W set mandatory thresholds for the down payment and repayment period on installment loans. Initially, these required household borrowers to pay at least 33 percent of the cost of a credit purchase up front (the down payment requirement) and repay the loan within a year. The restrictions were intended to hold down inflation even as the government relied heavily on debt to finance the Korean War effort. In France, similar restrictions on lending terms were introduced in 1954. From these similar starting points, French and American policy diverged. In the United States, support for credit controls quickly evaporated. In France, the policy was embraced and extended for nearly thirty years. French regulators made frequent adjustments to consumer-credit terms as macroeconomic conditions changed. In 1959, for example, as inflationary pressures mounted, the Banque de France briefly raised the down payment required on installment loans to 50 percent of the sales price.

Another reason for the divergence in attitudes toward credit in France and America was the divergent preferences of organized labor. For labor unions, government restrictions on the terms of installment lending posed a challenge because workers were especially sensitive to changes in the terms of installment credit. With lower income and savings, workers acutely felt changes in required down payments and repayment periods. When the mandatory minimum down payments on consumer loans were raised to combat inflation, workers disproportionately bore the burden of the contraction. Yet labor unions also worried about the impact of interest payments on the purchasing power of consumers. Hard-fought pay increases could be lost to new interest charges as workers took on new debts. And, to the extent that consumer credit stoked inflation, this could also hurt worker purchasing power. As Chester C. Davis, president of the U.S. Federal Reserve Bank, argued in 1941, when the United States first considered restricting the terms of installment loans, "What the low-income consumer really needs to fear – and which installment regulation helps to protect him from – is sky-rocketing prices which dip into his pocketbook and cut his real wages."[2]

American and French organized labor took opposite sides in this debate. American unions, and in particular the AFL and CIO, supported worker access to credit and objected to restrictions on lending terms. French unions, led by the communist CGT, opposed any extension of credit to workers, and thus

[2] Archives of the Federal Reserve Bank (FRB), St. Louis, Missouri. Chester C. Davis, president, Federal Reserve Bank of St. Louis, "Business Under Existing Emergency Conditions," address delivered at Meeting of the Chamber of Commerce Sales Managers Bureau Hotel Jefferson, October 3, 1941.

supported restrictions. These different labor views proved critical in pushing the narrative of consumer credit in different directions in the two countries.[3]

In response to these debates over the regulation of credit terms, consumer lenders in both France and America worked to redefine their sectors as integral to the postwar reconstruction project. They sought to defeat the image of consumer lending as a spur to irresponsible consumption by portraying loans as a source of discipline. In particular, lenders in both countries went to great lengths to make a link between credit and savings. They argued that credit was savings "after the fact," that repaying loans instilled a habit of savings, and that the purchase of durable goods was itself a form of savings. It its various forms, this linking of consumer borrowing to savings had the goal of reframing consumer loans as contributing to, not detracting from, industry and investment. Yet the very similarity of lender responses in the two countries raises questions about why national policies with respect to credit differed so much. To get at this, we must look beyond lender preferences toward the consensus that emerged between central bankers and labor unions in the two countries. This alliance, rather than the specific claims of lenders, drove a divergence in regulatory outcomes in the two countries.

Credit Controlled

For Americans, credit restrictions were born in wartime. In August 1941, under authority of the 1917 Trading with the Enemy Act, President Franklin Delano Roosevelt directed the Federal Reserve Board to restrict consumer credit terms. The restrictions were detailed under Regulation W of the Federal Reserve Act. With production diverted to the war effort, policymakers worried that consumer credit would drive demand to outstrip the limited supply of consumer goods. The initial wartime regulation, enacted as part of Roosevelt's "hold the line" program to manage inflation in the context of expansionary war spending, mandated a minimum 33 percent down payment and a twelve-month limit on repayment terms for credit sales. These restrictions were relaxed in November 1947. The Federal Reserve Board reinstituted Regulation W controls two more times: for a nine-month period from August 1948 to May 1949, and from September 1950 to May 1952. Three consecutive governors of the Federal Reserve – Marriner Eccles (1934–1948), Thomas McCabe (1948–1951), and William McChesney Martin (1951–1970) – all supported consumer credit restrictions as a means to hold down inflation.

Enforcing consumer credit terms under Regulation W was a thankless and challenging job. Especially when loans were linked to retail sales, lenders

[3] Ultimately, American unions came around to the French position. By the early 1970s, they concluded that liberal credit terms hurt workers by subjecting them to high interest rates and other unfavorable lending terms. By then, however, the terms of debate over credit had again shifted, with the focus of credit policy moving from its impact on workers to credit access for women, minorities, and the poor.

invented seemingly endless evasions. Retailers in some cases accepted payment on a charge card – to be paid off in a lump sum, and thus not covered by Regulation W – then later converted it into an installment loan. Some stores sold products "on approval," allowing customers to keep the product in their house while they accumulated the capital to pay for it. Other retailers issued multiple sales slips that were individually below the $6 threshold for meeting the mandatory down payment.[4] Because mortgages were exempt from Regulation W, mortgage lenders (including the U.S. Veterans Administration) increasingly allowed borrowers to package a range of household equipment with their home mortgages. These so-called package mortgages grew increasingly popular as wartime installment restrictions persisted.[5] Such financial innovation meant that enforcing Regulation W required constant adjustments. To ensure that retailers did not evade the rule by extending charge-account credit, for example, charge accounts were frozen if they were not paid within forty days. Over the course of World War II, Regulation W was amended sixty times. It nonetheless appears to have been effective. From 1939 to 1944, installment credit sales fell from 12 percent of sales in 1939 to 3 percent of sales in 1944. By contrast, unregulated charge accounts decreased from 23 percent to only 19 percent.[6] It was, as Federal Reserve Governor William McChesney Martin later acknowledged, an "unpleasant task" to administer, but nonetheless "effective and salutary in helping to counteract inflationary forces."[7]

With the end of World War II, the Federal Reserve argued that credit restrictions should be maintained at least until wartime producers had shifted production back to household goods. By 1947, a combination of bankers, industrialists, and labor groups were clamoring to have the credit restrictions loosened. Most of these highlighted the impact that the restrictions were having on the less-well off in society. A. E. Barit, president of Hudson Motor Car Company, argued that the high down-payment requirement hurt low-income customers that needed cars in order to get to work.[8] Northwestern Acceptance Company argued that restrictions on the duration of loans were hurting workers by making it hard to restructure delinquent accounts. A customer who was unable to pay in twelve monthly payments might avoid default if he or she were able to stretch repayment to twenty-four months, thereby lowering his

4 Edwin F. Gahan, "Evasions of Curbs on Credit Fought," *New York Times*, October 4, 1942.

5 Robert Paul Shay, *Regulation W: Experiment in Credit Control*, University of Maine Series, no. 67 (Orono, ME: University Press, 1953), 163.

6 Thomas F. Conroy, "Push Drive to Build Charge Accounts," *New York Times*, September 30, 1945.

7 FRB, Letter from Federal Reserve Board Chairman William McChesney Martin, Jr., July 9, 1951, to Honorable Burnet R. Maybank, Chairman Banking and Currency Committee, United States Senate, and Honorable Brent Spence, Chairman, Banking and Currency Committee, House of Representatives, Board of Governors of the Federal Reserve System, Washington, DC.

8 Meeting of the Board of Governors of the Federal Reserve System with the Presidents of the Federal Reserve Banks, Washington, DC, May 28, 1947, 5.

or her monthly payments.[9] Regulation W made such restructurings impossible. Organized labor argued that both term and down-payment restrictions meant that poorer workers would bear the brunt of monetary policy adjustments.[10]

In a response to these criticisms, the Federal Reserve countered that Regulation W was especially good for "people in the lower income groups" because they "stand to benefit more from the maintenance of economic stability than they would if there were no restraint upon the amounts of credit they might obtain."[11] Some dedicated consumer-finance companies strongly supported the Fed's down-payment and term restrictions on credit. These lenders, many of which purchased sales contracts from retailers, saw Regulation W as a way to ensure that retailers were not making irresponsible loans. They also had concerns about competitors, increasingly in the banking sector, that were willing to offer more liberal lending terms than the finance companies were comfortable offering.[12]

The resumption of hostilities with the Korean War provided a rationale for reinstating Regulation W under authority granted by Congress in the Defense Production Act of 1950. On September 18, "minutes" after Truman signed the Act, the Federal Reserve announced new installment-credit restrictions.[13] In some ways, the new credit terms had a smaller impact than earlier regulations. They covered only installment loans, meaning that store charge accounts and newly emerging revolving-credit accounts were not affected. They also treated different kinds of products differently, with the strictest treatment reserved for automobile manufacturers and distributors. New and used cars would require 33 percent down payments and be limited to fifteen-month financing. Other categories included household appliances (25 percent down, eighteen-month financing), furniture (10 percent down, eighteen-month financing), and home improvement loans (10 percent down, thirty-month financing).[14] A month later, on October 16, 1950, the terms were tightened further, reducing most repayment periods to fifteen months. The new terms generated intensive public criticism, which was initially directed at Congress. Organized labor objected that the new restrictions would push up unemployment.[15] Veterans' groups

9 FRB, meeting minutes, February 15, 1949, 260–261.

10 Thomas F. Conroy, "Business Divided on Regulation W," *New York Times*, January 30, 1944.

11 Meeting of the Board of Governors of the Federal Reserve System with the Presidents of the Federal Reserve Banks, Washington, DC, May 28, 1947, 3–5.

12 See, for example, *Control of Consumer Credit*, proceedings of the Conference (Philadelphia: University of Pennsylvania Press, 1947), 40, in which William Baldwin, the vice-president of GMAC, supports Regulation W and calls for stricter policing.

13 "Installment Buying Is Curbed on Autos, Home Appliances," *New York Times*, September 9, 1950.

14 "Installment Buying Is Curbed on Autos, Home Appliances," *New York Times*, September 9, 1950.

15 *Wall Street Journal*, December 9, 1950.

called for exemptions for disabled war veterans. Businessmen also objected.[16] The most vociferous objectors were automobile dealers, who suffered from the highest level of restraint.[17]

Growing pressure from constituents pitted the Federal Reserve against the powerful Banking and Currency Committees of the Senate and House of Representatives, and constituents increasingly accused the Federal Reserve of "needlessly thwarting business."[18] After holding hearings on Regulation W in July 1951, the congressional committees admonished the Federal Reserve to apply Regulation W with greater flexibility. The Federal Reserve balked. It responded that consumer installment credit was "not a type of credit which is directly essential for national defense."[19] On July 31, 1951, Congress acted directly, preempting the Fed's authority. It amended the Defense Production Act to place limits on installment terms that the Federal Reserve could impose.[20] Repayment periods were loosened from fifteen to eighteen months, and down payments were reduced – in the case of household appliances, from 25 percent to 15 percent.[21]

Ultimately, Regulation W fell victim to a broader struggle over the role of monetary policy in the United States. The Banking Act of 1935, which first centralized control over U.S. monetary policy with the Federal Reserve Board, gave the Board discretion over interest rates. Its autonomy was curtailed with the entry of the United States into World War II in 1942. Under expanded government borrowing to finance the war effort, the Fed committed to help finance expanded government borrowing through bond purchases that kept U.S. Treasury bill yields at 3/8 percent. The effect was to make the Federal Reserve subservient to budget policy set by the Treasury. Without discretion over the general interest rate, and in the face of high inflation (which reached 16 percent by 1947), direct restriction of consumer credit seemed to be one of

[16] George E. Cruikshank, "'W' Again?," *Wall Street Journal*, February 6, 1953.

[17] *Wall Street Journal*, July 21, 1951.

[18] FRB, Letter from Federal Reserve Board Chairman William McChesney Martin, Jr., July 9, 1951, to Honorable Burnet R. Maybank, Chairman Banking and Currency Committee, United States Senate, and Honorable Brent Spence, Chairman, Banking and Currency Committee, House of Representatives, Board of Governors of the Federal Reserve System, Washington, DC.

[19] FRB, Letter from Federal Reserve Board Chairman William McChesney Martin, Jr., July 9, 1951, to Honorable Burnet R. Maybank, Chairman Banking and Currency Committee, United States Senate, and Honorable Brent Spence, Chairman, Banking and Currency Committee, House of Representatives, Board of Governors of the Federal Reserve System, Washington, DC.

[20] See Pub. L. No. 82–96, 65 Stat. 131, as cited by Shay, "Consumer Credit Regulation: A Review and Response" (1966) (Federal Reserve Board, Staff Report no. 15 in "The International Economic Implications of Deregulating the U.S. Banking Industry," *American University Law Review* 25/84 (1981).

[21] *New York Times*, August 1, 1951.

the few tools available to the Federal Reserve. The Federal Reserve's embrace of Regulation W was in this sense a reflection of its broader weakness.

With new inflationary pressures caused by U.S. spending in the Korean War, the Federal Reserve launched a struggle with President Harry Truman to regain its autonomy. The culmination of that confrontation was the Treasury-Federal Reserve Accord of March 1951, in which the Federal Reserve formally gained independence in monetary policy. President Truman, who wished to maintain the interest-rate peg, immediately replaced pro-independence Fed Chairman Thomas McCabe with William McChesney Martin, whom he saw as an ally. As Leon Keyserling recalled, "Martin promptly double-crossed him," and defended an independent Federal Reserve.[22] By the terms of the deal, the Federal Reserve agreed to maintain the discount rate at a low 1.75 percent through the end of 1951.[23] By 1952, as the Fed regained authority to set interest rates at its discretion, sales-credit restrictions lost their allure as a tool for fighting inflation. The Fed rescinded Regulation W in August 1952.

Although Regulation W was not ever invoked again, president periodically contemplated it during periods of inflation. In 1953, President Eisenhower considered requesting that Congress give the Federal Reserve the authority to regulate consumer-credit terms again. Opposition from automakers and the United Auto Workers was vociferous. The six regional governors sitting on the Federal Reserve Board were evenly split on the reimposition of credit terms. No action was taken. As inflation heated up in 1956, the Economic Report of the President again recommended that Congress reinstate the Federal Reserve's authority to regulate terms of credit.[24] By that time, the Federal Reserve had rejected Regulation W as ineffective, and the Federal Reserve's authority ended with the expiration of the Defense Production Act. The Credit Control Act of 1969, passed during the Vietnam War, reinstated that authority.[25] It gave the Federal Reserve broad authority to regulate credit cards, and gave the president standby authority to authorize the Federal Reserve to regulate specific credit terms. President Nixon was opposed to imposing credit controls, and Arthur Burns, chairman of the Federal Reserve, ultimately had to convince Nixon to sign the law. Nixon did not immediately invoke the authority, which became virtually irrelevant when, in 1971, he moved to freeze wages and prices throughout the economy.

[22] Leon Keyserling, Truman Library Oral History Interview, May 3, 1971, 11 (cited in Robert L. Hetzel and Ralph F. Leach), "The Treasury-Fed Accord: A New Narrative Account," *Economic Quarterly* 87/1 (2001), 50.

[23] Robert L. Hetzel and Ralph F. Leach, "The Treasury-Fed Accord: A New Narrative Account," *Economic Quarterly* 87/1 (2001), 50.

[24] CNC, 1427200301, box 319: Secretariat Général du Conseil National du Crédit, États Unis, Mise à Place de la Politique de Crédit, July 1946–December 1966, Banque des Reglements Internationaux, 26eme Rapport Annuel, États-Unis, Crédit à la Consommation, June 11, 1956.

[25] Title II of Public Law 91–151 (1969).

Terms of Credit in France

In December 1945, with the country in chaos following liberation, France formed the National Credit Council (CNC) to help administer monetary policy for the Banque de France and to rationalize the banking sector.[26] Initially, consumer credit was left unregulated. In the fall of 1948, with mounting pressure from inflation, the CNC acted to restrict consumer credit. Virtually all consumer lending halted.[27] In 1952, credit was liberalized again, but the CNC also began discussions on how consumer credit might be regulated over the long term. In 1953, its Committee on Small Loans led a set of discussions focused on three potential problems related to consumer credit. First, by helping retailers maintain sales, credit could hurt price competition. Second, credit could encourage consumers to spend more than they could afford. And third, consumer credit could hurt economic growth by shifting investment toward consumer goods and away from capital investments.[28] Strikingly absent was any consideration of the potential welfare benefits of credit access or the boost it might provide to manufacturers.

Initially, the Committee on Small Loans proposed a "qualitative" approach to regulating consumer lending. The goal was to distinguish between loans for durable goods, which they would liberalize, and loans for nondurables, which they would restrict. Organized labor supported this approach, advocating the licensing only of those lenders who made loans for "goods that, economically speaking, are useful."[29] In practice, however, this distinction between durables and nondurables was hard to maintain. Coupon-credit lenders did not make any distinction between the two, and the economic unions created by associations of small retailers covered all kinds of products and services, apart from food. Merely qualitative restrictions on credit would leave so many exceptions that they were tantamount to full liberalization. In July 1954, the CNC abandoned its qualitative criteria and adopted a system of quantitative restrictions on the terms of credit modeled on those that had been adopted in the United States.

As in the United States, the new restrictions set minimum down payments and maximum repayment periods for consumer installment loans. Unlike in the United States, however, the new installment-term restrictions met with surprisingly little opposition. In part, this was because a relatively small share of

[26] Albert O. Hirschman and Robert V. Rosa, "Postwar Credit Controls in France," *Federal Reserve Bulletin* 35/4 (1949), 349.

[27] M. A. Kriz, "Credit Control in France," *The American Economic Review* 41/1 (1951), 86.

[28] CNC, 1427200301, box 111: Crédit à la Consommation et Vente au Crédit, Gilbert Mathieu, "Le Gouvernement Fixera-t-il un Taux d'Intérêt Maximum pour les Crédits Consentis aux Acheteurs" *Le Monde*, January 4–5, 1953.

[29] CNC, 1427200301, box 283, Comité National du Crédit, Comité du Crédit à Court Terme, December 1953–June 1961, Meeting of the Comité du Crédit à Court Terme, December 24, 1953, M. Drevelle, SNCF, 23.

sales at the time were dependent on credit. In 1953, only 19 percent of new and 10 percent of used car sales in France were on credit, and cars represented two-thirds of purchases made on credit.[30] For large retailers, another source of resistance in the United States, only 1 percent of sales were on credit.[31] Moreover, most lenders at the time were offering credit on terms that were already more stringent than the new controls. The captive auto finance houses DIN and DIAC both required a 50 percent down payment on personal car loans at the time.[32] La Semeuse required 40 percent down and offered a maximum of 6-month repayment.[33] When it began making loans in 1953, Cetelem required a 30 percent down payment.[34] Other lenders were entirely untouched. The economic unions of small retailers were legally exempted, and France's commercial banks were making virtually no consumer loans at the time. Hence, none of the major classes of lenders felt an immediate threat from the new controls. That situation quickly changed.

In May 1955, an administrative decree granted the CNC additional authority to alter the terms of installment credit as required by macroeconomic conditions.[35] From concern about a general overuse of credit, the CNC shifted to using credit terms as a tool for active macroeconomic management. Consumers were known to be relatively insensitive to interest rates. Policymakers thus feared they would respond more slowly to monetary adjustments than did businesses. This insensitivity implied that interest-rate adjustments would have to be more aggressive than would otherwise be merited if the terms of consumer lending could not be controlled directly. Monetary authorities also feared that businesses would subsidize consumer credit during times of monetary contraction in order to stabilize demand for their goods. These subsidies would push against central bank efforts to rein in demand, again dampening the impact of government monetary policy.

France's inspiration for using consumer-credit terms as a tool of macroeconomic policy came from Britain. Starting in 1952, the Conservative government of Winston Churchill had imposed down-payment and repayment restrictions on hire purchase contracts. The French embassy in Britain sent regular

30 "Le Developpement des Ventes à Crédit dans la Region du Nord," *Perspectives*, June 2, 1954; Jean Luc, "La Réglementation des Ventes à Tempérament de la Protection des Acheteurs," *Le Monde*, December 22, 1956.

31 Marius Allègre, "Étude du Crédit à la Consommation," *Conseil Économique*, March 4, 1954, 267–279.

32 CNC, 1427200301, box 111: Crédit à la Consommation et Vente au Crédit, "Enquête sur les Conditions Applizuées par les Entreprises Pratiquant le Financement des Ventes à Tempérament," July 8, 1953.

33 CNC, 1427200301, box 111: Crédit à la Consommation et Vente au Crédit, Correspondence, from Jacques Herisse, Commissaire de Police to Monsieur le Directeur de la Police Économique, "Vente à Crédit de Trousseaux et de Linge de Maison," 1957.

34 CHA, "Note Relative au Crédit à l'Équipement Électromènager," Internal memo, April 1953, 3.

35 "La Réglementation du Crédit à la Consommation Va Être Complétée," *Le Monde*, May 7, 1955.

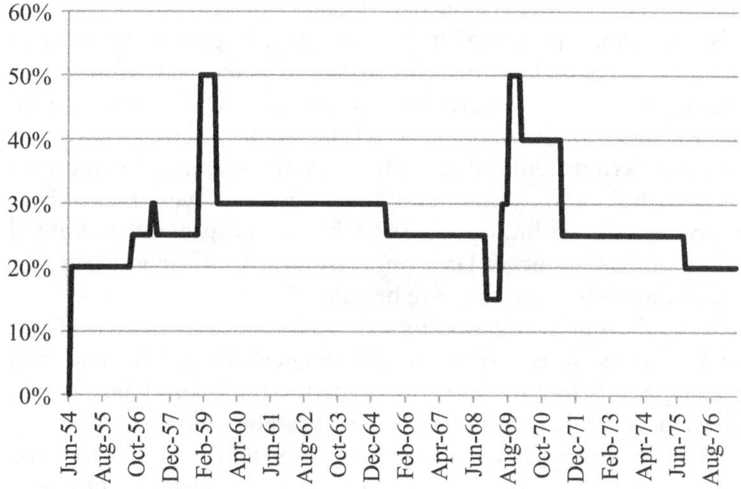

FIGURE 6.1. Minimum Down Payment on Installment Credit in France, 1954–1977

dispatches to the Banque de France reporting on the British experiment.[36] For Britain, hire purchase terms were intended to maintain the balance of trade by reducing imports of steel, on the one hand, and restraining inflation so as to encourage exports, on the other. For France, the focus was less on the balance of payments, because France maintained tight capital controls, and more on domestic industrial policy. Restrictions on consumer credit seemed to offer a means to match sustained spending on key industrial sectors with an inflation-fighting monetary policy.

The CNC adjusted installment-credit terms roughly a dozen times over the following two decades (see Figure 6.1). Twice it pushed mandatory down payments up to 50 percent of the sales price: first in 1958–1959 and again in 1968–1969. Repayment periods were also shortened. For automobiles, which received the strictest treatment, loan repayment periods were reduced to fifteen months.[37] These periods of tightening were brief, but seemingly effective. In the first episode, outstanding consumer credit fell from 1 percent of GDP before the control to 0.5 percent of GDP by the end.[38] But the broader economic impact seems to have been small. Credit still represented a small share of consumer demand at the time, and the temporary restraint evoked virtually no reaction from organized labor or manufacturers. The CNC's second move to tighten credit terms, in September 1969, came in the wake of the 1968 student/worker protests. Perhaps inevitably, it was more contested. First, consumer credit use

[36] See, for example: BdF/CDC, 1427200301, box 318, Grande Bretagne, Crédit à la Consommations, 1950–1968, Philippe Dargenton, Inspecteur des Finance, Ambassade de France à Londre, "Note sur le Crédit à la Consommation en Grande-Bretagne," August 12, 1954.

[37] "La Politique de Crédit à la Consommation Depuis 1958," *Actualités-Service: Économie et Finances* 22, June 1969, 4.

[38] "Le Crédit à la Consommation en France," *Agence Économique et Financière*, June 9, 1959.

in France had grown four times over the past decade, from 2.4 billion francs in 1959 to 11.6 billion francs in 1969.[39] It was also more important as a source of sales for manufacturers and retailers. By 1969, 30 percent of white goods and 45 percent of new cars were purchased on credit.[40] Again, cars received the toughest treatment, with down payments rising from 30 percent to 50 percent, and repayment periods reduced again from twenty-one months to fifteen months.[41] For household goods, minimum down payments were raised from 30 percent to 40 percent. To limit popular backlash, and provide additional incentives for households to put off large purchases, the CNC announced that the period of restraint would last only five months.[42]

The response to the tightening was mixed. As in the United States, critics noted that restricting access to loans with smaller down payments and longer repayment periods had the effect of targeting the poorest borrowers. Some leftists even accused French President Georges Pompidou of retaliating against the 1968 protestors by restricting credit in a way that especially targeted workers and the young.[43] Employers warned of the likely impact on business, especially small business. Léon Gingembre, founding president to the confederation of small and medium enterprises (CGPME), labeled the government effort "to reduce production by limiting consumption" as "very dangerous."[44] Consumer-finance companies warned that the restraint would induce retailers to offer their own credit, on highly unfavorable terms.[45] President Pompidou asserted that the restraints would help raise French savings, increase investment, and, by lowering domestic demand, push French companies to export.[46] In fact, the impact was not as dramatic as expected; new consumer lending was 10 percent lower in 1969 than in 1968.[47]

CNC control over credit terms endured for another decade, until it was eliminated by Economics Minister René Monory as part of an initial wave of economic deregulation in 1979. But the 1969 tightening was the last time it would be the primary focus of France's credit policy.[48] Partly because of charges that installment restrictions were discriminating against the poor

[39] Conseil National du Crédit, *Rapport pour l'Année 1959*, 1960; *Le Nouveau Journal*, September 30, 1970.

[40] *Le Monde*, August 30, 1969.

[41] "Les Restrictions du Crédit à la Consommation," *Les Échos*, September 1, 1969; "La Politique de Crédit à la Consommation Depuis 1958," *Actualités-Service: Économie et Finances* 22, June 1969, 4.

[42] Alain Weiller, "Les Restrictions d'Achats à Crédit ne Dureront que Cinq Mois," *France-Soir*, August 30, 1969.

[43] Jacques Kahn, "La France se Portera-t-elle Mieux Parce que les Jeunes Ménages Auront Plus de Mal à se Meubler?" *L'Humanité*, August 30, 1969.

[44] *Le Monde*, August 30, 1969.

[45] "Les Restrictions du Crédit à la Consommation," *Les Échos*, September 1, 1969.

[46] Alain Weiller, "Les Restrictions d'Achats à Crédit ne Dureront que Cinq Mois," *France-Soir*, August 30, 1969.

[47] *Les Échos*, January 20, 1970.

[48] *Le Monde*, April 26, 1979.

and partly out of concern that lenders were finding ways to evade the restrictions, the Banque de France began moving toward a more direct strategy for controlling credit growth. Beginning already in 1958, the Banque de France began experimenting with quantitative restrictions on credit extension that it called *encadrement de credit* (this was translated, infelicitously, as the "credit corset"). *Encadrement* was at first applied selectively – in 1958–1959, 1963–1965, and 1968–1970 – and primarily to commercial lending activities. It was applied to consumer loans for the first time in 1972, but then quickly became the main tool by which France reconciled the need to fight inflation with a continuing preoccupation with indicative economic planning.[49]

The adoption of encadrement changed the tone of business-government relations in the lending sector. Although the goal was to limit aggregate credit growth in consumer lending, annual credit volumes were allocated on a firm-by-firm basis.[50] The CNC granted each lending institution an annual quota for credit extension, allowing them broad discretion about how to meet the quota.[51] From 1973 to 1981, the average growth in consumer credit was 11 percent.[52] However, because the new quota was not allocated equally across lenders, it fostered a competition among firms to win the approval of the regulators. Lenders that complied with government goals and recommendations were given more generous growth margins. Cetelem, for example, was allocated an average credit growth rate of 17 percent over this period. Caught by the need to maintain government favor, these lenders were in a weak position to push against an increasingly stringent regulation of their sector.

Workers and Credit

These seemingly technical debates about credit regulation became the focus of intensive interest by other economic interests in society. In this broader debate, organized labor proved especially influential. In both France and America, consumer credit posed a conundrum for the labor unions. On the one hand, the short-term benefits of consumer credit were hard to deny. It allowed workers to purchase household goods such as refrigerators, washing machines, and

49 "Le Crédit à la Consommation," *Économie Geographie* 223 (March 1985), 15.
50 Henri Sterdyniak and Christian Vasseur, "Encadrement du Crédit et Politique Monétaire," *Observations et Diagnostiques Économiques* 11 (1985), 110.
51 *Le Monde*, January 7, 1989.
52 **Average Growth in Consumer Credit Extension under "Encadrement."**

1973	1974	1975	1976	1977	1978	1979	1980	1981
13%	12%	17%	10.5%	10%	10%	9%	7%	7%

CHA, "Orientation du Cetelem – Réseau Agréé – 1981," October 1980 (confidential) (AH-1991), 3–4.

automobiles. This became especially important with the rise of government-supported home loans that increasingly allowed workers to purchase houses that they then needed to furnish. Growth in consumer credit also drove a rapid growth in demand for the products of industrialization, especially automobiles and household equipment. The high demand in turn created new employment opportunities. On the other hand, labor unions worried that interest charged on the loans siphoned away income from spending, thereby lowering worker's purchasing power. In America, organized labor embraced the benefits of liberal credit access. In France, organized labor emphasized its costs for workers, and the peril it posed for the labor movement.

French Labor and Credit

Despite fractures in the French labor movement, virtually all labor groups opposed consumer credit. French socialist Max Léon, writing in 1956 in *L'Humanité*, captured the general tenor of their disapproval in describing consumer credit as "a system that generates comfortable profits for large firms and reduces the purchasing power of the customer."[53] His concern was that the interest paid on purchases increased the price that workers would pay for products. For French labor organizers, it was galling to see hard-fought wage gains lost to high-interest payments on consumer loans. The CGT warned that consumer credit was primarily "a means to slow the growth in direct revenue from work."[54] The union of rail workers, for example, opposed offering credit in the company commissary on the grounds that credit would "create fairly important reductions in the finances of workers."[55]

But there was also a secondary effect that worried France's labor leaders. Over the course of the 1950s, observers on both the right and the left noted that consumer credit deradicalized rank-and-file labor union members. By giving quick access to desirable consumer goods, it undermined trade union arguments that workers were not benefiting sufficiently from the postwar prosperity. Already in the late nineteenth century, credit from furniture magnate Dufayel was observed to keep the working classes "at home with family and furniture," and out of the radical café politics of the time.[56] Some postwar observers applauded this *embourgeoisement* of the working classes through credit.[57] Having gained the material benefits of industrialization, in the form of house, car, and television, workers appeared not to have much to protest

[53] Max Léon, "Rien à Payer," *L'Humanité*, July 3, 1956.

[54] Bulletin du Conseil Économique 24, October 24, 1956; René Creussol, "Le Developpement des Ventes à Crédit," *Économie et Politique* 22 (1956), 9.

[55] Bulletin du Conseil Économique 24, October 24, 1956; René Creussol, "Le Developpement des Ventes à Crédit," *Économie et Politique* 22 (1956), 9.

[56] Marjorie Anne Beale, "Mort à Crédit: The Credit Department Store and the Parisian Lower Classes, 1856–1920," Harvard History Department undergraduate thesis, 1982, 36.

[57] René Sédillot, *La Vie Française*, February 5, 1954.

against. The calming effect of material acquisition by the working classes was seen to promote social and political stability. Gabriel Veraldi wrote in *La Vie Française* in 1958: "The stability of the state requires, to a growing degree, the participation of workers in the benefits of progress. Consumer credit plays a social, economic, and political role of first order."[58]

For the French labor left, consumer credit looked like a form of social appeasement that ultimately could lead to a decline in trade union activism.[59] They interpreted the seeming passivity associated with credit not as a side-effect of material welfare but as response to the weight of obligations to pay monthly interest installments. Bearing up under an accumulation of debts, and the claim on future income that this implied, workers seemed to become more hesitant to risk losing their jobs and thus less willing to strike. Most critical was France's communist CGT, which from a high point in the immediate postwar years had by the mid-1950s lost much of its militant edge. Writing in 1956, one CGT representative to parliament saw credit as the problem: "The worker who has many debts to pay and who does not want to lose valuable objects, becomes less demanding; what he most wants above all is not to lose his position."[60] Socialist Max Léon observed that indebted workers were not only less likely to strike, but also more likely to accept overtime work.[61] Leftist commentator René Creussol argued that credit was offered by employers specifically to pacify the work force. "Employers hope that the need for regular repayment will cause workers to lose their combativeness and even, at the limit, their class consciousness, since they have to allocate a share of their salary at the end of each month toward paying their debts."[62] He argued that workers who did take out credit were reluctant to participate in strikes that had been unanimously supported by their peers. It was a concern that was echoed by organized labor across much of Europe.[63]

Even in the face of government credit restrictions, France's left remained decidedly uneasy about consumer credit. Michael Seidman, in his study of the

[58] Gabriel Veraldi, "Une Solution au Problème du Pouvoir d'Achat," *La Vie Française*, October 3, 1958.

[59] René Sedillot, "Le Crédit à la Consommation," *La Vie Française*, February 5, 1954.

[60] *Bulletin du Conseil Économique* 24, October 24, 1956, 502.

[61] Max Léon, "Rien à Payer," *L'Humanité*, July 3, 1956.

[62] René Creussol, "Le Developpement des Ventes à Crédit," *Économie et Politique* 22 (1956), 78–79.

[63] British Labour MP Aneurin (Nye) Bevan, who as health minister oversaw the creation of the National Health Service, articulated this concern that credit was de-radicalizing the left. In 1959, the year before he died, he described the failure of trade unionism to activate a new generation of younger workers: "Most of them are indebted, either from paying high mortgages to purchase a house, or to purchase household equipment, modern accessories or even for cars purchased on the installment plan. They bear two contradictory sentiments: satisfaction in seeing their material situation improve, and fear at not being able to pay the debts." *L'Express*, October 15, 1959. Cited in: Michel Drancourt, *Une Force Inconnue: Le Crédit* (Paris: Hachette, 1961), 180.

tensions between workers and students in France's 1968 protests, attributes some of the growing rift between the two factions to the large amount of debt held by workers. At the Renault factory, a center for worker protest, many of the older workers were burdened with mortgage and car payments, and younger workers were often behind on their payments.[64] Keeping up with payments was not necessarily compatible with sustained strike action. This concern about the impact of credit on workers was shared across the political spectrum. Anticommunist politician Jean-Paul David, founder of France's European Liberal Party, equated the indebtedness of French households with the unemployment that the students and workers were fighting against: "To encourage credit in order to relaunch growth is a good thing. To allow it to ruin those who do not know how to organize a budget, establish spending priorities, is as serious a fault of the state as it is to abandon hundreds of thousands of our compatriots to unemployment."[65] Whether out of concern about declining worker activism, or a more patrician attitude toward working-class imprudence, support for the idea of credit controls remained strong.

American Labor and Credit

For organized labor in the United States, the view of consumer credit could not have been more different. Labor union support for liberal worker access to credit traced its roots to the interwar period. In 1933, the American Federation of Labor came out in favor of the Russell Sage small loan legislation, arguing that "credit to persons of small incomes may be essential to tide over emergencies and to prevent the loss of a lifetime's savings."[66] It also supported the FHA Title I program for home-improvement loans. With the end of World War II, labor support for consumer credit was, if anything, stronger. This was partly because credit allowed workers to buy products that they had not been able to purchase during the war. When he visited U.S. consumer lenders in 1952, Cetelem's Boris Mera noted that the largest American workers organizations supported access to credit "because they give workers access to products."[67] Although organized labor did worry about the cost of credit, and would later dedicate significant political efforts to fighting high interest rates on consumer loans, in the early postwar period they overwhelmingly emphasized its benefits. J. Albert Woll, a labor lawyer who later joined the AFL-CIO, wrote in 1954: "So long as responsible sources of consumer credit are available at reasonable cost commensurate with the risk and expense of doing business, the family will rehabilitate itself with the perseverance and self-sacrifice typical

64 Michael Seidman, *The Imaginary Revolution: Parisian Students and Workers in 1968* (Wilmington: University of North Carolina Press, 2004), 232.

65 Jean-Paul David, "Une Carte Nationale de Crédit," *Bulletin d'Information – Parti Libéral Européen* 119, March 8, 1968.

66 *American Federationist*, April 1933, 345–346.

67 CHA, UFB, "Notes sur le Financement des Ventes à Crédit aux États-Unis," December 1952, 8.

of Americans."[68] But self-reliance was not the only purpose of credit. It also proved critical in sustaining workers, especially in the coal and steel mining sectors, through brutal early-postwar strike actions.

It is difficult to assess how important strike loans were to the success of labor mobilizations in the 1940s and 1950s. The best documented cases involved the strikes led by the United Mine Workers against U.S. Steel and its coal subsidiaries in western Pennsylvania and eastern Ohio and Pennsylvania. These were described by *Wall Street Journal* writer Edward Lally, whose reporting on the experiences of mine workers during periods of work stoppage included the household finances of mining families. His accounts reveal that, although strikers had access to several sources of potential public relief, including local charities, poor relief, and food distributed by the Department of Agriculture, most relied first and foremost on private credit.[69] Workers took out loans, either from banks or, more commonly, in the form of store credit from local retailers, to support themselves through protracted strike actions.

The bulk of credit to strikers was store credit. During the 1946 coal strikes in West Virginia and Eastern Ohio, a store owner in Wheeling, West Virginia, reported to Lally: "That merchants do 'carry' the miners in times of strike is axiomatic in coal communities."[70] Another store posted a sign in the window saying: "Your credit is as good now as it has been in the past."[71] For mines in remote areas, even the company store would extend credit to cover strikers during the strike. During a 1948 work stoppage at the Klondike field in Ronco, Pennsylvania, relating to pension negotiations, the Union Supply Company offered workers credit of $2–3 per family per day, and up to $5 per day for a large family. In case of a protracted strike, or series of strikes, the debt burden could become quite high. By late 1949, for example, coal strikers in western Pennsylvania were carrying as much as $800–1,000 in credit from the company store. One independent merchant announced that he was offering miners up to $2,000 in credit.[72] This was not an isolated case; a decade later, Lally reported that the Union Supply Co., the company store of U.S. Steel's Tennessee Iron, extended $672,000 to the 5,000 members of local 1013 during the 36-day Birmingham, Alabama, strike, for an average of $4 per worker per day.[73] For miners on an average monthly salary of $350, debt incurred over protracted strikes could take time to pay down. When the United Mine Workers tried to get coal miners back on strike in the fall of 1946, for example, many were still paying off debts from strikes the previous spring.[74]

68 J. Albert Woll, "Organized Labor Views of the Loan Shark Problem," *Law and Contemporary Problems* 19/1 (1954), 99.
69 Edward J. Lally, "Coal Strikers," *Wall Street Journal*, October 31, 1949.
70 Edward J. Lally, "Coal Country Slump," *Wall Street Journal*, November 27, 1946.
71 Edward J. Lally, "Coal Country Slump," *Wall Street Journal*, November 27, 1946.
72 Edward J. Lally, "Meet the Miner," *Wall Street Journal*, April 10, 1948.
73 *Wall Street Journal*, June 19, 1959.
74 Edward J. Lally, "Coal Country Slump," *Wall Street Journal*, November 27, 1946.

Some attributed the willingness of local stores to extend strike credit to a fear of retribution. "A hard-up miner denied credit when he has rough going would be likely to remember it when he was flush."[75] But there is little evidence for this sort of reprisal. Observing the 1949 coal strikes, Lally noted that of the thirty-four families cut off from credit by the Union Supply Co., thirty returned to do business with them after their strike.[76] It is more likely that offering store credit during strikes, even protracted strikes, was simply good business. Local stores were accustomed to providing workers with credit to buffer annual fluctuations in demand for workers at coal mines. For company stores, credit typically came in the form of scrip, a company-issued currency that allowed workers to make purchases in advance of their end-of-month paycheck.[77] Company stores enjoyed the added advantage of being able to extract repayment directly from the workers' paychecks.[78] Even among independent retailers, though, miners were known to be good credit risks. The credit these stores offered made them popular with workers even if they tended to charge higher prices and offer lower-quality goods.[79]

Over time, the steel and mining unions became more organized in their support of strike credit. The first example of explicit union support for worker strike credit in the United States was in the Youngstown, Ohio, steel strike of 1882. As part of a union effort to extend the strike, for which employers thought worker support was waning, the Amalgamated Association union agreed to secure an additional nine months of store credit for its workers.[80] By the post–World War II period, unions commonly negotiated with financial institutions for revised repayment terms for their members. In the steel strikes of 1959, steelworker locals in Western Pennsylvania and Eastern Illinois prearranged mortgage and debt moratoria with local banks and stores. This turned out to be important in mobilizing workers to strike, as the recession of 1958 had

[75] Price V. Fishback, *Soft Coal, Hard Choices: the Economic Welfare of Biuminous Coal Miners, 1890–1930*, 136.

[76] Edward J. Lally, "Meet the Miner," *Wall Street Journal*, April 10, 1948.

[77] Price V. Fishback, "Did Coal Miners 'Owe their Souls to the Company Store'? Theory and Evidence from the early 1900s," *Journal of Economic History* 46/4 (1986), 1018; Thomas G. Andrews, *Killing for Coal: America's Deadliest Labor War* (Cambridge, MA: Harvard University Press, 2008), 220–221.

[78] Price V. Fishback, *Soft Coal, Hard Choices: the Economic Welfare of Biuminous Coal Miners, 1890–1930*, 136.

[79] Lawrence R. Lynch, "The West Virginia Coal Strike," *Political Science Quarterly* 29/4 (1914), 656.

[80] *New York Times*, September 5, 1882; see also *Wall Street Journal*, May 3, 1912. More than 100 years later, this sort of loan guarantee was still being used by the National Education Association to support teacher-strike actions. From December 18, 1989, to February 28, 1990, the NEA's National Education Employees Assistance Fund loaned $1.28 million to the TerreBonne Education Association Federal Credit Union as collateral on loans to striking members of the Louisiana Education Assocation; $27,236 ended up having to be written off. Myron Lieberman, Charlene K.I. Haar, and Leo Troy, *The NEA and the AFT: Teacher Unions in Power and Politics* (Rockport, MA: Pro-Active Publications, 1994), 92.

left them short of work, and many workers were still repaying loans incurred to cover this down period. Where they were unable to negotiate moratoria, union locals would step in to support individual workers who were unable to keep up on their interest payments. "We'll pay," described one local union leader, "if a finance company's going to foreclose on a guy's house because he missed his last paycheck and can't pay."[81] Mostly, however, banks simply agreed to defer payments until the strike ended. During the protracted 1967 Anaconda copper mine strike in Butte, Montana, the local bank refused to foreclose on workers who held mortgages. The bank manager explained: "They'll make good once the strike ends."[82]

Reimagining Credit as Thrift

For French and American lenders, the evolution of the national narrative surrounding consumer credit from the pre–World War II emphasis on welfare to the postwar emphasis on industrial growth posed a special challenge. So long as credit had been about welfare and worker self-reliance, broader access to credit was easy to interpret as socially positive. With a new postwar emphasis on the link to industrial growth, however, the interwar narrative that had helped transform small lending into a legitimate and socially useful business once again came under threat. To the extent that postwar industrial policy entailed savings and investment, thrift and discipline, it was possible once again to see credit as a social cost rather than a benefit. This possibility led lenders in France and the United States to re-narrate the logic and public purpose of consumer loans. In the new narrative – one that was strikingly similar in both countries – credit was reimagined as a tool to promote savings, thrift, and discipline.

In France, such arguments played a central role in public debates about the degree to which credit should be liberalized or regulated. The relatively small cadre of consumer-finance companies worked to portray consumer credit as beneficial for both French workers and industry. Their case was grounded in three related arguments. First, they argued that consumer credit would provide a "spark" that would ignite a rapid growth in product and consumption of modern household goods.[83] The idea was that credit could launch a virtuous cycle: new demand would drive new production, this would create new manufacturing jobs, and those would in turn increase demand further.[84] Looking back in 1955, the consumer group UFC gave its endorsement to the virtuous-cycle argument. By then, Cetelem alone had funded 150,000 households to buy stoves and refrigerators using more than 7 billion francs

[81] *Wall Street Journal*, June 19, 1959.

[82] Michael K. Drapkin, "Strikebound Town," *Wall Street Journal*, November 30, 1967.

[83] CHA, "Le Démarrage du CETELEM," July 8, 1983.

[84] CHA, UFB, "Note Relative à la Vente à Crédit des Biens d'Équipement Électro-Ménager," January 3, 1953.

of credit. As France's leading consumer association acknowledged: "Those goods would certainly not have been purchased, and therefore not produced, if it had not been for [Cetelem]."[85] Even non-borrowers benefited, because the growth in scale permitted by new credit sales lowered the price of goods for everyone.[86]

The second and related case made by lenders was that consumer credit would be beneficial for French families. Lenders pointed out that the French government had supported mortgages to promote home sales but had not made provisions for the homeowners to furnish their new houses. Trade unions, while skeptical of consumer credit generally, supported credit for household equipment. In 1956, only 9 percent of French workers had refrigerators, 5 percent had washing machines, and only 24 percent even had hot water.[87] Lenders also clearly suggested that a well-furnished home could cure perceived social ills of the middle-class family. Cetelem, in making the case for greater credit access, argued that "the social interest in this effort is too evident... keeping women in the home; reducing the difficulties of finding domestic help; fighting the attraction of the café."[88] They also argued that credit provided families with a means to hedge against potential inflation: "The salaried worker [is] able, thanks to this mechanism, to have a specific good at a specific time, while fixing definitely at that date the purchasing power of a salary that risks to not follow – or only to follow far behind – the rhythm of a new decline of the money."[89] High inflation in the early 1950s made this sort of argument particularly compelling, and in any case dramatically reduced the interest burden of fixed-rate installment loans. In the longer-term, the expectation was that credit would help restrain inflation, as goods for which there is credit will enjoy a greater volume, greater economies of scale, and therefore lower prices.[90]

But the most important argument that France's consumer lenders made was to equate credit with savings. For Cetelem, portraying consumer credit as savings was central to its identity from the very founding of the company. Jacques de Fouchier, the head of Cetelem's holding company, Compagnie Bancaire, acknowledged the perception that household borrowing could hurt the economy: "Household savings is, directly or indirectly, the source for capital markets.... It could seem that there was a conflict between the behavior of

[85] Union Fédérale de la Consommation, *Bulletin Mensuel d'Information* 29 (1955), 47.
[86] Jean Chicoye, "Les Achats à Crédit," *Revue de l'Action Populaire* 140 (July–August 1960), 794.
[87] Max Léon, "Rien à Payer," *L'Humanité*, July 3, 1956.
[88] CHA, UFB, "Note Relative à la Vente à Crédit des Biens d'Équipement Électro-Ménager," October 9, 1952.
[89] CHA, UFB, "Note Relative à la Vente à Crédit des Biens d'Équipement Électro-Ménager," October 9, 1952.
[90] Pierre Locardel, "L'Extension du Crédit à la Consommation Sera Reservé à Certains Articles Utilitaires," *Le Figaro*, April 14, 1953.

households [in borrowing on credit] and the financial health of the productive economy." He noted that this conflict was only apparent, however, because "the act of credit... implies a process of savings in the form of reimbursement.... The savings follows the investment."[91] This idea that credit was equivalent to savings – that it was, as Cetelem's founder Jean Chicoye called it, "directed savings" – lay at the very heart of Cetelem's corporate image.[92] Cetelem's early promotional material, targeted as much at the regulatory authorities on which they relied for approval as to potential borrowers, emphasized credit as a tool for economic virtue: "Buying on credit means agreeing in advance to save while enjoying immediately the productive capital that is household equipment: it is therefore an act of good management."[93]

In the somewhat puritanical culture of early Cetelem, what mattered about installment buying was the discipline it imposed. For families, credit became a training tool for responsible financial management. The need to make fixed monthly payments instilled virtuous patterns of thrift that would endure even after the loan was repaid. In its early promotional material to Frigidaire, for which Cetelem hoped to provide credit, it emphasized that installment payment "instills a habit of saving by the buyer."[94] Nor was it likely that income not used for installment payments would go toward savings. It warned that families that were forced to wait long enough to save for a major expense might simply give up and end up spending their income on current consumption.[95] "Nothing guarantees the amount used to reimburse the credit would have been saved," Chicoye warned. More likely, it would have gone to "other purchases for which the useful character would have certainly been questionable."[96] As an object lesson, Cetelem often compared the level of installment credit sold in France to the (comparable) level of household expenditures on gambling.[97] In the late 1950s, the French government commissioned a study to see what effect installment credit was having in countries with higher levels of credit use than those found in France. In a study of borrowers in Canada, Australia, and Britain, researchers concluded that installment credit allowed people to plan

91 CHA, Michel de Fouchier, "Les Prets aux Particuliers et l'Épargne," presentation to the international group for the study of the problem of savings, October 1967, 1.

92 Jean Chicoye, "Les Achats à Crédit," *Revue de l'Action Populaire* 140 (July–August 1960), 786–798.

93 CHA, Promotional material for launch of Cetelem, "Note d'Information Concernant le CETELEM," September 1953, 2.

94 CHA, "Pourquoi Vendre à Crédit?" Document prepared for presentation at Frigidaire (c. 1959).

95 CHA, Michel de Fouchier, "Les Prets aux Particuliers et l'Épargne," presentation to the international group for the study of the problem of savings, October 1967, 1.

96 Jean Chicoye, "Les Achats à Crédit," *Revue de l'Action Populaire* 140 (July–August 1960), 797.

97 CHA, AH 1979, E-10, Études et Planification, "Le Crédit à l'Equipement des Particuliers," January 8, 1979, 12.

financially, and that this induced "a greater effort in their professional [lives] and a more precise organization of their own budgets."[98]

Advocates in the consumer-lending sector often went further, arguing that credit *was* savings. Politically, the intent was to link consumer credit to the national project of postwar reconstruction. If borrowing was helping increase savings, rather than reduce it, then credit was abetting postwar industrial redevelopment. Henri Dhavernas, the head of Diner's Club in France, was typical in his rhetoric when he announced in 1968: "The French will understand, like Americans have, that credit is the modern form of savings."[99] Exactly what this sort of claim meant differed from observer to observer. Cetelem's de Fouchier, speaking in 1967 before the International Study Group on the Problem of Savings, noted that countries with higher consumer borrowing did not necessarily have lower savings rates. France, after all, had low consumer borrowing and household savings of 7.5 percent of disposable income; the United States had high consumer borrowing and household savings of 10.1 percent.[100] Others argued, somewhat evasively, that installment credit equaled savings in the form of products rather than money. And there was at least some recognition that consumers might borrow and save at the same time. In 1962, the French bank Crédit Lyonnais approached Cetelem to invite it to open independent kiosks within the Crédit Lyonnais branch offices. It argued such an arrangement would benefit both parties: Cetelem would benefit from preferred access to its customers, and Crédit Lyonnais would be able to attract new depositors from among Cetelem's clients.[101] The idea, which was eventually shelved, mirrored the experience of U.S. banks, which enjoyed a growth in deposits when they introduced consumer-lending products.

Credit and Discipline in America

American consumer lenders echoed their French counterparts in making the case that consumer credit increased household savings and therefore investment. Their argument, conveyed concisely in a 1959 pamphlet prepared by the Colorado Consumer Finance Association, was that "credit encourages thrift."[102] Almost since they have existed, American consumer lenders have linked credit products with savings plans. These lending products took a variety of forms. Arthur Morris, who introduced the first "Morris" installment plan in the United States in 1910, allowed borrowers who continued to pay

98 "Le Crédit à la Consommation en Grande-Bretagne, au Canada et en Australie," *Notes et Études Documentaires*, no. 2697, La Documentation Française, September 6, 1960, 25.

99 Maurice Roy, "La Guerre des Cartes est Déclarée," *L'Éxpress*, March 4, 1968.

100 CHA, Michel de Fouchier, "Les Prets aux Particuliers et l'Épargne," presentation to the international group for the study of the problem of savings, October 1967, 1.

101 CHA, Jean Chicoye, "Compte-Rendu d'Entretien avec Monsieur Bloch-Laine du Crédit Lyonnais," April 14, 1970, D90.

102 RLDM, box 58, folder 13, Colorado Consumer Finance Association, "Consumer Credit Is Building Colorado," pamphlet, c. 1959, 4.

their monthly installment beyond the period of the loan to earn interest of 5 percent on those deposits. "By these operations [the borrower] has learned thrift, and probably for the first time has become a property holder."[103] They also attributed the relative calmness of the American labor movement to the pacifying effects of credit. Writing in 1929, just as the Great Depression was taking hold, John Walker, CEO of the Morris Plan Corporation, emphasized the role of lending in forestalling worker radicalization: "The deafness of American labor to the wiles of the Soviet and Communistic propagandists is due to the fact that ... they have acquired, or are acquiring, property of one sort or another through the instrumentality of Consumer Credit."[104]

By the 1950s, the idea of credit as savings was part of a broader political gambit to recast consumer credit as promoting, rather than detracting from, industrialization. The goal for consumer lenders was to portray their line of business as economically productive and socially respectable. In 1958, the banking-industry magazine *American Banker* declared a minor revolution in home economics: "Americans have learned to save a new way – they save their money in durable goods which they buy on the installment plan."[105] They also emphasized the discipline imposed by credit: "The typical installment borrower today is not an improvident man with small income.... He has committed himself to a regimen of small monthly payments for the purpose of acquiring an equity. To him these payments are essentially savings.... It is an investment in life itself."[106] Postwar credit advocates also repeated the argument that credit thwarted communism. Willam J. Cheyney, who would later become head of the lender-affiliated National Foundation for Consumer Credit, described consumer credit as a bulwark against the preeminent scourge of the 1950s. Writing in 1952, as McCarthyism was beginning to take hold, Cheyney imagined a world without consumer credit: "If it hadn't happened, wouldn't these people likely have their tongues out for Communism – any ism – instead of private enterprise?"[107]

This emphasis on credit as savings might have been purely a marketing stance, except that there was some evidence that credit and savings actually were connected, if in complicated ways. One of the surprising but seemingly universal findings in the new postwar consumer credit markets was the tendency

[103] *The Morris Plan of Industrial Loans and Investments* (New York: Industrial Finance Corporation, 1915), 10.

[104] AJM, box 6, The Morris Plan Corporation of America, 1925–1967, "Address of John R. Walker, President of the Morris Plan Corporation of America," July 2, 1929, 7.

[105] Otto Lorenz, associate editor, *American Banker*, "Installment Credit Leads to New Form of Savings," *1957 Consumer Credit Symposium* (New York: Consolidated Reporting Company, 1958), 98.

[106] Louis J. Asterita, deputy manager, American Bankers Association, "Installment Credit – A Safe Investment for Commercial Banks," *1957 Consumer Credit Symposium* (New York: Consolidated Reporting Company, 1958), 42.

[107] William J. Cheyney, *The Growth of an Idea* (Washington, DC: National Foundation for Consumer Credit, 1952), 67.

for households to save and borrow at the same time. In one early inquiry into this phenomenon, a U.S. retail survey in 1945 asked whether store owners thought consumers would in general buy on credit even if they had sufficient savings to pay without credit. Of the retailers who expressed an opinion, 75 percent answered yes: consumers would borrow in order not to erode their own savings.[108] In a set of consumer surveys conducted by University of Michigan researcher George Katona in 1964, fully a third of installment buyers reported having sufficient savings to pay with cash, but preferred to use credit.[109] In his 1960 study of the auto-lending sector, Allen Jung reported the same phenomenon. At that time, U.S. auto loans averaged 11 percent APR and savings accounts were capped at 3 percent. Yet many consumers who had sufficient savings nonetheless preferred to purchase on credit because, in Jung's interpretation, "savings are hard to replace."[110] American banks, as they increasingly entered the consumer-lending business in the 1950s, noted the same surprising behavior. A San Francisco banker expressed amazement that average consumers were "buying more on credit and laying away even more in savings."[111] A prominent banker in Chicago, describing a customer who borrowed $2,000 to visit Europe even though he had $5,000 'in the till,' emphasized the need to maintain financial discipline: "The average family is reluctant to use savings for some of the luxuries of life because he [sic] knows he won't put it back."[112] And Otto Lorenz, a writer with *American Banker*, described "instances clear across the United States of individuals who borrow from the personal loan departments in banks, march straight across the lobby and deposit the proceeds in their savings accounts where they let the cash lie undisturbed year after year." Why? "The personal loan installment obligation is a debt which 'makes' them save."[113]

American consumer advocates also saw installment credit as, if not equivalent to savings, at least a good second-best option for households that could not manage to save on their own. For example, the merits and risks of consumer credit were laid out in a series of educational pamphlets prepared by university home economics departments for use by their agricultural extension programs. What is interesting about these brochures is the spirit of "budgetism"

[108] Not all retailers offered credit; hence, 42 percent of respondents were uncertain, 45 percent responded yes, and 15 percent responded no. "Post-War Credits Draw Mixed Views," *New York Times*, March 19, 1945.

[109] George Katona, *The Mass Consumption Society* (New York: McGraw-Hill, 1964), 235.

[110] Allen F. Jung, "Price Policy and Discounts in the Medium- and High-Priced Car Market," *Journal of Business* 33/4 (1960), 346–347.

[111] Robert Frost, "Note of Confidence Sounded on Quality of Credit," *New York Times*, July 11, 1965.

[112] Robert Frost, "Note of Confidence Sounded on Quality of Credit," *New York Times*, July 11, 1965.

[113] Otto Lorenz, associate editor, *American Banker*, "Installment Credit Leads to New Form of Savings," *1957 Consumer Credit Symposium* (New York: Consolidated Reporting Company, 1958), 98–99.

they embraced. The University of Michigan agricultural extension program recommended that "not more than 20% of your take-home pay should go for installments."[114] A credit brochure from the Auburn University Extension Services admonished: "It is wise to sign no contract to pay out more each month on unpaid balances than the total set aside for installment buying."[115] For home economists, what mattered about installment credit was the share of the monthly budget that was dedicated to repayment. They also embraced the idea of credit as a second best alternative to savings. A pamphlet from the Agricultural Extension Service at Purdue University observed: "Many people who do not have the self discipline [sic] to save money can control their spending when they are in debt. By obligating themselves for payments, they can accumulate some of the things they want."[116] A brochure from the Agricultural Extension Service of the Texas A&M elaborated: "Some families find it difficult to save regularly and pay cash for the things they want. By buying 'on time,' these families commit themselves to setting aside a certain amount of money each week or month for items they buy."[117]

Credit and Coalitions

With the end of World War II, consumer credit sat at the crossroads of two goals: satisfying pent-up consumer demand and ensuring the transition to postwar industrial production. In the United States, a confluence of interests led economic and political actors to view those two goals as fundamentally compatible. In what was understood as a virtuous cycle, credit drove new demand that increased production scale and efficiency, driving prices down and wages up. With liberal access to credit, everyone benefited. In France, observers drew the opposite conclusions. In the view that emerged during the early 1950s in France, consumer credit risked crowding out industrial investment. Not only would lower investment hurt productivity, but they saw excess consumer demand as driving inflation, which would raise prices and hurt exports. Hence France tightly controlled the market for consumer credit, but not primarily for reasons of social welfare. Rather, they feared that liberalized consumer credit would be counterproductive in terms of promoting economic growth.

Two factors led France and the United States to draw these starkly opposite conclusions. The first was a set of three differences related to the role of

[114] RLDM, box 58, folder 8, "Consumer Credit – Friend or Foe," University of Michigan, 1957.

[115] RLDM, box 58, folder 12, "Close-Ups of Consumer Credit," Auburn University Extension Service, Circular 568, c. 1962, 9.

[116] RLDM, box 58, folder 11, "A Dollar Down: Some Facts about Credit," Agricultural Extension Service, Purdue University, Circular 786, December 1962, 7.

[117] RLDM, box 58, folder 11, Wanda Barkley, Elsie Short, and Eula Newman, "Using Consumer Credit," Agricultural and Mechanical College of Texas, Texas Agricultural Extension Service, c. 1960, 3.

France's developmental state. Faced with major reconstruction efforts, and a goal of guiding industrial development by focusing on key sectors, France's government was in the position of overseeing the allocation of capital while also managing inflation. In this context, consumer credit provided a logical buffer. Because French consumer credit was still at a low level, industry initially did not object to the relatively modest impact of managed credit on its sales. Finally, French commercial banks in the 1950s were deeply indifferent to consumer lending, and put up no resistance to controls. In the United States, the situation was nearly reversed. With the White House accord of 1951 granting the Federal Reserve autonomy from the Treasury, the country moved to a single interest-rate tool for setting monetary policy. Granted autonomy, credit controls that remained popular with the White House were no longer desired by the Fed. Also, business opposition to credit rationing exerted heavy pressure on Congressmen to liberalize. Not just the powerful auto sector and its dealers but also American banks increasingly saw credit controls as a drag on business.

The divide between French and American attitudes toward credit in the wake of World War II also had its roots in different attitudes to consumer credit by organized labor. In general, French trade unions viewed consumer credit with deep skepticism. They emphasized the extra costs that high interest payments imposed on workers, and worried about the tendency for credit to de-radicalize the workforce. By contrast, American trade unions were broadly committed to worker use of credit for consumption. Although they recognized that it reduced their purchasing power over time, they also understood that workers who were trying to furnish new houses and start new families wanted access to the benefits of the very industrialization they were helping build. And, especially in the steel and mining sectors, consumer credit in the form of bank loans and sales credit was an important tool in the fight for new workplace rights. Some social observers did eventually note the role of credit in restraining worker protest. Writing in 1978, David Caplovitz argued: "The growth of the American family's contractual obligations has made it less tolerant of risk-taking and more committed to job security. Just as the growth of bureaucracy has facilitated the development of consumer credit, so consumer credit would seem to help socialize individuals to bureaucratic employment."[118] But, far more than in France, labor groups in the United States viewed access to credit as a necessary, if not entirely desirable, worker's right.

In the United States, labor eventually became disenchanted with the supposed virtues of credit. By the early 1980s, organized labor had entirely changed its view. The AFL-CIO called for the Credit Control Act, which had expired in 1982, to be reauthorized on the grounds that restricting consumer credit would allow the Federal Reserve to keep interest rates lower, helping industry and

[118] David Caplovitz, "The Social Benefits and Costs of Consumer Credit," in Royston Miles Goode, *Consumer Credit*, United Kingdom Comparative Law Series, vol. 3, 1978, 133.

employment.[119] Indeed, it pointed to the French experience with *encadrement*, which would itself soon be abolished, to argue for the effectiveness of consumer-credit controls. Henry Schlechter, head of monetary policy for the AFL-CIO, argued that the French approach "helped it make progress toward modernizing its industrial base and increasing its exports."[120] The Reagan administration was entirely unresponsive to the proposal, and in 1983 even the French eliminated their controls.

In France, the ability to selectively allocate credit across lending institutions and sectors also had unintended consequences. One of these was to drive France's commercial banks to experiment with consumer lending in the early 1970s. Bank-issued personal loans were exempted from the installment restrictions and did not fall under the *encadrement* that restricted lending growth by consumer-finance companies. This gave banks an advantage during periods of tight credit limits. Banks also had new incentives at the time to seek alternative sources of profit. Administrative restrictions on commercial loans had pushed French companies to seek non-bank forms of funding, including issuing stocks and bonds.[121] In 1972 and 1973, personal loans briefly surpassed installment lending as the dominant form of consumer credit. The experiment, however, was short-lived. In 1974, the CNC extended *encadrement* to personal lending, and bank-sponsored personal-lending programs diminished. At the same time, banks became discouraged by unusually high defaults on their consumer loans, and reduced their lending levels.[122] Sobered by these losses, they had to wait another decade before making a new attempt to enter the consumer-lending market.

[119] George Meany Memorial Archives (GMMA), National Labor College, Silver Spring, MD. RG98–002, series 1, number 8/19, Credit, 1969–1983, Statement by the AFL-CIO Executive Council on *Tight Money*, February 15, 1982.

[120] GMMA, RG21–002, series 29, number 12/32, Statement of Henry B. Schechter, Director, Office of Housing and Monetary Policy, AFL-CIO, on Major Banking and Consumer Protection Laws and Service Capabilities of the Financing Industry before the Committee on Banking, Housing, and Urban Affairs, United States Senate, May 18, 1981, 3.

[121] P. Dubarle and R. Mouchotte, "Le Comportement des Entreprises en Periode d'Encadrement du Crédit," *Revue Économique* 24/2 (1973), 310–313.

[122] Alain Chatriot, "Protéger le Consommateur Contre Lui-Même: La Régulation du Crédit à la Consommation," *Vingtième Siècle* 91 (2006), 99.

7

The Politics of Usury

Usury laws are the oldest and most common response to societal concerns about the high cost of consumer lending. They are politically attractive in that they seem to draw a hard line against exploitative lending. Where they have been used, they are supported by a coalition of religious conservatives and pro-welfare liberals. As often as they have been employed, though, usury laws have been equally criticized. Two strains of critique have dominated. France's liberal Finance Minister Anne-Robert-Jacques Turgot (1775), for example, decried interest-rate caps as an infringement on private contracts.[1] British utilitarian Jeremy Bentham (1787), by contrast, argued against interest rate caps primarily on the grounds that restricting access to financial markets hurt the poor.[2] Both critiques point to an apparent dilemma: interest rate caps seem to sacrifice access to credit in the interest of consumer protection. Yet, for small lenders in the postwar period, the reality of usury regulation was more nuanced, and the apparent policy dilemma of access versus protection more complicated.

The practical problem with interest-rate caps was that small loans were by their nature expensive to administer. Any interest rate that felt acceptable to the public – the biblical rate of 6 percent was a common reference point – made most small loans uneconomical. The fact that small lending still happened was a testimony to the ease with which the true costs of lending could be hidden. One way was through noninterest charges. Fees for late payments, agent commissions, credit insurance, and the reporting of interest as a discount were all common practices that had been accepted by regulators in order to allow lenders to charge higher effective interest rates than state usury caps seemed to allow. These workarounds meant that usury caps came at the cost

[1] Anne-Robert-Jacques Turgot, *Les Prêts d'Argent* (Paris: 1775).

[2] Jeremy Bentham, *In Defense of Usury* (London: Payne and Foss, 1787).

of transparency, because they made it harder for consumers to assess and compare the total costs of loans. The second way to hide high interest charges was through cross-subsidies. When loans were tied to the sale of a specific product, revenue from the sale could be used to offset a lower interest rate charged to the consumer. Frequently, this meant that cash customers were subsidizing credit customers. Lenders also commonly provided a cross-subsidy among their borrowers, with the profits from larger loans going to offset losses from administering smaller loans. These options meant that usury caps did not typically reduce access. Rather, they forced lenders to choose between disguising the high costs of loans, at the cost of transparency, and subsidizing the loan activity from another line of business, at the cost of fairness. This implied a trilemma for national interest-rate policy: among the goals of low interest rates, transparency, and fairness, only two of the three could reasonably be achieved.

Usury legislation in France and the United States confounds common cultural arguments about national approaches to markets. In the United States, usury caps were, for most of the twentieth century, publicly popular and politically perilous. Legislators and courts found narrow exemptions from strict state usury laws, but they refused to eliminate them outright even when they were unrealistically low. In France, regulators discussed the imposition of a usury cap in the 1950s and decided that this sort of regulation would be too difficult to police. When a cap was eventually imposed, in 1966, it was set generously high, and designed in a way that was more market driven than the American fixed-rate cap. As commercial interest rates rose in France, its usury legislation allowed consumer-lending rates to increase as well. Within the bounds of these interest-rate caps, the French government also repeatedly intervened to insulate consumer lenders from the worst impacts of the usury cap. When lenders made "innovations" that allowed lenders to evade the usury caps – including leasing and rent-to-own retailing – the government typically found that they were legal. French attitudes toward credit prices were more market oriented than their American counterparts.

Usury in America

The United States emerged from World War II with a complex patchwork of state usury laws. More than half had small-loan laws based on the Russell Sage initiatives of the 1920s. But for retailers and banks launching into personal and installment lending in the postwar period, the loan-size cap on state small-lending laws was typically too low. To give them access to reasonable interest rates in states where 6 percent or 8 percent usury caps were still on the law books, most states adopted regulatory innovations in the 1940s and 1950s that pushed effective interest-rate caps up to 12–18 percent. Three basic strategies were employed. A few states simply increased the size of the loan to which their original small-loan laws applied – in one case from $300 up to $10,000.

A second set of states set different usury caps for different loan sizes. The Massachusetts Small Loan Law was typical of this approach. It allowed 2.5 percent per month for loans of up to $200, 2 percent per month up to $600, 1.75 percent up to $1,000, and 0.75 percent for loans of more than $1,000.[3] The challenge with multiple usury caps was their complexity in application. For a loan of $800 in Massachusetts, the first $200 was still capped at 2.5 percent, the next $400 at 2 percent, and the remaining $200 at 1.75 percent. For the consumer, calculating the effective interest-rate cap on any loan was virtually impossible.

The third approach was to allow some combination of discounting, "add-ons," and fees. The 1949 Florida Consumer Finance Act was typical of this approach. For consumer installment loans, it provided for a discount of up to 10 percent, a monthly "carrying charge" of $0.20 per $25 of a loan, plus a past-due fee of 5 percent. Together, this could amount to an APR of 40 percent – only slightly less than the 3.5 percent per month rate (42 percent per year) that it replaced.[4] An alternative to the discount method was the add-on approach, in which a service charge was added to the amount of the loan. The Kansas Sales Finance Act, passed in 1958, was typical of the add-on method. Non-auto credit was limited to $8 per $100, plus a $0.50 monthly fee for the first $50 of loan and an additional $0.25 fee for each additional $50.[5]

In the late 1960s, a struggle broke out over how these laws should be reformed. The principle impetus for reform was not the diversity of work-arounds that were adopted, although that diversity was impressive. Because most lenders at that time operated exclusively within single states, differences in state usury laws did not impose a significant burden. Rather, pressure for reform came from three sources: consumer advocates, legal reformers, and retailers. Political pressure for change also came from public outcry that appeared to originate partly in the 1969 federal Truth in Lending Act, requiring consumer lenders of all types to express interest charges as APRs.

Prior to that law, retailers had found ways to understate the actual cost of credit. For installment sales, retailers borrowed the discounting strategies used by commercial banks. They expressed the cost of the loan in terms of the price-premium customers would pay on a product in order to cover the cost of credit. The trick was that the loan was amortized over the period of installment

[3] National Consumer Law Center (NCLC) Records, Hale Library, Kansas State University, Manhattan, KS, box 8, folder (060.275), William Willier and Paul Garrity, "Proposal for Urgently Needed Small Loans Regulation Concerning Rewriting Slow Paying Small Loans onto Quasi Open-End Terms," December 29, 1969.

[4] John Kilgore, "Capital Comments," *Tallahassee Democrat*, July 21, 1949.

[5] Auto loans received special treatment, with rates of $7 per $100 (12.9 percent APR) for new cars, $10 per $100 (18.5 percent APR) for used cars less than two years old, and $13 per $100 (24 percent) for older cars. RLDM, box 8, folder 4, Preliminary Bill, "Kansas Sales Finance Act," 1958; RLDM, box 8, folder 4, Richard L. D. Morse, "Consumer Finance Charges – Quotations Compared," 1958.

payments, so that the consumer was actually paying interest on only half of the full amount borrowed. A customer paying a 10 percent price premium was in reality paying 20 percent interest. Interest rates for revolving accounts were typically expressed on a monthly basis, at 1.5 percent or 2 percent. In either case, retailers were insulated from most state usury laws based on court findings that their lending fell under the common-law "time-price" doctrine. The time-price doctrine allowed products to be sold at two different prices: one price for a cash sale and another, higher price for a credit or "time" sale. Although a clear infringement on the principle of the usury statutes, most state courts nonetheless upheld the time-price doctrine in deference to the growing installment sales sector.

By the late 1960s, large U.S. retailers began pushing for state legislation that would clarify the legality of their revolving accounts. Up until then, most states had allowed them to interpret revolving loans as installment loans, and this meant that they fell under the time-price doctrine and thus were immune to state usury caps.[6] But if courts concluded that revolving accounts were loans rather than installment sales, then for most states, retailers would need to be licensed as small lenders.[7] The first sign of trouble came in 1968, when the Attorney General of Oregon ruled that bank credit cards were loan transactions and thus subject to usury law.[8] By 1969, a series of individual and class-action state court cases filed against retailers offering sales credit had made their way to state supreme courts. In early cases in Massachusetts and Tennessee, the courts held that revolving accounts did not fall under state usury restrictions.[9] In similar cases in Wisconsin and South Dakota against retailers, state courts found that revolving credit *was* subject to usury caps.[10] In a usury case against an Iowa retailer, the courts found that revolving credit was subject to usury restrictions, but that both parties had to "have a common purpose in evading the usury law."[11] The decision implied that past retail lending would be exempted, but left open the possibility that future retail loans could be found usurious. Even in states in which no precedent had been established, class-action cases were being filed against retailers that were potentially costly. By 1971, JC Penney was facing class-action laws suits in four states (California, Colorado, South

[6] RLDM, box 212, folder 12, Richard L. D. Morse, statement before the Subcommittee of the Kansas Senate Committee on Financial Institutions, December 18, 1969, 2.

[7] Robert Braucher Papers (RBP), Harvard Law School Library, Cambridge, MA, box 33, file 2, Letter from Walter Malcolm, NCCUSL, to William Wemple, Chairman of the Banking Committee of the American Bar Association, August 27, 1968.

[8] RBP, box 33, file 2, Letter from Walter Malcolm, NCCUSL, to William Wemple, Chairman of the Banking Committee of the American Bar Association, August 27, 1968.

[9] *Denis v. Sears, Roebuck & Co.*, 1969, 223, Tenn. 410, 446 S.W. 2d 260; *Uni-Serv Corp. of Mass. v. Commissioner of Banks*, 349 Mass. 283, 207 NE 2n 906.

[10] Opinion, Hon. Roy D. Burns, Judge, in the Supreme Court of the State of South Dakota, *Stanley Rollinger v. J. C. Penney Company*, December 15, 1971.

[11] Findings of Fact and Conclusions of Law Filed by the District Court of the State of Iowa, January 24, 1972. Equity 74765, *State of Iowa v. Younker Brothers, Inc.*

Dakota, and Wisconsin). In an internal review, it estimated its potential liability in the Wisconsin case alone at $60 million.[12]

For states in which legislation specifically set interest-rate caps for installment loans – typically at 1.5 percent per month, or 18 percent per year – new legislative initiatives were being considered that would reduce those caps. One of the first of these was in Washington State, where the AFL-CIO sponsored ballot referendum 245, which lowered the retail lending rate to 1 percent per month. Pennsylvania followed with legislation that reduced top monthly rates to 1.25 percent per month.[13] For retailers, these legal cases and new state laws posed a potentially serious challenge. Although many retailers had been accustomed to subsidizing their lending programs out of sales revenue, the cost of offering consumer loans at 12 percent was simply too high. When Minnesota passed legislation reducing the ceiling on revolving credit charges from 1.5 percent to 1 percent per month, the Gamble-Skogmo group, which operated three different chain stores in Minnesota and Wisconsin, discontinued its revolving credit plans. Gamble-Skogmo claimed that under the new law, it would be losing ten cents on every dollar of credit sales.[14]

Retailers responded to these legal and legislative challenges by organizing. In December 1968, JC Penney launched Operation: Credit Project, a set of state and national outreach initiatives coordinated with other retailers.[15] Penney's top management was a combination of traveling store managers, who moved periodically from store to store, and fixed store managers, who often became important figures in their communities. This second set of managers began to reach out to their local counterparts, and to make contact with local legislators. JC Penney also initiated contact with the other two large national retail chains, Montgomery Ward and Sears. Their representatives met annually to discuss lobbying strategies and select priority states to target. The goal was initially primarily defensive: "to protect the remaining states as quickly as possible."[16] They targeted Maine, for example, which was a relatively small retail market. In 1971, the Maine legislature was considering an especially restrictive credit code, and the retailers all feared that legislative success would embolden other states to pursue similar restrictions.[17] They also reached out to national

[12] JCPCR, Credit Matters, July 1971, Final Draft [report to the Penney board of directors, drafted by Robert J. Devine], October 8, 1971.

[13] JCPCR, Credit Matters, July 1971, Final Draft [report to the Penney board of directors, drafted by Robert J. Devine], October 8, 1971.

[14] John Greenwald, "Gamble-Skogmo Ends Revolving Charge; Others Tightening Credit," *Minneapolis Star*, December 22, 1971.

[15] JCPCR, Credit Matters, July 1971, Final Draft [report to the Penney board of directors, drafted by Robert J. Devine], October 8, 1971.

[16] JCPCR, Credit Matters, Correspondence, From R. J. Devine to W. G. Hocker, "Re: Meeting of National Credit Coordinators" – Legislation 1971–1972.

[17] JCPCR, Credit Matters, July 1971, Intra-Company Correspondence, R. J. Devine, Meeting of National Steering Committee on UCCC – November 3, 1971.

policymakers in Washington, DC, where Senator William Proxmire, a Democrat from Wisconsin, was proposing legislation that would impose a nationwide interest-rate cap.

The retailers' message for state and national policymakers had two parts. The first part was that they were not actually making any money on their credit services. To make this case, JC Penney in 1970 broke with the standard practice in the highly secretive lending industry and disclosed financial data on the interest income and expenses of its credit unit. It revealed a service charge income the prior year of $96 million and lending-related costs of $116.6 million.[18] The cost of interest ($49.8 million) was less than half the total cost of consumer loans, outweighed by operating costs ($45.5 million) and provisions for nonpayments ($21.3 million). In 1972, it even invited members of the Connecticut legislature to visit Penney's Dallas regional credit office in order to understand the difficulty and expenses of providing credit.[19] Other stores followed Penney's lead. Manchester's Department Stores in Wisconsin, forced by recent state legislation to lower its interest rates from 1.5 percent per month to 1 percent per month, testified that its credit program was now a large net cost. In 1970, service-charge (interest payment) revenue was $262,411, whereas the cost of providing the credit that generated this revenue was $363,323.[20] Any additional losses caused by lowering interest-rate caps, it warned, would have to be recovered through increased product prices. It pointed to a study showing that retail prices in the state of Washington had jumped when the interest cap was lowered from 1.5 percent to 1 percent. Opponents countered with the example of Louisiana, where a retailer interest rate cap of 10 percent per annum seemed not to have led to increased prices.

The second part of the retail group's message was that aggressive interest-rate caps would unfairly favor bank lenders over retail lenders. Banks had significant noninterest sources of income for their credit programs that retailers did not have. Consumer paid an annual card fee. Banks also earned a fee from retailers that was equal in the early 1970s to 3–6 percent of the sales price of the product.[21] State laws that contemplated capping lending rates at 1 percent per month (12 percent APR) would therefore favor banks over retailers. For banks, which were trying to break into retail credit markets, these caps offered a way in. Writing to Senator Proxmire in 1971, JC Penney CEO Mil Batten argued: "The consumer will not benefit from the elimination of retail credit as a viable competitive force . . . the customer unknowingly pays

18 JC Penney, *Annual Report*, 1970.

19 JCPCR, Credit Matters, July 1971, Letter from Robert Percell to E. G. Cole, January 10, 1972.

20 JCPCR, Credit Matters, July 1971, Testimony of Stewart Manchester of Manchester's Department Stores before the Wisconsin Senate Advisory Committee on the UCCC on December 18, 1970.

21 "The Credit Crunch," *Penney News*, April–May 1971, section II.

the bank discount in addition to the bank's finance charge."[22] Robert W. Johnson, a journalist and strong advocate of retailers, argued that retailers were being hurt by an expectation of free credit: "Retailers' historical practices have handicapped them from a legislative point of view. Having offered 'free' credit for at least two centuries, why should retailers now charge for this service?"[23]

State consumer advocates worried that usury policies were being pushed by the out-of-state interests of the large consumer-finance companies and retail chains. Although retailers argued that they were losing money on credit, local advocates of more stringent interest rate ceilings argued that they were simply not accounting for all of the benefits they earned from their lending programs. Credit, like advertising, was not supposed to earn a profit directly. Rather, the benefits were felt in their main line of business: in added sales driven by the availability of credit, reputation, regular contact with customers that made sophisticated direct-marketing campaigns possible, and the lower cost of business loans secured against their consumer-credit portfolios.[24] They questioned why retailers, who repeatedly expressed concern about imposing the costs of their lending programs on their cash customers, nonetheless did not require interest payments from their thirty-day charge-card customers.[25] These concerns appeared to be vindicated when a 1974 investor prospectus from Sears showed that 50 percent of Sears's profit came from its credit business.[26]

The Uniform Consumer-Credit Code

The third and critical set of actors involved in the American usury debate was a group of socially active legal scholars that pushed for reforms that married interest-rate liberalization with consumer-protection policies emphasizing

[22] C. T. Stewart Collection (CTSC), DeGolyer Library, Southern Methodist University, Dallas, TX, Credit Matters – Federal Legislation and Issues, Letter from W. M. Batten to Senator William W. Proxmire, February 24, 1971, 3.

[23] JCPCR, Credit Matters, July 1971, Robert W. Johnson and Edgar A. Pessemier, Report on Long-Term Strategy for Retail Credit, 1971, 8–9.

[24] Because retailers had few assets, banks granted them expensive unsecured loans. Credit receivables gave banks an asset to secure their lending, and this lowered their lending rates. NCLC, box 2, folder 35, Mark Leymaster, Statement Concerning Regulation of Retail Credit Usury Ceilings, January 14, 1982, 3–4; Testimony of Steven C. Dilley before the Insurance and Banking Committee (Wisconsin) in Opposition to Bill S-263 (UCCC) on Monday, September 13, 1971.

[25] RLDM, box 211, folder 31, Letter from William E. Ryan to Richard L. D. Morse, March 29, 1974; Paul Zagorski, associate editor of *Everybody's Money* and member of the board of directors of Wisconsin's Consumers League, Testimony to Senate Committee on UCCC Bill, September 10, 1971.

[26] RLDM, box 211, folder 31, Letter from Richard L. D. Morse to William E. Ryan, April 3, 1974.

transparency and fairness. Their idea, drawn directly from the Russell Sage campaigns of the 1920s and 1930s, was that restrictive state-level interest-rate caps were limiting credit access and impeding price competition. To bring credit to poor consumers, the government had to bring competition to the consumer-lending sector. From the late 1960s to the early 1970s, activist lawyers and legal scholars pushed for state-by-state adoption of a Uniform Consumer Credit Code (UCCC). They argued that competition would naturally promote both a reduction in interest rates and an extension of credit to the worthy poor. What was required of legislation was to ensure that the competition was fair and transparent. The UCCC was formally endorsed by the American Bar Association.

The idea of the UCCC was to create greater competition among lenders, with the expectation that this competition would lead to lower interest rates. It removed licensing requirements for all lenders except those making loans of more than 18 percent.[27] It capped consumer loans at a peak level of 36 percent and mortgages at 10 percent. Revolving accounts were capped at 24 percent for balances below $500 and 18 percent for anything above. In exchange for the higher interest-rate caps, the UCCC imposed consumer protections, including limits on wage garnishment, a three-day cancelation window for doorstep selling, prohibitions of false advertising, the principle of unconscionability in consumer contracts, and an end to the holder-in-due-course doctrine (see discussion later in the chapter).[28] By 1971, versions of the UCCC had been adopted in Utah, Idaho, Oklahoma, Indiana, and Wyoming.[29] Fights over proposed UCCC legislation were still raging in other states.

The lawyers on the UCCC committee of the National Conference of Commissions of Uniform State Laws had originally intended to do away with usury caps altogether. State usury laws were, they argued, "so riddled with exceptions that they provide only spotted and residual coverage that is highly haphazard but, nevertheless, is baneful to both creditors and debtors."[30] Robert W. Johnson, a staunch advocate of the UCCC, argued that usury caps forced cash buyers to subsidize credit buyers. He explained: "If you push down the portion of the time price allocable to the finance charge, he must raise his cash price."[31]

27 James J. White and Frank W. Munger, "Consumer Sensitivity to Interest Rates: An Empirical Study of New-Car Buyers and Auto Loans," *Michigan Law Review* 69/7 (1971), 1209.

28 "The Credit Crunch," *Penney News*, April–May 1971, section II, 14–15; Richard L. D. Morse and William I. Fasse, "Where Is the Consumer in the Uniform Consumer Credit Code?" *Journal of Home Economics* 66 (1970), 68.

29 "The Credit Crunch," *Penney News*, April–May 1971, section II.

30 RBP, box 33, file 2, Letter from Walter Malcolm, NCCUSL, to William Wemple, Chairman of the Banking Committee of the American Bar Association, August 27, 1968.

31 RBP, box 33, file 4, Statement by Robert W. Johnson on the Uniform Consumer Credit Code, before the Subcommittee on Consumer Affairs, House Committee on Banking and Currency, February 26, 1969, 4.

These criticisms were probably accurate. That the UCCC included interest-rate caps at all was a political expedient: an acknowledgment of the continued popularity of usury laws. As Johnson noted, "Political realism suggests that state legislators would not accept the Code without rate ceilings."[32] Part of the problem was opposition from organized labor. The AFL-CIO assailed the UCCC for allowing higher interest rates. The economist Paul Samuelson, who was a vocal advocate of the UCCC, seemed to recognize the need for retaining some form of usury ceiling: "The proposed maximum rate schedules of the proposed Uniform Consumer Credit Code are schedules that the economy can live with – which is more than can be said for the hodgepodge that has hitherto characterized our history."[33]

Although its drafters accepted the political necessity of incorporating a set of interest-rate caps, the core idea of the UCCC was that competition would cause interest rates to fall. Walter Malcolm, president of the National Conference of Commissioners on Uniform State Laws, explained: "[The] underlying principle [is] that the economic forces of free enterprise and supply and demand should set rates through competition under and within maximum ceilings prescribed."[34] To ensure that happened, the UCCC provided for unlicensed entry in consumer lending. For states that required a lender to be licensed, these provisions would be abolished. With more entrants, greater competition should drive down lending rates more effectively. This provision for free entrance became a major obstacle to support from banks, which still faced licensing restrictions under banking law.

Retailers and sales finance companies became strong advocates of the UCCC.[35] In 1970, the big three retail lenders, plus GMAC and Household Finance, created a National Steering Committee on the UCCC. This group set priorities for states to target for lobbying and public-relations efforts.[36] What was critical about the UCCC was that it offered counterproposals to stem the rising tide of populist state laws that were lowering interest-rate caps. It was, ultimately, a tool in the larger retail struggle against growing pressure from bank credit card lenders. After a particularly grueling struggle to push UCCC legislation, the Montana Retail Association wrote to Robert Braucher, one of the UCCC's drafters: "We gave it [UCCC bill] our best, which wasn't good enough. We are only proud of the fact that the retailers of Montana were not

32 RBP, box 33, file 4, Statement by Robert W. Johnson on the Uniform Consumer Credit Code, before the Subcommittee on Consumer Affaris, House Committee on Banking and Currency, February 26, 1969, 3.

33 Paul Samuelson, Statement before the Committee of the Judiciary of the General Court of Massachusetts in support of the Uniform Consumer Credit Code, January 29, 1969.

34 RBP, box 33, file 2, Letter from Walter Malcolm, NCCUSL, to William Wemple, Chairman of the Banking Committee of the American Bar Association, August 27, 1968, 5.

35 RBP, box 34, file 1, Letter from Harold Read to Nathaniel Butler, December 20, 1968.

36 JCPCR, Credit Matters, July 1971, Intra-Company Correspondence, R. J. Devine, Meeting of National Steering Committee on UCCC, November 3, 1971.

subjected to vicious condemnation and ridicule as were the bankers... of our State during the debate."[37]

The UCCC was opposed by consumer groups, Legal Aid, AFL-CIO, the United Auto Workers, local consumer groups, and a majority of Democratic representatives. It was even opposed by Virginia Knauer, Nixon's special assistant for consumer affairs.[38] All accused it of being drafted by and for industry.[39] Wright Patman, Democratic chair of the House of Representatives Banking Committee, was deeply critical of the high-interest-rate caps allowed in the UCCC and the lack of transparency in pricing (the UCCC permitted some fees to be excluded).[40] Senator Estes Kefauver ridiculed the UCCC proposal as "charity at 42%." Consumer advocate Richard Morse argued that the high interest rates it allowed would "fan the fires of inflation and have the greatest impact on those who can afford it least."[41] Organized labor worried that the higher interest rates allowed under the draft legislation would hurt the poor. The AFL-CIO noted, in a stark reversal of its early post–World War II position on credit: "Raising rates to encourage easier credit for low-income families not only would raise rates for everybody else but would be self-defeating for the low-income families."[42] George Meany, leader of the AFL-CIO, referred to Robert W. Johnson, the UCCC's most vocal public supporter, as "the chief theoretical apologist for the outrageously high credit finance charges which the Code would permit to be exacted from consumers."[43]

Another vocal opponent of the UCCC was the National Consumer Law Center (NCLC), a nonprofit organization that represented low-income consumers. The NCLC was launched in 1967 at Boston University with a sizeable grant from the federal Office of Economic Opportunity. Its initial task was to study the likely impact of the UCCC on the poor. Its researchers questioned

37 RBP, box 34, file 1, Letter from Socs Vratis, Executive Vice President, Montana Retail Association, to Robert Braucher, February 12, 1969.

38 RLDM, box 211, folder 38, "Statement of the Consumer Federation of America before the Subcommittee on the Uniform Consumer Credit Code of the Iowa Legislative Council," November 25, 1969.

39 RBP, box 34, file 1, Letter from Harold Read, National Conference of Commissioners on Uniform State Laws, to Roger S. Barrett, Vice President, Household Finance Corporation, March 10, 1969.

40 RBP, box 33, file 2, Letter from Wright Patman, Chairman of the House of Representatives Committee on Banking and Currency, to Betty Furness, Special Assistant to the President for Consumer Affairs, October 2, 1968.

41 RLDM, box 211, folder 38, "Statement of the Consumer Federation of America before the Subcommittee on the Uniform Consumer Credit Code of the Iowa Legislative Council," November 25, 1969, 2.

42 GMMA, Sidney Margolius, "Consumers: A Twist in the Credit Pitch," *Consumer: The Uphill Fight*, 1973, AFL-CIO pamphlet, 1973.

43 GMMA, RG RG13-006, series 2, number 1/2, National Commission on Consumer Finance, 1972, Letter from George Meany to Anne Draper and Dick Warden, November 18, 1969.

the idea that competition would lead to lower interest rates, arguing that "demonstrated consumer behavior suggests that this assumption is open to serious challenge."[44] They noted that low-income consumers had historically shown themselves to be almost entirely unresponsive to lower interest rates.[45] And they criticized the UCCC for not limiting the allowable maturities of loans. Some of the greatest abuses of poor consumers, they found, occurred when lenders needlessly extended the term of the loan, often without any reduction in monthly payments.[46] The NCLC went so far as to draft its own, highly consumer-friendly alternative to the UCCC, called the National Credit Act (NCA). Wisconsin was the only state to adopt a version of the NCA.[47]

Unexpectedly, the strongest voice and financial backing to block adoption of the UCCC came from bankers' associations. Their opposition was surprising in part because they had been some of the early sponsors of the UCCC. The bulk of financial support for the UCCC project between 1964 and 1968 came from banks (48 percent) and consumer-finance companies (22 percent).[48] As late as 1968, the American Industrial Bankers Association announced its support for the UCCC.[49] All of this changed with the passage of the National Truth in Lending Act in 1968. Initially, the UCCC committee had proposed requiring lenders to provide consumers with the dollar amount of the finance charge, rather than stating the simple interest rate.[50] As in their struggle against Russell Sage in the 1940s, America's banks were still pricing their loans using the discount or loan-plus-fee format. With the passage of the federal Truth in Lending legislation that mandated a simple annual percentage rate, banks and consumer-loan companies united in opposing the UCCC.[51]

Three additional consumer-friendly provisions of the UCCC were of special concern to banks. Theses dealt with the holder-in-due-course doctrine, deficiency judgments, and free entry.[52] The holder-in-due-course doctrine

44 NCLC, box 2, folder 38, Blair C. Shick, Statement before the Subcommittee on Consumer Credit of the U.S. Banking, Housing and Urban Affairs Committee on the Report of the National Commission on Consumer Finance, May 17, 1973, 5.

45 NCLC, box 8, folder 22, William E. Boyd, "National Consumer Act and the Uniform Consumer Credit Code – A Comparison and Critique," c. 1970, 3–4.

46 NCLC, box 8, folder 28, W. D. Warren, Memorandum to UCCC Committee and Staff, February 7, 1970.

47 NCLC, box 2, folder 38, Blair C. Shick, Statement before the Subcommittee on Consumer Credit of the U.S. Banking, Housing and Urban Affairs Committee on the Report of the National Commission on Consumer Finance, May 17, 1973.

48 RBP, box 33, file 2, Analysis of Contributions to Consumer Credit Project, 1964–September 1930, 1968.

49 RBP, box 35, file 3, Max A. Denney, AIBA, Resolution Pertaining to the Proposed Universal Consumer Credit Code, June 26, 1968.

50 RBP, box 35, file 4, Robert L. Jordan, William D. Warren, Staff Memorandum, "Report for May 1965 Meeting," 1965, 13.

51 RBP, box 34, file 1, Letter from Socs Vratis, Executive Vice President, Montana Retail Association, to Robert Braucher, February 12, 1969.

52 RBP, box 33, file 5, Robert W. Johnson and George W. Hettenhouse, "The Uniform Consumer Credit Code – A Threat to Banks?" draft manuscript, August 23, 1968, 2.

formally separated loan contracts from sales contracts. For banks, it meant that their right to enforce credit contracts, especially contracts that had been discounted from retailers, was not diminished by the prior behavior of the seller. If a refrigerator that was sold on credit failed, the bank that had purchased the loan still enjoyed full rights to enforce the repayment of the loan. A second area of concern was with so-called deficiency judgments. Deficiency judgments allowed banks to make an additional claim on a debtor if the property against which the loan was secured did not have sufficient resale value to cover the cost of the loan. The practice of deficiency judgements was criticized by consumer advocates, who argued that lenders did not try to sell seized collateral for its full market value. The UCCC would have weakened creditor rights both under holder-in-due-course doctrine and in cases of insufficient collateral.

Most vexing for banks, however, was the UCCC provision for free entry. Any state adopting the UCCC would have to abolish its licensing requirements for lending, although lenders would have to register with state authorities.[53] Banks were strongly opposed to the free entry provision of the law, on the grounds that banks were subject to state banking laws, in particular laws promoting unit banking, that did not allow them to enjoy the benefits of free entry.[54] Whereas retailers and small lenders were free to open as many lending facilities as they wished, banks could not. The American Bankers Association (ABA) pushed for the UCCC to be modified to adopt the "convenience and advantage" licensing standard that had been incorporated into the earlier Russell Sage Small Loan legislation. UCCC advocates criticized the ABA's proposal, calling licensing and control of entry the Maginot Line of consumer credit.[55] It would, they believed, "deprive consumers of the primary protection contemplated by the UCCC from excessive rates."[56]

At the heart of the bankers' opposition to the UCCC, however, was a concern about their competitive struggle with retailers over the future of American consumer credit. As one banking association representative, speaking before the [House] Special Committee on Consumer Credit in 1968, explained: "The Code does not and cannot increase the powers of the banking industry with respect to entering new fields of business (e.g., direct retail sales of goods)."[57] As retailers constantly noted, banks could afford to operate under lower interest-rate caps because they enjoyed alternative income from retailer and customer

53 GMMA, RG RG13–006, series 2, number 1/17, Uniform Consumer Credit Code: AFL-CIO Position, 1968–1974, Anne Draper, Economist, AFL-CIO Department of Research, "Background Statement on the UCCC," February 7, 1969.

54 RBP, box 33, file 5, Letter from James Northam to Alfred A. Buerger, et al., December 20, 1968.

55 RBP, box 33, file 2, Letter from Walter Malcolm, NCCUSL, to William Wemple, Chairman of the Banking Committee of the American Bar Association, August 27, 1968, 12.

56 RBP, box 33, file 2, Letter from Walter Malcolm, NCCUSL, to William Wemple, Chairman of the Banking Committee of the American Bar Association, August 27, 1968, 6.

57 RBP, box 33, file 5, Robert W. Johnson and George W. Hettenhouse, "The Uniform Consumer Credit Code – A Threat to Banks?" draft manuscript, August 23, 1968, 3.

fees. By supporting more restrictive rates, banks hoped to squeeze at least smaller retailers out of the lending business. Senator Robert Taft, speaking in 1971, warned that interest-rate caps could "make chaos of the existing and viable competitive relationships among retailers, banks, small loan companies, and other credit grantors."[58] His message was that lower rates might hurt banks, but they would certainly hurt retail creditors more. With retailers gone, banks would then raise rates again, and customers would suffer. Ultimately, that is exactly what happened. By the time state-level usury laws were relaxed, beginning in 1978, many American retailers had already given up their own store-credit programs.

Usury in France

Unlike the United States, where long-standing, low fixed usury caps forced most lenders toward evasion, France first adopted usury caps only in 1966. This seems to have allowed it to approach usury regulation in a way that was responsive to the economic challenges that modern consumer lenders faced. One of the big problems stemmed from macroeconomic fluctuations. As interest rates and inflation cycled up and down, the impact of fixed usury caps on lenders also changed, sometimes dramatically. The very inflexibility of usury limits that made them politically attractive also made them challenging to comply with during periods of economic instability. What is striking about the French experience is how little regulators heeded the usury caps that they did put in place. Their major goal was to stabilize the level of lending activities, rather than to define a specific cost of lending that was deemed inherently legitimate. French usury caps were deployed flexibly to support the lending practices of the responsible consumer lenders.

How could a meaningful usury cap also buffer lenders from macroeconomic volatility? In general, national regulators have experimented with three means to avoid dramatic loan-portfolio adjustments as inflation and interest rates changed with the business cycle. One approach, pioneered in Germany, set usury ceilings for consumer lending at a predefined percentage above the average rate at which businesses were able to borrow. This technique had the advantage of allowing consumer lending to adjust for interest rate and inflation shifts while still blocking especially high interest rates. A second approach tied current lending ceilings, often broken into risk categories, to past average historic lending rates for the same kinds of loans. Because current caps were tied to previous-quarter lending rates, this approach insulated consumer lenders from having to dramatically contract their portfolio. And because it set rate caps by risk class, it allowed lenders to charge more for riskier loans. What it sacrificed was the flexibility to charge significantly more to cover small, un-risky

[58] Senator Robert Taft, 92nd Congress, 1st Session, volume 117, no. 125. Cong. Rec S13113, August 4, 1971.

loans. A third approach was to set a general standard of fairness or exploitation then allow courts or regulatory agencies to interpret what this might mean.

France's postwar experience with usury caps embraced, at different times, all three of these strategies. Until 1966, usury was defined by a general legal standard established by law on August 8, 1935, that defined the concept of usury vaguely in terms of "good faith." In practice, usury was rarely employed as a legal argument.[59] From 1966 until 1989, usury rates for consumption were set at twice the level of average corporate bond rates. A final set of reforms in 1989 moved to a more complex set of interest-rate caps that set the peak rate for different risk classes on the basis of the average rate for that class in the prior quarter. What is striking about this postwar regulatory trajectory is how little impact it had on actual lending practice. The problem was not one of enforcement – although the risk of pushing borrowers into the black lending market is commonly adduced as a reason to avoid usury limits. The conundrum of usury caps was that a mechanical limit unconnected to other economic indicators could create – as U.S. states would discover in the late 1970s – artificial credit scarcity. Yet interest ceiling formulas that were more attentive to cycles in inflation and discount rates were subject to regulatory manipulation that undermined the social purpose of the regulation.

Unlike the United States, France did not have a deep historical tradition of usury laws. Revolutionaries under the First Republic briefly experimented with usury caps in 1792, then removed them as impractical. They did not return until 1935, when the legal notion of usury was introduced by ministerial decree.[60] The next time usury caps were seriously examined was with the liberalization of consumer credit in 1953. As they adopted restictions on the terms of installment loans, the National Credit Council (CNC) also contemplated whether, and at what level, interest rates should be capped. Ultimately they decided not to act, for two main reasons.

Most French lenders at the time had two sources of income: direct interest payment from borrowing consumers, and fees paid by retailers in the form of discounting of loans by third-party lenders. Door-to-door sales relied especially heavily on retailer subsidies. In the case of economic unions, the CNC noted: "The interest rate is only a part of income of these companies. [Economic unions] survive not only on the interest they charge to borrowers but thanks to fees paid by the retailers."[61] Another doorstep lender, La Semeuse, was charging 1 percent to coupon customers in the 1950s and discounting retailers 13 percent when they cashed in the coupons.[62] Because retailers agreed not

[59] René Sedillot, "Le Crédit à la Consommation," *La Vie Française*, February 5, 1954.

[60] René Sedillot, "Le Crédit à la Consommation," *La Vie Française*, February 5, 1954.

[61] CNC, 1427200301, box 283, Comité National du Crédit, Comité du Crédit à Court Terme, December 1953–June 1961, Réunion du Comité du Crédit à Court Terme, December 24, 1953, 13.

[62] CNC, 1427200301, box 111: Crédit à la Consommation et Vente à Crédit, Direction du Crédit, Documention et Statistiques, Crédit à la Consommation, October 1952.

to raise prices for coupon customers, it meant that cash customers were in effect subsidizing credit customers through the higher prices they were paying for their products. Manufacturers were also frequently called upon to support some of the costs of credit. The most common form of manufacturer subsidy for credit was the captive industry lender. These dominated in the automobile sector, but were also used by early household electronics manufacturers such as Philips. But independent consumer finance companies also found ways of taxing manufacturers in order to subsidize consumer loans.

Cetelem found indirect ways to displace costs onto both retailers and manufacturers. Retailers were required to keep a security deposit with Cetelem equal to 7.5 percent of sales, and cover any losses up to 20 percent of the initial value of the loan. Manufacturers whose products Cetelem helped finance were also asked to contribute. Most agreed to accept a ninety-day delay in payment, a considerable savings on a one-year loan.[63] These extra sources of income, from retailers and manufacturers, would remain an important source of revenue for consumer lenders through the 1970s. For Cetelem it would only be in 1982 that the flow of cross-subsidies between retailers and credit providers would reverse. In that year, the fees that Cetelem had begun paying retailers to promote their credit products outweighed the fees they had traditionally received from retailers to provide their customers with credit.

The second source of cross-subsidy for small loans was from large-loan borrowers. Even for the most efficient lenders, making small loans under interest-rate caps typically required subsidizing their small-loan portfolio from their profitable large loans. Not all lenders agreed to do this. Many automobile finance companies stayed outside of the small-loan market for this reason. But a surprising number of lenders accepted making small loans, even though these had to be subsidized. They had a variety of reasons for doing so. Retailers subsidized small borrowers to promote sales or lure new customers. Banks subsidized small loans in order to draw in new depositors or best competing local banks. Many lenders also seem to have felt a social obligation to provide small loans, even if these were unprofitable. This meant that debates about usury caps had complex distributional implications. On the one hand, usury caps were likely to push the smallest borrowers into the hands of extra-legal lenders. On the other hand, for small borrowers who were able to secure a loan, the loan was heavily subsidized from the interest on larger loans.

[63] Conditions varied by manufacturers and product type, but on a one-year installment loan with a 25 percent down payment and a declining balance, the 90-day grace period provided more than half (58 percent) of the capital required for the loan. For example, a product sold for 150 francs would require a loan of 120 francs. Because monthly payments reduced the principal that needed to be financed, the heaviest capital requirement fell during the early months of the loan. Over the first three months, the loan would actually generate free cash for Cetelem. Given sufficient growth in outstanding loans, it was frequently possible to finance their entire capital requirements out of accounts payable and retained earnings. CHA, "Note Relative au Crédit à l'Équipement Électromènager," Internal Memo, April 1953, 4.

Thus usury caps seemed to pose two challenges. On the one hand, the CNC did not have the ability to monitor the revenue that lenders received from retailers to offset the low interest rates they charged customers.[64] If the usury cap was set too low, CNC suspected that lenders could simply shift more of their costs onto retailers and manufacturers. This engendered problems of pricing transparency. On the other hand, credit rationing by way of usury caps felt unfair to poorer borrowers. The basic cost structure of lending meant that usury caps would disproportionately hurt not consumers who were higher credit risks, but consumers who tended to take out smaller loans. As the CNC noted, a usury cap would "heavily penalize the borrowers of modest means."[65] Unwilling to give in on either transparency or fairness, the CNC concluded that usury caps were unworkable. This position did not last long. France quickly took up efforts to regulate consumer interest rates. But, each time France moved to regulate usury rates more aggressively, it also confronted new costs in terms of transparency and fairness.

A Flexible Rate Cap

The first formal restriction on usury caps came with the law of May 20, 1955. It defined a usurer as "anyone who provides a conventional loan whose total payment exceeds by 50% the payment requested by lenders in good faith for operations of the same type bearing the same risks." The penalties were intended to be heavy. Any party found guilty had to return the excess credit charged, with the possibility of imprisonment and a fine from 24,000 to 24 million francs. Penalties could also include the closing of stores that offered usurious credit, and the revocation of business licenses.[66] In practice, few cases were ever filed.

A decade later, French legislators returned to address the failure of their earlier usury legislation. The new law of December 1966 tied consumer-lending rates directly to the rate for commercial lending. Consumer lenders were not opposed to an interest-rate cap, but had concerns about how it had been

64 Conditions varied by manufacturers and product type, but on a one-year installment loan with a 25 percent down payment and a declining balance, the 90-day grace period provided more than half (58 percent) of the capital required for the loan. For example, a product sold for 150 francs would require a loan of 120 francs. Because monthly payments reduced the principal that needed to be financed, the heaviest capital requirement fell during the early months of the loan. Over the first three months, the loan would actually generate free cash for Cetelem. Given sufficient growth in outstanding loans, it was frequently possible to finance their entire capital requirements out of accounts payable and retained earnings. CHA, "Note Relative au Crédit à l'Équipement Électromènager," Internal Memo, April 1953, 4.

65 CNC, 1427200301, box 283, Comité National du Crédit, Comité du Crédit à Court Terme, December 1953–Juin 1961, Conseil National de Crédit, "Tarifs de Financement et Ventes à Temperament," Rapport Presenté par le Comité du Crédit à Court Terme, July 10, 1961, 3.

66 François Bruel, "Pour Réprimer les Taux Usuraires dans les Ventes à Temperament," *Combat*, October 13, 1956.

designed. The new law set usury in consumer loans at 200 percent of the commercial bond rate. In 1967, when the commercial bond rate was 7 percent, the usury cap was 14.12 percent. Consumer lenders were not happy about this. First, consumer lenders funded themselves 80 percent on the money market, mainly with short-term bank loans, and not from bonds.[67] They argued that the interbank rate would provide a more appropriate baseline for any interest-rate cap than the commercial bond rate.

Of far greater concern was the creation of a single global cap for all loans. Many lenders still used a formula for consumer loan rates that included a base interest rate plus a set of fees. This approach allowed them to charge higher effective interest rates on small loans, which were more expensive to administer. The 1966 legislation seemed to break with this approach. It called instead for the usury cap to target the "effective total rate" of interest (*taux effectif global*, or TEG). With bank borrowing at 6 percent and a cap for the TEG set at 14 percent, lenders did not have enough remaining interest income to cover their administrative costs. Unsure how to proceed, lenders began reviewing their estimated 5 million outstanding consumer-loan contracts.[68] They also sought leeway in how they calculated the TEG. In May 1967, the government relented. A letter from the Minister of Justice (Garde des Sceaux) clarified that lenders would be allowed to exempt certain fees from their interest-rate calculation. To ensure that this exemption did not become a loophole through which any interest rate could pass, the government set a cap on permissible fees. Lenders would be allowed to exclude from their interest rate a filing fee (*perception forfaitaire*) of 100 francs and a monthly charge (*frais d'échéance*) of 2 francs per month.[69] The move was justified as an effort to separate the service cost of a loan from the credit cost.[70]

By the mid-1970s, the weaknesses of the bond-linked usury formula were becoming clear. In 1975, as commercial bond rates rose through 12 percent, the consumer-credit usury cap topped 24 percent. This lending rate was seen as excessive, even before lenders added the permitted administrative fees.[71] Raymond Barre, appointed finance minister in 1976, began the practice of negotiating voluntary interest-rate caps (so-called *taux afférents*) directly with the Professional Association of Finance Companies (APEF) and the bankers' association AFB.[72] Under implicit threat from *encadrement* – the practice by which the government in 1972 began to limit credit extension on a lender-by-lender basis – consumer lenders made a good-faith effort to restrain

[67] Florence Paricard, "Consommation: Le Taux de Crédit Doit Baisser," *La Vie Française*, March 30, 1986.
[68] *Combat*, March 29, 1967.
[69] *Combat*, March 29, 1967.
[70] CHA, Economics Ministry, Rapport du Groupe de Travail sur la Réforme du Crédit à la Consommation, March 1979 (N.00), 31–2.
[71] *Le Monde*, June 5, 1975.
[72] *La Vie Française*, December 23, 1978.

their lending rates below the rising usury cap. Initially, voluntary caps were only modestly lower. In 1978, when the legal cap was 23.08 percent, the negotiated cap was 21.3 percent.[73] By the spring of 1979, the spread had grown. Although rising bond rates had driven the statutory cap up to 24 percent, Minister Monory had negotiated a dramatic reduction in the voluntary cap to 17 percent.[74] Despite these gains, the exclusion of fees from this voluntary cap continued to bother consumer advocates. Apparently low voluntary rates could quickly escalate when fees were added. The effect was especially strong for small loans, for which a full accounting of costs brought the effective annualized interest rate up to nearly 40 percent. And because small loans were used disproportionately by the poor, the fee system hid the deeply regressive costs of borrowing. Moreover, it was nearly impossible to directly compare lending costs. And, without directly comparable prices, it was difficult for consumers to shop around for cheaper loans.

In the summer of 1979, Monory again required that consumer creditors include all fees in their interest-rate calculation.[75] The idea was that consumers should have a single number, the TEG, that would include the full costs of credit. Monory's decision was disputed even within the Economics Ministry. Critics warned that the requirement could actually reduce transparency by forcing lenders to hide costs rather than reveal them. A report of the ministerial working group on consumer-credit reform warned: "It seems likely that in most cases the producer or seller, or both, would absorb the cost difference between the rate charged [to] the client and the real rate required by the financial institution."[76] The Centre d'Information et d'Étude du Crédit argued that the reform would force lenders to lend at lower rates, effectively cutting off smaller loans that helped the poor.[77] Monory responded by loosening the voluntary interest-rate cap to allow room for lenders to cover their costs.

In one unexpected way, Monory's reform would end up benefiting the consumer-lending sector. The adoption of a true TEG, one that incorporated all of the costs of the loan, occurred just in time for the staggering increase in lending costs that followed the high inflation of 1980 and 1981. By the fall of 1980, when the statutory consumer-credit usury cap reached 30 percent, consumer lenders voluntarily agreed not to exceed 25.7 percent. By the peak of commercial bond rates, in mid-1981, the voluntary cap reached a staggering 28.4 percent, which was still significantly lower than the peak statutory rate of 35.38 percent.[78] The surprise for consumer lenders was that demand

[73] *La Vie Française*, December 23, 1978.

[74] *Maintenant*, May 7, 1979.

[75] Yves Messarovitch, "Le Taux de l'Usure en Défaut," *Le Figaro*, June 20, 1986; *Le Monde*, June 20, 1986.

[76] CHA, Economics Ministry, Rapport du Groupe de Travail sur la Réforme du Crédit à la Consommation, March 1979 (N.00), 34.

[77] Forum International, July 10, 1979.

[78] *Le Monde*, June 20, 1986.

for consumer loans was unaffected even by interest charges that exceeded 25 percent – a level that had long been considered a symbolic threshold for consumers. So long as the real costs of loans had been hidden, it was difficult to know if borrowers agreed to pay more because they did not understand the full costs, or because they were willing to pay such high rates. With Monory's move to unitary pricing, there could be no doubt about consumer psychology. The resulting insights, along with financial deregulation, inaugurated a period of high-interest-rate lending beginning in the mid-1980s.

The high inflation of the early 1980s revealed the benefits of France's more flexible approach to usury. Whereas in the United States, inflationary pressures of 1980–1981 put intense pressure on states to relax their usury caps, France's linking of consumer rate caps to commercial bond rates proved more flexible. However, this flexibility came at a cost. First, because it set a single cap for all loans, lenders had to subsidize their more expensive small-loan portfolio with profits from larger loans. This raised the issue of fairness.

Second, commercial bond rates proved to be quite volatile. When bond rates fell rapidly, as they did in 1987, consumer lenders were forced to pull back on credit extension. Bond rates in 1987 fell 3 percent in a single year. This meant that the consumer-lending usury cap, at twice the commercial bond rate, had to decline by a full 6 percent, from 23.5 percent to 17.5 percent. Because many of the outstanding consumer loans had interest rates within this range, a large percentage of loan contracts would have to be reevaluated. Lenders warned that this could result in a dramatic contraction in lending. Especially hard hit would be their small-loan portfolios, as these loans were the most expensive to administer.

Faced with the prospect of severe credit rationing during a period of relative economic prosperity, then-Economics Minister Édouard Balladur considered his options. One idea was to have producers pitch in for the cost of the interest-rate reduction, because they were expected to benefit from the lower rates. Ultimately, Balladur opted to undo Monory's transparency effort. Lenders would once again be allowed to exempt administrative fees from the TEG calculation, and the value of those fees would once again have to be set by statute.[79] Separating out the fee again not only allowed lenders effectively to exceed the usury cap, but it also returned France to a system in which consumers could not easily assess or compare actual interest rates. The reintroduction of fees also disproportionately raised the cost for smaller loans. For larger loans, the one-off fee had a relatively small impact on interest rates. For smaller loans, the administrative fee could push a 17 percent loan, which formally conformed with the new usury cap, to an actual interest rate of between 23 percent and 25 percent. One major lender argued that even this higher rate did not nearly reflect the real cost of administering their smallest and riskiest loans, which they estimated at closer to 40 percent.[80]

[79] *Libération*, January 19, 1988.

[80] Yves Mamou, "L'Usure des Taux," *Le Monde Affaires*, June 10, 1989.

Balladur's usury problems were not over. In 1988, a rise in the bond market pushed the usury cap back up again, to 21 percent. Consumer groups argued that, with higher rates, all service charges should once again be incorporated into the usury rate. Under the new cap, if fees were kept apart, effective interest rates could rise to 27 percent for the smallest class of loans.[81] Traditionally, consumer-lending companies had received fees from the retailers for which they provided installment credit. As late as 1980, Cetelem received commissions on its installment-credit contracts with retailers amounting to 58 million francs. By 1987, that relationship had reversed. Cetelem was no longer earning any fees from retailers. And French banks, which, since financial deregulation in the mid-1980s, had pushed hard to break into the installment credit business, were offering generous fees back to retailers in order to get credit customers.[82] In 1988, retailers were receiving between 1.4 percent (for furniture dealers) and 4.5 percent (for used car dealers) back from banks and consumer-credit companies as fees. Unless retailers and distributors were willing to give up this new source of revenue, lenders had relatively little room to reduce the interest rates they charged. Rather than antagonize retailers they were trying to woo, France's banks approached the finance ministry for relief. As one banker explained: "We went crying to the finance minister, who has a softer heart than the retailers."[83]

As one crisis followed another, the need for more fundamental reform became clear. Any new usury-cap law would have to abandon the commercial-bond target. It would also have to address the very different cost structure of different-size loans. France's Minister of Consumption Jean Arthuis proposed that interest rates for consumer loans be separated into different risk categories. The idea of multiple interest-rate caps had long been advocated by consumer lenders. Noting that a single usury cap forced them to cross-subsidize more expensive small loans from the profits they made on less-costly large loans, lenders argued that they were forced to penalize their most creditworthy customers. It would also allow them to do away with fees, thereby reintroducing full transparency to interest rates.

Arthuis's proposal would base current interest-rate caps, broken out into risk categories, on the rate from the prior financial quarter for each category. Using a survey of all lenders, the Banque de France would determine this historical baseline. The new usury caps would then be set at 50 percent above the historical average. Almost all French consumer groups, including the Union Française des Consommateurs (UFC) and the Association Force Oeuvrier Consommateur (AFOC), approved of the new formula. There were two exceptions. The Communist-affiliate Indecosa-CGT argued that rates should be set on the

81 *Le Matin*, December 10, 1987.

82 Claude Soula, "Crédit: Les Banquiers Defendent Leurs Acquis," *Libération*, December 16, 1987.

83 Claude Soula, "Crédit: Les Banquiers Defendent Leurs Acquis," *Libération*, December 16, 1987.

basis of the real costs of making loans rather than on existing market rates.[84] The family-oriented Confédération Syndicale du Cadre de Vie (CSCV) worried that the new formula would lead to a gradual ratcheting-up of interest rates over time.[85] Both groups were skeptical that competition in consumer lending would ever lead to lower interest rates. Reine-Claude Madère, head of CSCV, noted: "Credit providers tend to stick to the ceiling level. It is the least solvent clients who will be the most affected."[86]

Early evidence suggested that the new formula would almost certainly cause a jump in rates in the short-term. In an experimental survey run in the region of the Pays de la Loire, the Banque de France found that rates on the riskiest classes of loans might increase to a peak of 33 percent. This was significantly above the 25 percent rate, including fees, that was charged under the existing sytem.[87] The size of this increase would depend critically on the number and specific definitions of risk classes that were chosen. The more narrowly the high-risk lending categories were circumscribed, and the larger their number, the higher this interest-rate bump was likely to be for the smallest and riskiest loan classes. Among the lending community, specialized lenders pushed for risk groupings that would allow them to offer higher rates. Automobile lenders, for example, pushed for used car loans to be broken out as a separate risk category, as these typically involved significantly higher risk and also higher average interest rates. Non-auto consumer lenders advocated separate categories for personal loans, which tended to be offered by banks and have lower rates, from revolving credit, which tended to be offered by consumer-finance companies and have higher rates. Consumer groups wanted risk groups to be specified on the basis of loan size alone, with different usury ceilings calculated for loans of less than 10,000 francs, between 10,000 and 20,000 francs, and more than 20,000 francs.[88] The users' committee of the CNC called for three separate categories distinguished by type of purchase: investments (cars and white goods), furnishings (including furniture and entertainment), and daily expenses.[89] Ultimately, the CNC settled on six risk categories, including three for consumer mortgages (large, small, and home equity) and three for consumer credit (loans below 10,000 francs, loans above 10,000 francs, and revolving credit). The new non-mortgage usury limits, which took effect in 1990, were set at 25.45 percent, 19.39 percent, and

84 Michel Madieu, "Consommation: Le Revenu Confisqué," *Révolution*, November 17–23, 1989, 26–27.
85 Christophe Boltanski and Pacal Riche, "Endettement: Le Spectre de l'Usure," *Liberation*, May 4, 1990.
86 Christophe Boltanski and Pacal Riche, "Endettement: Le Spectre de l'Usure," *Liberation*, May 4, 1990.
87 Christophe Boltanski and Pacal Riche, "Endettement: Le Spectre de l'Usure," *Liberation*, May 4, 1990.
88 Christophe Boltanski and Pacal Riche, "Endettement: Le Spectre de l'Usure," *Liberation*, May 4, 1990.
89 *Lç Monde*, May 5, 1990.

22.19 percent, respectively.[90] The choice to segregate revolving credit was especially significant, as it allowed French lenders to expand rapidly in that area without having to worry about the differential costs of managing the more complex revolving accounts.

Usury and the Morality of Lending

How French and American regulators approached interest rate caps raises common challenges but surprising differences of approach. One surprise is the way in which American policymakers moralized interest-rate caps. Faced with the realities of consumer-lending costs, politicians nonetheless pushed for more restrictive rates. In France, by contrast, usury caps were a technical regulatory tool. The CNC initially considered imposing a rate cap, but decided that the technical challenges of administering the rate were simply too great. When they did impose a rate, first in 1966 and then again in 1989, regulators worked closely with lenders to devise formulas that would minimally disrupt their credit activities. Why was France, with its Catholic heritage and traditional skepticism of markets, able to treat usury as a narrow technical matter, while the United States, with its embrace of markets, emphasized a moralization of usury?

The reason had to do with the ways in which American elites had come to see consumer credit as promoting social goals. If consumer credit was a market-based tool for social welfare, then it had to be constrained in ways that emphasized social justice. Even in the breach, clear and strict state usury laws made a political statement that socially damaging consumer lending would not be accepted. Some of the most important credit innovations in the United States were legal devices that allowed lenders to make consumer loans appear to conform to the strict ethical standards embodied in state-level usury statutes. For France, expectations of consumer credit were lower. No policymakers were making the case that consumer credit would enrich or enoble the working classes or poor. Indeed, for most of the early postwar period, consumer credit was viewed as a sort of market distortion that allocated capital away from useful investments in production. From the French regulator's perspective, the problem with credit markets was not that they were unfair, but that they were economically inefficient. And the solution to that problem was to limit the size of markets by restricting the amount of credit that lenders could offer.

90 *Le Figaro-Économie*, September 17, 1990.

8

Credit for Being American

By the 1960s, the coalition in support of greater credit access in America was changing. American labor was becoming less enthusiastic about the virtues of consumer credit. It worried that high interest rates were disproportionately hurting poorer workers, and so fought the progressive liberalization of state usury caps. It sought legislation that would limit creative and misleading lending practices, including ballooning loans, wage garnishment, and loans secured against anything other than the product purchased on credit. More generally, it argued against promoting further credit access. Labor activist Sidney Margolis, writing in 1973, warned: "The one thing most debt-ridden families don't need is still easier credit. Raising rates to encourage easier credit... would be self-defeating for the low-income families."[1] But just as labor was becoming disenchanted with credit, other rights groups began seizing on credit access as part of a broader campaign that pushed the idea of economic citizenship. By shifting the terms of the discourse about credit from one of economic welfare to one of economic rights, these groups helped promote the idea of credit access even as the social costs of debt were becoming apparent.

The first rights-based groups to mobilize actively around credit access were poor urban blacks. In a series of public-private initiatives, coordinated through the federal Office of Economic Opportunity and nonprofit Urban Coalition, retailers, banks, and local governments experimented with supporting credit to poor welfare recipients who could not pass standard creditworthiness tests. This movement found its most compelling expression in the National Welfare Rights Organization (NWRO), a grassroots organization of welfare mothers that rallied around the cause of retail credit access. The NWRO was followed

[1] GMMA, RG34-002, series 1, number 17/7, "Consumers: A Twist in the Credit Pitch," AFL-CIO pamphlet, 1973.

by the women's movement. For middle-class white women the NWRO credit campaign strongly evoked their own credit struggles. From the early 1970s, the National Organization for Women (NOW) spearheaded a campaign to secure personal credit ratings for women. This battle was won with the passage of the Equal Credit Opportunity Act (ECOA) of 1974. The NOW victory in turn opened the door for poor urban blacks. In 1977, an amendment to ECOA extended the definition of discrimination to include not just sex but also race. In the same year, the Community Reinvestment Act (CRA) required banks to lend in the communities where they took deposits. Within the space of ten years, credit had been reenvisioned as an encompassing economic right in America.

Credit and the Urban Crisis

From 1964 to 1968, American cities were swept up in a wave of urban ghetto riots. The largest of these were the Harlem riots in 1964, the Los Angeles Watts riots in 1965, the south-side Chicago riots of 1966, and the Newark riots in 1967. But these were only the most heavily publicized events. During this time, hundreds of thousands of the black urban poor participated in 329 separate incidents in 257 American cities.[2] In 1968, the National Advisory Commission on Civil Disorders was formed to investigate the cause of these riots. Headed by Illinois governor Otto Kerner, the Commission produced a study – the Kerner Report – that suggested that urban black disorder could be quelled by greater integration into American capitalism: "Rather than rejecting the American system, [the rioters] were anxious to obtain a place for themselves in it."[3] A centerpiece of this effort was the provision of consumer credit.

The focus on consumer credit as a matter of social justice had its roots in David Caplovitz's deeply influential 1963 study of urban product markets, *The Poor Pay More*, in which he documented the usurious and unfair practices of retailers in Harlem. Inspired in part by Caplovitz's study, the Federal Trade Commission (FTC) in 1965 launched a similar study of poor retailing and credit in Washington, DC.[4] Its findings were strikingly similar. They triggered a set of quiet but consequential law-and-order initiatives to more actively regulate and police the consumer and credit transactions involving the urban poor.[5] Many of the consumer-credit policies that emerged in the early 1970s, including

[2] Lizabeth Cohen, *A Consumers' Republic: The Politics of Mass Consumption in Postwar America* (New York: Vintage Books, 2003), 356.

[3] Kerner Commission, *Report of the National Advisory Commission on Civil Disorders*, 1968, 7.

[4] Federal Trade Commision, *Economic Report on Credit and Retail Sales Practices of DC Retailers*, 1967.

[5] Mary Gardiner Jones, "The Inner City Marketplace: The Need for Law and Order," *George Washington Law Review* 37 (1969), 1015.

a cooling-off period for doorstep lending (1972), were rooted in the FTC initiative.[6]

The conclusions of the Kerner Report suggested that one solution to the problem of ghetto riots was not merely a policing of urban markets, but an active extension of credit markets to the urban poor. The linking of consumer credit to social justice certainly had its critics. Caplovitz himself coined the term "compensatory consumption" to describe the tendency for the consumption of durables to compensate for blocked social mobility.[7] The newly emerging black power movement was also deeply critical of the impact of credit. Stokely Carmichael (Kwame Ture) later described the impact: "[Through credit] the black community is sapped senseless of what economic resources it does have."[8] But the move to extend credit held deep appeal for white, middle-class Americans. Especially for upper-middle-class white women, who were in the midst of their own battle to secure access to consumer credit, the idea that credit could bring justice to the urban poor held deep resonance.

The earliest efforts to promote consumer credit for the poor were a set of limited-income credit unions (LICUs) initiated and supported by the Office of Economic Opportunity (OEO) in the framework of President Lyndon Johnson's War on Poverty. By 1968, there were 300 such unions, including 9 in Washington, DC, alone, founded with a mission to serve "low income and other disadvantaged people."[9] Over the next two years, as attention focused on credit for the urban poor, their numbers doubled. About half of these worked directly with the OEO.[10] There were also eighty state-chartered community development banks, most of which also worked with the OEO.[11] The idea of these new banks was to allow the urban poor the support to meet their own borrowing needs. They were initiated with considerable federal and local financial support, but they were expected to become self-sufficient over time. Some of these were highly innovative. In New York, the Consumer Action Program of Bedford Stuyvesant branched out to create a cooperative housing union as well as a merchant's cooperative.[12]

6 Mary Gardiner Jones, "The Federal Trade Commission in 1968: Times of Turmoil and Response," *Journal of Public Policy and Marketing* 7 (1988), 5.

7 David Caplovitz, *The Poor Pay More* (New York: Free Press, 1967), 13.

8 Kwame Ture and Charles V. Hamilton, *Black Power: The Politics of Liberation* (New York: Vintage, 1992), 20.

9 The Urban Coalition, *Consumer Credit and the Low Income Consumer*, Preliminary Report, ii.

10 Thomas F. Cargill, "Credit Unions and the Low-Income Consumer," *Journal of Consumer Affairs* 7/1 (1973), 69.

11 William G. Kaye and Assoc., *Consumer Credit and the Low Income Consumer: A Study of Selected Activities by Commercial Banks, Credit Unions and Retailers to Make Consumer Credit, Consumer Counseling and Consumer Education Available to Low Income Persons* (Rockville, MD: The Urban Coalition, 1969), 28.

12 The Urban Coalition, *Consumer Credit and the Low Income Consumer*, Preliminary Report, ii.

The goal was for the LICUs to become self-sustaining, but they faced two major challenges. First, because they drew on deposits from the local, and predominantly poor, community, they were poorly capitalized. Taken together, the 629 LICUs operating in 1970 provided $40 million in consumer credit that year. Cumulatively, LICUs had by 1973 lent $307 million since their founding.[13] Given the millions of poor Americans who sought access to consumer credit, this volume of lending was not nearly adequate. Second, lending to the poor was expensive. Part of the problem came from heightened levels of late payment and nonpayment. As of 1968, 8.3 percent of LICU loans were at least two months in arrears.[14] Even more costly than the late and nonpayments was the high cost of administering small loans. The average loan offered by the LICUs in 1968 was $372, compared to the average loan by the black-owned Freedom National Bank's Harlem branch, which was $1,500.[15] In part, that was simply because poorer consumers borrowed for different kinds of goods. A survey of credit extended by LICUs in 1968 showed that a far higher share of loans (59 percent) were borrowed to purchase non-durables than was the case (44 percent) for traditional credit unions.[16] One study found that LICUs required twice as many staff as traditional credit unions. As William Kaye noted in his 1969 survey of low-income lending: "[i]t is uneconomical for banks to make the very small loans which are likely to be the type of loan needed by low-income persons."[17] For many of the LICUs founded in the 1960s, this hard reality proved impossible to overcome. Of the approximately 400 OEO-affiliated credit unions created at the time, only 100 remained in 1990.[18]

As the high cost of Lyndon Johnson's War on Poverty became apparent, first Johnson and then President Richard Nixon began to seek new, inexpensive ways for the federal government to support the poor. Nixon called on private companies to take on a share of the welfare burden. Democrats, too, embraced the idea of credit extension as socially progressive but also cost effective. The problem was that the urban poor needed access to more credit than they could accumulate themselves through credit unions, even if their operations were being subsidized. One way or another, outside capital would have to be brought

[13] Thomas F. Cargill, "Credit Unions and the Low-Income Consumer," *Journal of Consumer Affairs* 7/1 (1973), 69.

[14] 1968 Annual Report of the Bureau of Federal Credit Unions, 1969.

[15] William G. Kaye and Assoc., *Consumer Credit*, 5, 23.

[16] William G. Kaye and Assoc., *Consumer Credit*, 75.

[17] William G. Kaye and Assoc., *Consumer Credit*, 5.

[18] The 1990s would see a resurgence of limited-income credit unions, with their numbers rising to 538 in 1999. John Isbister, "The Lending Performance of Community Development Credit Unions," Report Commissioned by the Regents of the University of California, 1992; Charles D. Tansey, "Community Development Credit Unions: An Emerging Player in Low Income Communities," *Capital Xchange*, September 2001, retrieved from www.brookings.edu/articles/2001/09metropolitanpolicy_tansey.aspx.

into the poor urban neighborhoods. One proposal, introduced in the Senate in 1970, would have created a set of National Development Banks, capitalized by the government and managed as nonprofit financial institutions.[19] Far more influential, however, was the idea of a public-private partnership proposed by Democratic Senator William Proxmire, chair of the Senate Subcommittee on Financial Institutions. This scheme, called the Community Credit Expansion Act, was modeled loosely on the FHA Title I program. It would have used Department of Housing and Urban Development funds to secure up to 80 percent of loans offered by private lenders in poor neighborhoods.[20] As written, the bill would have capped interest at 1 percent per month and applied to installment but not revolving credit.[21] Fiscal austerity under Nixon, along with concerns that securing loans to the poor could prove expensive, left the Proxmire proposal with insufficient support to pass.

By the time federal legislation was being debated, local governments, nongovernmental organizations, and private companies were already experimenting with alternative approaches to "ghetto credit" on the basis of public-private partnerships. In Boston's Operation Creditworthy, three local department stores were approached by three federally sponsored LICUs and asked to grant credit to members. Under the program, the treasurers of the credit unions proposed a list of depositors that they certified as being creditworthy. In case of repayment problems, the credit unions agreed to help with collections.[22] Filene's, Gilchrist's, and Jordan Marsh agreed to participate, offering initial loans of $50.[23] To their surprise, the stores discovered that half of the applicants already had a credit account with at least one of three participating stores.[24] In another experiment, retail giant Montgomery Ward began working with the welfare department of Denver, Colorado, to extend credit to welfare recipients.[25] It was in part because of their favorable first impression of the Denver program that they were so open to a similar proposal from the National Welfare Rights Organization (see below).

Banks also experimented with extending credit to the poor. In 1967, Marine Midlands Trust formed an independent Community Development Division to promote private loans to poor urban blacks. They experimented making a small

[19] Fred C. Alvine, "Black Business Development," *Journal of Marketing* 34/2 (1970), 6.

[20] Senator William Proxmire, "Introduction of the Community Credit Expansion Act," *Congressional Record*, May 13, 1969, S 5090.

[21] CTSC, box 8, Memorandum from A.W. Driver to W.G. Hocker, "Community Credit Expansion Act and Penney Testimony," January 29, 1970.

[22] William G. Kaye and Assoc., *Consumer Credit*, 43.

[23] The Urban Coalition, *Consumer Credit and the Low Income Consumer*, Preliminary Report, 45.

[24] Records of the National Welfare Rights Organization (NWRO), Moorland-Spingarn Research Center, Howard University, Washington, DC, box 2247, Montgomery Ward, Presentation to Be Made by Eugene Keeney, President of American Retail Federation, at Urban Coalition Meeting of 11/20/69.

[25] NWRO, box 2118, Consumer Credit for Welfare Recipients.

number of so-called character loans to minorities who had initially been denied credit through their conventional credit-evaluation process.[26] New evaluations would be conducted on the basis of a set of credit standards written by the Federal Housing Authority to promote minority mortgage access under the 1968 Housing Act. The idea of these standards was to emphasize current ability and willingness to pay over past repayment record, as past repayments were influenced by a number of factors outside of the control of the poor.[27] High administrative costs were a recurring problem. One city that responded to this concern was Newark, New Jersey. In the wake of dramatic black urban riots of 1968, city officials created the Newark Bank Program. The program offered banks $34 per loan to cover the processing costs of lending to poor urban blacks, regardless of the size of the loan. A group of five private banks agreed to participate and began offering loans to the urban poor at 6.5 percent.[28] Nonetheless, a combination of high cost and slow repayment eventually led most of these innovative small lenders to close.

Credit for Welfare Recipients

One of the most widespread and highly publicized efforts to extend credit to the urban poor was launched not by the government or private business, but by a nonprofit grassroots organization: the National Welfare Rights Organization (NWRO). The NWRO campaign focused on credit access as a way to bridge the seemingly distant worlds of the white middle class and poor urban blacks. The NWRO was founded by academic-turned-activist George Wiley. Wiley was especially interested in the challenges of mobilizing welfare recipients. Having pursued graduate work in chemistry at Berkeley and taken a teaching position at Syracuse University, he represented the institutional branch of the black movement that embraced ties with middle-class whites. In 1966, he lost his bid to head the Congress on Racial Equality to Floyd McKissick, who moved that organization toward the more radical vision of black power. Wiley brought to the NWRO the view that poor blacks needed support from liberal whites: "We're practical politicians and our politics use white liberal support."[29]

Wiley was also friends with Richard Cloward, and deeply influenced by his research with Frances Fox Piven into the sources of urban poverty.[30] In 1966, Cloward and Piven published an article in *The Nation* in which they outlined a "crisis strategy" for promoting fundamental social and economic

26 William G. Kaye and Assoc., *Consumer Credit*, 20.
27 William G. Kaye and Assoc., *Consumer Credit*, 21.
28 William G. Kaye and Assoc., *Consumer Credit*, 23.
29 *Washington Post*, May 3, 1970.
30 Their most famous work, *Poor People's Movements*, dedicates considerable analysis to the rise and fall of the NWRO.

political reform.[31] Their idea was to work within the existing welfare system, promoting access to welfare benefits for those who were already formally covered but not receiving their benefits. Economically, the strategy focused on consumption rather than production. Politically, their idea, what they referred to as the "break the bank" strategy, was to overwhelm the state with welfare claims, then use the ensuing crisis to create a guaranteed minimum income.[32] Wiley's target audience was single mothers who were recipients of Aid for Families with Dependent Children (AFDC) welfare support. Working with this group, he hoped to get them to mobilize in order to secure access by the poor to welfare benefits. The idea was to embrace a highly individualistic view of social welfare, not challenge the system.[33] In addition to the members who were welfare recipients, 10 percent of the NWRO's members were activists. They were youth, both black and white, and an estimated three-quarters were volunteers supported through President John F. Kennedy's domestic volunteer program, VISTA.[34]

In 1969, the NWRO launched a campaign to get retailers to offer credit to its members.[35] The campaign was clearly inspired by Caplovitz's study of credit in Harlem. Their case against retailers who refused to offer credit to the urban poor was twofold. First, credit was a practical necessity. As Wiley explained: "The need for credit is a budgetary need.... Admittedly, credit costs money, but credit is like a telephone or an automobile – it is to be considered a necessity, in the context of our material standard of living."[36] The need was especially strong for welfare recipients, who had low incomes and also faced restrictions on the amount of savings they could hold. For large necessities, they were forced to rely on credit. If the reputable large stores refused to offer them credit, Wiley argued, "those poor are forced to buy from ghetto merchants with their exorbitant prices and exploitive credit practices."[37] Rather than blame urban loan sharks, they focused attention on retail lenders who had seemingly abandoned the poor urban borrower to that fate.

[31] Richard Cloward and Frances Fox Piven, "The Weight of the Poor: A Strategy to End Poverty," *The Nation*, May 2, 1966.

[32] Jack L. Roach and Janet K. Roach, "Income Rights, Mothers' Rights, or Workers' Rights? Collective Action Frames, Organizational Ideologies, and the American Welfare Rights Movement," *Social Problems* 50/2 (2003), 304.

[33] William Howard Whitaker, "The Determinants of Social Movement Success: A Study of the National Welfare Rights Organization," PhD Dissertation, Brandeis University, 1970, 246.

[34] Frances Fox Piven and Richard A. Cloward, *Poor People's Movements: Why They Succeed, How They Fail* (New York: Vintage Books, 1979), 293.

[35] CTSC, box 8, Credit Matters – Federal Legislation and Issues, Letter from W. G. Hocker to All Store Managers, April 24, 1969.

[36] Cited in Felicia Ann Kornbluh, "A Right to Welfare? Poor Women, Professionals, and Poverty Programs, 1935–1975," Dissertation, Princeton University, 2000, 425.

[37] NWRO, box 2105, George A. Wiley, "Statement to the Senate Banking and Currency Committee," January 14, 1970.

The critical leap made by the NWRO was from an argument on the basis of need to one about rights, and on equality of opportunity rather than equality of income.[38] The image of credit as a right resonated strongly with middle-class concerns about credit access, and especially with the women's movement's effort to secure access to credit independent of their husbands. The view was embodied in the NWRO slogan: "Give us Credit for being American."[39] This idea, that credit should be automatic, implied that those who were not receiving credit were being discriminated against. The NWRO pointed out that AFDC mothers faced specific challenges that creditors did not take into account in granting credit. Many single mothers were turned down for credit, they argued, because they had no credit rating of their own, independent of husbands who may have abandoned them or ruined their own credit. They also accused retailers of entirely abandoning urban areas, even though they contained significant populations that were creditworthy. By shifting the rhetoric of welfare from entitlement to fundamental rights, the NWRO was able to broaden the appeal of the movement.

Although the NWRO portrayed credit as a universal right, it also seemed to have expected that credit access for the poor would not need to be subsidized. On the one hand, welfare recipients had a regular income, and they tended not to move around. Both of these things should have tended to make them good credit risks.[40] The agreements they signed with retailers included a monthly rate of 1.5 percent, which was the standard rate for most retail credit. Yet in correspondence with their retail collaborators they accepted the idea that this rate could be increased if default rates under the program required it.[41] Indeed, Wiley appears to have felt that retailers would find that welfare credit customers would open a new and profitable market. In a letter to Montgomery Ward setting the terms of their joint lending experiment, Wiley claimed: "The criteria for success should be whether or not Montgomery Ward realizes a profit from the program."[42] Internal correspondence suggests that the NWRO was willing to be flexible about interest rates, offering higher rates should higher-than-expected default rates make this necessary. The idea that credit to the poor should be profitable was reflected in the NWRO's campaign to win

38 Andrea Jule Sachs, "The Politics of Poverty: Race, Class, Motherhood, and the National Welfare Rights Organization, 1965–1975," Dissertation, University of Minnesota, 2001, 172.

39 NWRO, box 2038, Sears, Handwritten Note with Slogans for the Sears Campaign (author unknown).

40 Eliot Janeway, "Credit Cards for Welfare Clients," *Social Service Outlook* 4/9, November 1969, 10.

41 The Urban Coalition, *Consumer Credit and the Low Income Consumer*, Preliminary Report, 47.

42 NWRO, box 2038, Montgomery Ward, Letter from Etta Horn, Chairman of the NWRO Ways and Means Committee, to Ashley de Shazor, Vice President for Credit, Montgomery Ward, September 10, 1069.

over Sears shareholders. Its shareholder mailings argued that Sears's discrimination against the poor "is hurting the nation, the company and your financial interests."[43]

There was a powerful organizational logic for the NWRO to emphasize access to credit. The organization funded itself through member dues, assessed at $1 per member per year. To maintain its central lobbying efforts (in 1969 its budget was $900,000), it needed to attract paying membership from a constituency – welfare mothers – that was not easy to mobilize. Critical to the retail-credit strategy was the provision that stores offer credit on the basis of a letter of reference from the local WRO. Wiley called this approval process a "dignified and human procedure for screening out poor credit risks." He also emphasized that members receiving a letter of reference would have "demonstrated their responsibility by participating in the organization for at least a 3-month period."[44] Whatever the merits of this organizational emphasis for evaluating creditworthiness, the letter of reference was a valuable tool for mobilizing membership. NWRO promotional material for its Sears campaign referred to the reference letter as "a way to encourage recipients to join your WRO after an agreement is reached."[45] The Philadelphia WRO reported a doubling of its membership after signing agreements for credit from two major downtown department stores.[46] The leadership also suggested that, because the amount of credit available initially would only allow twenty-five accounts per local WRO, new members would have incentives to mobilize. "Only with continued action will there be enough credit for an expanded membership."[47] And, to promote the national effort, local WROs were discouraged from signing any deals with their local Sears branch until a nationwide agreement had been reached.[48]

The signature effort in the credit campaign was its action against Sears. The NWRO approached Sears in the spring of 1969 to request that it provide $150 revolving credit accounts to members bearing a reference letter from their local WRO. The accounts would be repaid in fixed $5 monthly payments, and the NWRO would bear zero liability in case of nonpayment.[49] When Sears declined its proposal, the NWRO mobilized a series of protest actions against its stores nationwide. Local WROs in twenty-one cities staged Sears shop-ins, in which customers rang up a large number of products and then applied for "collective" credit. When they were turned down, they left their carts full of goods at the checkout counters, blocking the store. In Chicago,

43 NWRO, box 2038, Sears, "Statement to Sears Stockholders."
44 NWRO, box 2105, George A. Wiley, "Statement to the Senate Banking and Currency Committee," January 14, 1970.
45 NWRO, box 2038, Sears, "Call to Action," 4.
46 NWRO, box 2038, Sears, Nationwide Sears Credit Campaign, 3.
47 NWRO, box 2038, NWRO Group Credit Guidelines
48 NWRO, box 2038, Sears, "Call to Action," 4.
49 NWRO, box 2038, Sears, Letter to the Management of Sears Roebuck & Co., April 1 1969.

they interrupted a Sears fashion show, walking on stage in old clothes they described as "welfare fashions." They targeted members of Sears's board of directors who were employed at universities where students might be induced to put pressure on them.[50] And when a number of Sears shareholders assigned proxies to the NWRO, they were able to gain access to and protest at the May 1969 Sears shareholder meeting in Chicago.[51] A few local Sears stores did agree to work with the NWRO: in Winston-Salem and Cincinnati, for example.[52] Most did not, and the protests went on for nearly two years.

It is clear from the internal documents of the NWRO that the choice of Sears was as much strategic as on principle. Wiley did not necessarily expect Sears to concede quickly. It served instead as a publicity stunt, a tool for mobilizing, and an implicit threat to other businesses it approached. Promotional material sent to local WROs noted that the campaign against Sears could spur membership and "soften up other downtown stores."[53] It was even used as a threat in another campaign being waged by the NWRO at the time, in which it requested that manufacturers of household goods give it discount coupons to distribute to welfare recipients. Typical of its correspondence was a letter to Proctor and Gamble (P&G). It reminded P&G management of the Sears campaign, then warned: "At our May 23rd meeting, we will consider if any action should be taken against Proctor and Gamble."[54]

Whether because of the Sears threat or for other reasons, other retailers were far more amenable to the NWRO's experimental lending program. A number of the mid-sized retail chains, including Wannamaker's, Lerner, Lit Brothers, and Lane Bryant (women's apparel), came to lending agreements with the NWRO.[55] By 1970, larger retailers such as Gimbels, Federated Department Stores, and Abraham and Straus had all signed nationwide credit agreements with the NWRO.[56] One of the earliest and most significant of the agreements was with America's third-largest retail chain, Montgomery Ward. After an amicable set of discussions in the fall of 1969, Ward agreed to a pilot program in which it would offer $100 each to 3,000 NWRO members in nine urban areas: Baltimore, Washington, Cleveland, Chicago, Kansas City, Los Angeles, Detroit, Dallas, and Oakland.[57] Ward's one stipulation was that it would not

50 NWRO, box 2038, Sears Research, Memo from David Lloyd-Jones to Tom Sampson, NWRO, April 30, 1969.

51 NWRO, box 2038, Other Organizations in Sears Action.

52 NWRO, box 2038, Sears, "Boycott Stepped-Up in Over 62 Cities," *WRO's in Action* 1/1 (April 1969).

53 NWRO, box 2038, Sears, "Call to Action."

54 NWRO, box 2038, Consumer Credit, Letter to H. J. Morgens, President, Proctor and Gamble Co., from George A. Wiley, May 16, 1969.

55 Felicia Ann Kornbluh, "A Right to Welfare? Poor Women, Professionals, and Poverty Programs, 1935–1975," Dissertation, Princeton University, 2000, 414.

56 *Wall Street Journal*, December 9, 1969; *New York Times*, May 9, 1970.

57 NWRO, box 2105, George A. Wiley, "Statement to the Senate Banking and Currency Committee," January 14, 1970; *Wall Street Journal*, December 9, 1969.

automatically approve the welfare recipients referred by the NWRO, but would also subject them to its own internal evaluation for creditworthiness. In some ways, it was a natural extension of Ward's strategy of moving downmarket in order to expand its customer base. Ward's president, Edward Donnell, called the NWRO initiative "a worthwhile step to make Ward's services uniformly available to all financially responsible consumers."[58] The program began in January 1970 and ran for one year.[59] It was understood that the program would be evaluated at the end of one year on the basis of the delinquency performance of the participants.[60]

Not everyone was supportive of the NWRO's credit project. Consistent with its founder's apprehension about consumer credit, JC Penney responded to its advances by explaining that it did not offer credit on a group basis, and citing its "obligation to assure the wise use of credit and to help avoid credit overextension."[61] Penney also argued that any change in the criteria it used to evaluate credit applications would raise its overall credit costs, and that this would lead to higher product prices paid by all of its customers.[62] Individuals who wrote to the NWRO stressed similar criticisms, if more tartly. One correspondent wrote: "It eludes me why Sears or any other department store has any need to extend credit to welfare recipients for any item. Unfortunate, yes; importunate, no."[63] Another wrote: "I think your demands are absurd! You only perpetuate the 'do nothing – live off someone else' theory."[64] A third respondent predicted: "We'll only end up paying more money, and have more problems than we have."[65]

By 1970, the experimental welfare lending programs were starting to generate results, and the results were uniformly disappointing. After the first six months of its experimental collaboration with the NWRO, Montgomery Ward reported that it had 413 active accounts, 22 percent with late payments, accounting for 10.8 percent of the total outstanding balance.[66] The Marine Midlands Trust Community Development Division had made only twenty-five loans, but these were experiencing 12 percent–15 percent delinquencies,

58 NWRO, box 2247, Montgomery Ward, Press Release, Montgomery Ward, December 8, 1969.

59 NWRO, box 2247, Montgomery Ward, Letter from Ashley D. DeShazor, Vice President for Credit at Montgomery Ward, to George A. Wiley, NWRO, September 15, 1970.

60 *Wall Street Journal*, December 9, 1969.

61 NWRO, box 2038, Penney's Credit, Letter to George Wiley from Wallis Hocker, General Credit Manager, JC Penney, April 21, 1969.

62 CTSC, box 8, Memorandum from A. W. Driver to W. G. Hocker, "Community Credit Expansion Act and Penney Testimony," January 29, 1970.

63 NWRO, box 2038, Mail, Letter from C. B. Fischer to NSWRO, July 3, 1969.

64 NWRO, box 2038, Mail, Response to Solicitation for Support for the Sears Campaign.

65 NWRO, box 2038, Correspondence with People about Sears, Letter from M. K. [illegible] to George Wiley, April 3, 1969.

66 NWRO, box 2247, Montgomery Ward, Letter from Ashley D. DeShazor, Vice President for Credit at Montgomery Ward, to George A. Wiley, NWRO, September 15, 1970.

compared to 1.15 percent for its overall consumer-lending portfolio.[67] A study of Philadelphia's eight-bank minority lending program, the Job Loan and Urban Venture Corporation of Philadelphia, found on the basis of its 848 loan applications and 270 loans, issued from April 1968 to January 1970, that 79 were more than two months late and 41 had been written off.[68]

In 1971, the Arden House Conference on Public Welfare, a business association dedicated to New York welfare policy, became interested in the prospects of a credit-based approach to urban welfare. In a survey of existing welfare lending programs conducted in 1971, it found a poor record of repayment.[69] In the twelve programs it evaluated, nonpayment rates ranged from 4 percent to 56 percent. A retailer in Philadelphia that had offered 677 small loans of $50–$75 to members of the local WRO reported 62 accounts forwarded to collections, accounting for 10 percent of the total $46,000 in credit sales. A New York bank that had made loans through five branches "in a ghetto area" to borrowers who had previously been denied credit reported a bad-debt ratio of 14 percent.[70] In an internal memo, the Arden House Credit Committee reported: "Not one firm had found their program successful. Many lost substantial amounts because of high loss ratios." Out of concern that these findings would "humiliate" the proponents of the welfare lending movement, the results of the survey were never published.[71]

Women and Credit

The plight of women in credit markets became the focus of a social and political campaign in 1972. This was stimulated initially by a wave of letters sent in response to an editorial in *Ms. Magazine*, in which the author described her experience applying for an American Express card.[72] In the same year, the National Organization for Women (NOW) formed its Credit Task Force, the Center for Women's Policy Studies received a Ford Foundation grant to study sex discrimination in credit, and the National Commission on Consumer Finance held hearings on the availability of credit to women.[73] Volumes of letters written to *Ms. Magazine* and NOW document the broad-based

[67] William G. Kaye and Assoc., *Consumer Credit*, 20.

[68] Robert H. Edelstein, "Improving the Selection of Credit Risks: An Analysis of a Commercial Bank Minority Lending Program," *Journal of Finance* 30/1 (1975), 39.

[69] This group would become one of the big proponents of the earned-income tax credit.

[70] JCPCR, Credit Matters, July 1971, Memo, from Subcommittee on Credit for Low Income Families, to Arden House Credit Committee, "Credit for Low Income Families," September 1, 1971.

[71] JCPCR, Credit Matters, July 1971, Arden House Consumer Credit Committee, Minutes of the Meeting of November 29, 1971.

[72] "Where Credit Is Due," *Ms. Magazine*, October 1972.

[73] Flora Davis, ed., *Moving the Mountain: The Women's Movement in America since 1960* (Champaign, IL: University of Illinois Press, 1999), 149.

discrimination women faced in credit markets. Thanks to these letters, we know an enormous amount about the discrimination they faced. The three most common classes of grievances pertained to marriage, pregnancy, and divorce.

The largest share of complaints concerned the credit plight of married women, who faced a series of discriminatory and degrading lending practices. First, women who had access to credit prior to marriage commonly lost it upon marriage. In a letter received by a woman in Baltimore, Maryland, in March 1973, Bank of America wrote: "We are in receipt of notice of your recent marriage and wish to congratulate you and your husband. We regret that we must therefore delete your BankAmericard account number # [blacked out] which is in your maiden name."[74] The woman was invited to reapply for credit in her husband's name. JC Penney explained this practice as a matter of efficiency. They argued that because husbands typically paid the monthly credit bill, matching their payment with their wives' accounts "becomes an expensive nightmare." They also explained that issuing credit in the husband's name was a convenience, giving them credit automatically at the store when their wives opened an account.[75] For women, the practice often meant that they lost their own good credit rating to less-creditworthy husbands. Most credit-rating agencies at the time also merged women's credit files with their husbands when they were married. One woman complained of her ex-husband: "I have always had good credit then married a no-good money-hungry man who used my good credit standing so he could get credit."[76]

Two of the national credit card brands – BankAmericard and American Express – became the focus of specific condemnation by women's groups. Bank of America regularly changed the names of married women applicants to the names of their husbands. In one case, when a husband complained about the practice, the credit representative explained to him that its naming policy was a "response to male vanity."[77] American Express did little better. In 1973, an American Express campaign to court women only stirred up greater resentment. Its national advertising campaign listed among the "good reasons to give your wife an American Express Card:... Shopping (You don't have to go along anymore)."[78] A survey conducted by NOW in 1972 found that the national-chain retailers also rarely extended credit to women. Of eighty women who had applied for credit under their own names at one of three large

74 Records of the National Organization for Women (NOW), Schlesinger Library, Harvard University, Cambridge, MA, box 209, folder 75, Sharyn Campbell, "Newsletter of the National Task Force on Credit, Finance and Taxes," National Organization for Women, c. 1973.

75 JCPCR, Credit Matters, July 1971, Final Draft [report to the Penney board of directors, drafted by Robert J. Devine], October 8, 1971.

76 NOW, box 44, file 31, Letter Susan Onaitis (NOW), September 1, 1972.

77 Records of Ms. Magazine (MS), Schlesinger Library, Harvard University, Cambridge, MA, carton 1, file 1, Letter to Ms. October 25, 1972.

78 MS, box 1, folder 8, "Letters to the Editor," *Ms. Magazine*.

New York retail chains (Spiegel, Sears Roebuck, and Korvett), only ten were granted credit. Credit applications for the Belk-Matthews Department Store chain in Georgia did not even have a space for the wife to enter her salary.[79] The one brighter spot in women's access to credit was MasterCharge. More than a third of women who applied for credit from banks that participated in the MasterCharge network – specifically, Chemical, Marine Midland, and Manufacturers Hannover Trust – were granted credit.[80]

Even without a specific intent to discriminate against women, women's groups charged that legal and structural factors led to a credit system that was inherently biased against women. In most credit-rating schemes, creditworthiness was tied to wages and education, two areas in which women already faced unfair treatment.[81] Most scoring schemes also factored in a person's phone exchange (a practice that would later be made illegal). Because telephone companies charged extra to list two names, the majority of married women were simply not listed.[82] In some states, legal provisions discouraged lenders from granting credit to married women. Until it was superseded by reform legislation in 1975, for example, California law deemed that community property was "under the management and control of the husband." Lenders argued that such community-property provisions would hamper collections if they did not have a husband's approval for credit applications by married women.[83]

One of NOW's most trenchant criticisms was that discrimination against married women in credit markets was being incorporated into new regulations that were intended to protect consumers. One example was the Uniform Consumer Credit Code (version 5) that was being considered in state legislatures. Because the Code allowed a higher interest rate for smaller loans – in recognition of the high fixed costs of consumer lending – it also banned lenders from making multiple loans to the same family. UCCC drafters feared that a single lender would make multiple loans that would result in a higher overall interest charge than they would have enjoyed as a single lump loan. NOW objected that the ban on multiple agreements made it illegal for married women to take out credit in their own name if their husbands had already borrowed in theirs. Sharyn Campbell, coordinator of NOWs Credit Task Force, warned UCCC advocate Robert W. Johnson: "It is essential to the cause for equal credit opportunity that legislators refrain from enacting statutes that will perpetuate

79 NOW, box 45, file 38, Letter to William M. Matthews, VP, Belk-Matthews Department Stores, Macon, GA, August 9, 1974.

80 NOW, box 45, file 31, NOW, "New York Credit Survey" 1972.

81 National Association of Working Women (NAWW) Records, Schlesinger Library, Harvard University, Cambridge, MA, file 1286, 9 to 5 Organization for Women Office Workers, "Report on the Credit Project," July 2, 1980, 2.

82 NOW, box 209, folder 40, NOW, "Women and Credit," Internal Report, January 1973, 2.

83 NOW, box 211, file 8, Michele D. Stratton and Nancy J. Peterson, *Women and Credit*, National Organization for Women, San Francisco chapter, August 1974, 5.

the already complicated legal framework surrounding the extension of credit to married women."[84]

Married women who were of childbearing age faced a special kind of discrimination that the National Organization for Women described as a "morbid preoccupation of creditors with pregnancy."[85] Banks regularly discounted women's wages in credit applications out of concern that working women who had children would experience an interruption of their income and potentially leave the workforce permanently. This sort of salary discrimination was sanctioned by government policy. Until passage of the Equal Credit Opportunity Act (ECOA), the banking guidelines of the FDIC called for the "exclusion of one half of the wife's income in determining effective income for a mortgage."[86] For FHA loans, a wife's salary was typically not counted at all prior to 1965.[87] Many banks continued to use these practices until they were banned by ECOA.

In order to have their income counted as part of the application for a loan, women commonly had to provide additional assurances concerning the likelihood of pregnancy. Typical of the accounts of many applicants was a married woman in North Carolina who was required by Cameron Brown Bank to sign a document certifying "that I am not pregnant and do not plan to become pregnant in the near future. If I should become pregnant, I will return to work."[88] Other women were required to show medical proof they had had hysterectomies.[89] Such letters appear to have been extremely common in the industry, with lending professionals referring to them casually as "pill letters" or "baby letters."[90] In an editorial to *Glamour* magazine that helped galvanize women around credit discrimination, Carole de Saram, NOW's first coordinator for the Credit Task Force, warned: "The banks are stepping into the bedrooms of America."[91]

Accounts of the contracts that bankers required women to sign were in some cases so shocking that they became a central part of NOW's case for credit reform. One example of this sort of extreme intrusion into the private lives of a young couple was related to NOW by Ellen Sheer.[92] Both Sheer and her husband worked, and they hoped to purchase a house. Sheer's husband had been in the military service, and this qualified the couple for a loan guarantee

[84] NOW, box 30, file 59, Letter from Sharyn Campbell to Robert W. Johnson, February 21, 1974.

[85] NOW, box 209, folder 40, NOW, "Women and Credit," Internal Report, January 1973, 3.

[86] NOW, box 30, file 59, Lynne C. Litwiller, "Report of the Taxes and Credit Task Force," October 1972.

[87] NOW, box 209, folder 40, NOW, "Women and Credit," Internal Report, January 1973, 3.

[88] NOW, box 211, file 41, Billie Venable Sessoms, Suzanne Nelsen, and Patricia Smith, "A Preliminary Report on Women and Credit," National Organization for Women, Durham, NC chapter, October 15, 1973, 11.

[89] NOW, box 45, file 31, NOW, "New York Credit Survey," 1972.

[90] NOW, box 45, file 19, Letter from [name omitted for confidentiality] to Amy Scupi, NOW, Washington, DC.

[91] NOW, box 45, file 31, "You Won't Get Credit for Being a Woman," *Glamour*, November 1972.

[92] Name disguised.

offered through the Veterans Administration. In order to buy the house they wanted, the couple needed the mortgage broker to include both of their salaries at their full values in the credit application. Their mortgage broker eventually agreed to do so, on condition that the couple submit three documents relating to possible future pregnancy. Sheer describes these:

> 1) Two letters from my gynaecologist [*sic*] – one stating that I was under his supervision in birth control. The other had to state that because of the condition of my ovaries, it would be difficult for me to become pregnant even without birth control; 2) My husband's notarized statement that if I should become pregnant, he would agree to an abortion. And if for some reason I had to stop taking the pill, that he would have a vasectomy performed; 3) My notarized statement that if I should become pregnant, I would agree to an abortion. And if for some reason I had to stop taking the pill, that I would agree to my husband's vasectomy."[93]

To be sure that the applicants understood what they were signing, the lender read them each provision out loud before they signed for the loan.

The end of marriage, through divorce or death of a spouse, created a new set of problems for women. The practice of merging women's credit information into their husbands' accounts when they were married meant that women who were divorced or widowed were left with no credit history of their own. They were forced to establish a new credit rating at a time of acute financial hardship. For divorced mothers who sought credit in their own names, alimony and childcare payments were frequently not considered as income in loan applications. A survey by NOW of banks in Durham, North Carolina, found that only half accepted these as valid sources of income, on the grounds that they were not regular payments.[94] JC Penney explained that they did not consider child support payments for fear of being perceived as "taking food out of a child's mouth."[95] As late as 1978, four years after the practice had been banned, the FTC fined Bloomingdales for not considering alimony and childcare in evaluating credit applications.[96]

Although single women typically fared better than their married counterparts, they were certainly not immune to credit discrimination. In many cases, the rationale for denying credit was blatantly sexist. A woman applying for an educational loan was rejected on the grounds that women change their majors too often.[97] Another single woman applying for a mortgage was told

93 NOW, box 45, file 19, Letter from [name omitted for confidentiality] to Amy Scupi, NOW, Washington, DC.

94 NOW, box 211, file 41, Billie Venable Sessoms, Suzanne Nelsen, and Patricia Smith, "A Preliminary Report on Women and Cedit," National Organization for Women, Durham, NC chapter, October 15, 1973, 10.

95 NOW, box 211, file 41, Billie Venable Sessoms, Suzanne Nelsen, and Patricia Smith, "A Preliminary Report on Women and Cedit," National Organization for Women, Durham, NC chapter, October 15, 1973, 7.

96 NAWW, file 1286, 9 to 5 Organization for Women Office Workers, "Report on the Credit Project," July 2, 1980, 3.

97 NOW, box 44, file 32, Letter from [name omitted for confidentiality] to Lynne C. Litwiller, October 26, 1972.

that women were unreliable risks as homeowners "because it is assumed they cannot maintain property and perform simple repairs to prevent loss in value in case of foreclosure."[98]

The response to these grievances came quickly in the form of the Equal Credit Opportunity Act (ECOA), passed in October 1974. The act itself banned credit discrimination on the basis of sex or marital status. Title VII of the act, which was applied as Regulation B of the Federal Reserve, addressed many of the grievances that NOW and other women's groups had highlighted. Regulation B banned lenders from either requesting information about pregnancy or including it in risk analyses; required lenders to allow spouses to open separate accounts and credit-rating agencies to maintain two separate ratings; banned discounting of income – although it still permitted lenders to consider the "probable continuity" of income; and banned the termination of credit accounts when women changed their name or marital status.[99]

With the passage of ECOA, women's groups mobilized to make a reality of women's new protections against discrimination in credit markets. Both national groups such as NOW and local organizations such as 9 to 5 mobilized to help women build their own credit. Local groups were encouraged to set up tables at malls and even within retail stores to provide information on credit and help women fill out credit applications. NOW circulated guidelines for establishing a credit rating. Women were instructed to make sure they did not put their spouse's name on the application, nor include any information about their spouse.[100] They were also told to open an account with a local retailer, carry credit for six months, open another retail account, carry credit with them for six months, and, only then, apply for credit from one of the national credit cards.[101]

One response to the challenges women faced in establishing a credit record took the form of a movement to create "feminist credit unions."[102] The first of these was launched at the suggestion of Gloria Steinem in 1974 in Dallas, Texas. By 1976, there were eighteen sister institutions around the country, including three in Texas, with a combined $3 million in assets. Unlike women's banks, which made loans to business women but operated on a for-profit basis, the feminist credit unions had a social goal. After depositing 15 percent of the amount to be borrowed, a depositor could take out a loan without a prior credit rating. As one user reported, "Coming in each month to make my payment is like visiting with friends." However, as quickly as it formed, the movement

[98] NOW, box 209, folder 40, NOW, "Women and Credit," Internal Report, January 1973, 1.

[99] Laurie D. Zelon, "Equal Credit: Promise or Reality?" *Harvard Civil Rights–Civil Liberties Law Review* 11 (1976), 191–197.

[100] NOW, box 209, folder 74, Cynthia Harrison, "Preparation Sheet for NOW Credit Education Project," National NOW Credit Committee (c. 1978).

[101] NOW, box 209, folder 74, Cynthia Harrison, "Preparation Sheet for NOW Credit Education Project," National NOW Credit Committee (c. 1978).

[102] NAWW, file 1287, Letter from Elaine A. Wozniak, Feminist Federal Credit Union, to Ann Donner, Credit Rights Coordinator, 9 to 5, May 22, 1980.

fragmented. Some groups, organized as the Feminist National Network, sought to mobilize at the national level to influence policy; other groups, organized as the Feminist National Alliance, wanted to focus their energies on local education and lending. Of the two dozen feminist credit unions that had been formed by the early 1980s, only three survived to the end of the century.[103]

Credit advocacy groups also played an important role in ongoing fights among credit regulators. The Federal Reserve Board, charged with enforcing ECOA, faced pressure from lenders to weaken restrictions on consumer credit.[104] Under lobbying from Sears and Roebuck, the Federal Reserve Board in 1977 proposed diluting Regulation B to allow lenders to discount certain classes of income, including alimony and child support. In an unusually public fight between government agencies, the FTC, which was charged with monitoring lender compliance, contacted women's groups and asked them to apply political pressure in order to block the change. Writing to 9 to 5, they warned: "Your help is needed to insure that this does not occur!"[105]

Credit Markets and Social Welfare

Unlike the NWRO, NOW was careful to portray credit as a privilege rather than a right. In its educational material on credit discrimination, it systematically warned that "nobody has a right to credit, and discrimination in granting credit based on sex is often hard to prove."[106] Still, letters to NOW from its membership show that women clearly perceived the connection between their credit plight and that of urban blacks. A divorced woman in Santa Monica who was turned down for an educational loan noted with surprise the resonance that prior debates about red-lining and black credit access had for the women's movement. "The reluctance of banks to grant loans to blacks – 'high-risk loans' – has been documented elsewhere. I guess I just hadn't thought about these implications for women."[107]

Despite the clear resonance, NOW was careful to maintain its distance from the urban-black movement to secure credit. In 1974, for example, NOW was approached by an LA-based community organization called the Center

[103] *Sistershares*, Newsletter of the Massachusetts Feminist Federal Credit Union, volume 2, nos. 1–4, 1976–1977; see also http://www.feministcu.org/about%20CFCU.htm. Accessed June 19, 2009.

[104] NOW, box 30, file 59, Susan Onaitis, "Federal Reserve Board Regulations," News from the National Organization for Women (c. 1974).

[105] NAWW, File 1287, Letter from Lois Pines, Regional Director, FTC, to 9 to 5, June 6, 1979.

[106] NOW, box 211, file 8, Michele D. Stratton and Nancy J. Peterson, *Women and Credit*, National Organization for Women, San Francisco chapter, August 1974, 12; see also: NOW, box 211, file 41, Billie Venable Sessoms, Suzanne Nelsen, and Patricia Smith, "A Preliminary Report on Women and Credit," National Organization for Women, Durham, NC chapter, October 15, 1973, 1.

[107] NOW, box 44, file 32, Case History, Santa Monica, California, February 27, 1972.

for New Corporate Priorities (CNCP). Its founder, James Lowery, had been pushing for greater government participation in urban and minority credit markets, and he proposed the formation of a new National Task Force on Credit Policy to address credit access among urban minorities. The proposed Task Force would marry the credit concerns of women and minorities through a program that included what it called "affirmative lending" for traditionally marginalized groups.[108] Given NOW's active promotion of women's access to credit, Lowery hoped they could join forces.[109] NOW declined to participate. In an internal memo, former Credit Task Force coordinator Sharyn Campbell argued that joining with CNCP would be a distraction: "The incidence of sex discrimination in the extension of credit has been reduced considerably thanks to feminist organizations without the help of public interest groups. I question the value of diffusing our strength with this sort of task force where it does not have a great deal to offer us."[110]

As originally passed in 1974, ECOA focused narrowly on the discrimination concerns of women. This legislation later became the armature for an extension of fair credit access to other groups. Amendments to ECOA in 1977 broadened the range of prohibited forms of discrimination from sex and marital status to age, race, color, religion, national origin, political affiliation, and receipt of public assistance benefits. The elderly were a critical case, as they were reliable re-payers. The amended ECOA stated that credit could not be denied on the grounds that it was not possible to secure life insurance – a common justification at the time for denying credit to the elderly.[111] In the same year, Congress passed the Community Reinvestment Act (CRA) requiring banks to lend in the communities in which they operated. CRA specifically banned redlining, the practice of incorporating zip codes or telephone exchanges in credit scoring formulas.

In many ways, Cloward and Piven's crisis strategy proved prescient. Although researchers continued to dispute the importance of grassroots mobilization in increasing the welfare rolls during this period, the rising financial burden of the welfare state did indeed induce a radical shift in the way Americans thought about welfare. It was in this period that the subsequent marrying of markets and welfare had its historical roots. New welfare institutions embraced markets through tools such as the earned-income tax credit, introduced in 1975, which tied welfare support to employment. Welfare-to-work provisions, begun under the Omnibus Budget Reconciliation Act of 1981,

[108] NOW, box 30, file 59, Center for New Corporate Priorities, "Proposal for a National Task Force on Credit Policy," c. 1974.

[109] NOW, box 30, file 59, Letter from Jim Lowery, Director of the Center for New Corporate Priorities, to Sharyn Campbell, NOW, May 13, 1974.

[110] NOW, box 30, file 59, Letter from Sharyn Campbell to Karen DeCrow, President of NOW, on Occasion of her Resignation as Task Force Coordinator on Credit, August 28, 1974.

[111] NCLC, box 4, folder 16, "Access to Credit: Special Problems of the Elderly," A Report Prepared for the AARP, September 1987, 3.

required that welfare recipients seek work.[112] This movement culminated with the 1996 welfare reform adopted by President Bill Clinton that, among many provisions, replaced Aid for Families with Dependent Childrent (AFDC) with a welfare-to-work program called Temporary Aid for Needy Families (TANF). The fundamental reassessment that Cloward and Piven hoped would result from a swelling of the welfare rolls led in a direction they had not foreseen.

The Move to Credit Liberalization

The rising idea of credit as an economic right, and the coalition of left and right activists behind it, laid the intellectual groundwork for a liberalization of the consumer lending sector that ultimately drove its profitability and expansion during the 1990s and 2000s. The most important of these reforms was the elimination of usury caps.

The first blow to usury caps came from the 1978 Supreme Court ruling in *Marquette Nat. Bank v. First of Omaha Svc. Corp.*, which allowed out-of-state credit card lenders to retain state-of-origin usury rules. In the case, Marquette National Bank of Minnesota had filed claim against First of Omaha for charging 18 percent interest, which was permitted under Nebraska state law, to its credit card customers in Minnesota, where usury caps limited interest rates to 12 percent. Marquette at the time was charging its customers 12 percent interest, plus a $10 fee to cover expenses. Apart from the differences in interest rate and fees, the services were the same: revolving credit cards that were both affiliated with the BankAmericard (Visa) network. The defendants argued that the National Bank Act (Rev.Stat. § 5197, as amended, 12 U.S.C. § 85) preempted state usury laws (Minn.Stat. § 48.185 [1978]) for states in which they were not located. The relevant passage of the law, Section 85, read: "Any association may take, receive, reserve, and charge on any loan or discount made, or upon any notes, bills of exchange, or other evidences of debt, interest at the rate allowed by the laws of the State, Territory, or District where the bank is located." Because the Nebraska bank operated no branch banks in Minnesota, the court found that it was not considered to be located in Minnesota. Justice William Brennan noted: "Minnesota residents were always free to visit Nebraska and receive loans in that State." He argued that the intent of the original 1864 National Bank Act was to create a "national banking system"; any change in section 85 should therefore be made by Congress, not judicial interpretation.[113]

What is surprising in retrospect is how uncontroversial the *Marquette* decision was at the time. Support in the Supreme Court was unanimous. A combination of high inflation caused by the oil embargo of 1973 and a set of successful legal battles fought at the state level meant that many states by the

112 Andreas Cebulla, Karl Ashworth, David Greenberg, and Robert Walker, *Welfare-to-Work: New Labour and the US Experience* (London: Ashgate, 2005), 6.

113 *Marquette Nat. Bank v. First of Omaha Svc. Corp.*, 439 U.S. 299 (1978), No. 77–1265.

mid-1970s were moving away from reforms that would tighten usury caps. Many, in fact, were embracing a 1.75 percent per month (21 percent APR) rate that would allow larger retailers to operate their consumer-lending branches profitably. In addition, the fact that the case focused on national banks made it seem unthreatening, as these banks were reputable and highly regulated. If, by dint of the ruling, national banks took lending business from less-regulated small lenders, then that was likely to benefit rather than injure consumers. The Supreme Court's 1978 ruling of 9–0 in *Marquette* was in this sense a ratification of struggles that had already played out at the state level.

If usury liberalization was already in the cards, a second move to liberalize interest rates was largely accidental. As a result of consumer protection policies put in place earlier in the century, most state loan laws prohibited lenders from changing interest rates on outstanding loans. In 1980, President Jimmy Carter removed those restrictions. This opened the way for interest-rate adjustments that became a key tool for modern credit cards. Ironically, the liberalization had roots in Carter's concern that consumers were borrowing too much.

In 1978, as inflation reached 9.4 percent, AFL-CIO President George Meany encouraged Carter to impose restrictions on credit, an authority he had been granted by the Credit Control Act (CCA) passed in 1972 under the Nixon administration. In a strong reversal of labor's earlier support for liberal credit access, Meany argued that tightening consumer credit was a better alternative "to the extremes of either tight money/high interest rates, or wage and price controls."[114] Former Fed chairman Arthur Burns had called the CCA "one of the worst pieces of legislation ever written by Congress."[115] But his successor, Paul Volcker, supported consumer-credit controls as part of a broader project to control inflation. Eschewing traditional Regulation W-style controls on installment down payment and repayment periods, on March 14 Carter imposed a 15 percent capital requirement on revolving credit card loans. The Federal Reserve Board also created a federal provision that the terms of consumer credit could be changed so long as borrowers received thirty-day notification. Their goal was to reduce borrowing by exposing consumers to the current high interest rates. The reform seemed to work. Lenders immediately began increasing charges on credit card accounts, including the imposition of annual fees. By April 1980, consumer-credit purchases had begun to fall dramatically. Observers were surprised by the rapid decline in lending. By June, the economy was contracting, and in July the Fed began to phase out the new capital requirements.

Even with the end of the period of high inflation, however, most lenders retained the new fees and higher interest rates they had imposed under the CCA.

114 Cited in Stacey L. Schreft, "Credit Controls: 1980," *Economic Review of the Federal Reserve Bank of Richmond* (November/December 1990), 28.

115 Cited in Stacey L. Schreft, "Credit Controls: 1980," *Economic Review of the Federal Reserve Bank of Richmond* (November/December 1990), 34.

They also retained the right to alter credit contracts so long as they provided thirty-day notice. These two changes in lending practice, precipitated as the unplanned consequence of Carter's credit-control experiment, helped reshape the economics of consumer lending. First, as inflation came under control and interest rates declined in the early 1980s, lenders found that the growing wedge between capital costs and user payments drove ever-greater profitability. Second, lenders were now able to increase rates as consumer-credit worthiness deteriorated. From this moment, the riskiest borrowers were transformed into the most profitable borrowers. As with so many other sectors, deregulation of the consumer-credit sector thus had its roots in the Carter administration. The consequences of these decisions, however, were not foreseen. To the contrary, policies intended to slow demand for credit had the exact opposite effect in the long term.

The new reforms also had an immediate impact on competition between retail and bank lenders. Suddenly, national banks enjoyed an unprecedented advantage in competition against retailers and state banks. Both state and federal regulators responded quickly to level the playing field. A provision added to the 1980 Depository Institutions Deregulation and Monetary Control Act (PL 96–221) extended the *Marquette* state-of-origin policy to all state banks insured by the Federal Deposit Insurance Corporation (Section 501). In order to untie the hands of retail lenders and local finance companies that competed with banks, most states also changed their usury policies. By the end of 1981, forty-five states had either raised their usury-rate ceilings for consumer loans or eliminated them altogether.

For states that retained usury laws, smaller local lenders found that they could partner with out-of-state banks to provide loans that exceeded local interest-rate caps. A new industry of state-level small lending was born. Tax preparers began working with banks to make tax refund anticipation loans (RALs). RALs had APRs of 150 percent–300 percent and were used especially by low-income recipients of the Earned Income Tax Credit. Payday and auto title lenders, whose loans ranged up to 390 percent, also partnered with out-of-state federally chartered and FDIC banks to exempt themselves from state usury laws.[116] The Consumer Federation of America lamented: "The result is a set of usury laws that should make a finance company proud."[117]

Marquette left open a range of questions about the scope of state regulatory authority over national banks that were not settled until the 1990s. In 1996, the Supreme Court heard the appeal of *Smiley v. Citibank*, in which a New Jersey man had argued that the late fees charged by Citibank violated the state law restricting late fees. Banks, which in the debates leading up to the 1968 truth in lending legislation had argued that fees should be treated separately

[116] Michael S. Barr, "Banking the Poor," *Yale Journal of Regulation* 21 (2004), 161–173.

[117] RLDM, box 212, folder 24, Letter from the Consumer Federation of America to the Senate Banking Committee, June 17, 1982.

from interest charges, now argued that they were equivalent to interest and thus covered by the *Marquette* precedent. When the Supreme Court found in favor of Citibank, credit card use of late fees expanded from an average late fee of $12 in 1996 to $29 in 2002.[118] Similar cases explored the ability of state regulators to dictate minimum repayment rates. In 2000, the California legislature passed legislation requiring credit card issuers to include a warning on monthly statements that paying only the minimum balance would increase their principal. In *ABA v. Lockyer* (2002), the American Bankers Association (ABA) sued the Attorney General of California, alleging that the law infringed on a different provision of the National Bank Act that provides for "all such incidental powers as should be necessary to carry out the business of banking."[119] The ABA prevailed, arguing that the cost of printing such a warning made the law "overly burdensome" on banks and was therefore preempted by the National Bank Act itself.

This ad hoc set of court rulings was consolidated in 2004, when the Office of the Comptroller of the Currency issued new rules that preempted state regulation of a wide range of nationally chartered bank activities, including use of noninterest charges, credit account management, mandatory disclosures, and interest rates and fees.[120] The final stones in the foundation of America's liberal consumer credit markets had been laid.

[118] Mark Furletti, "Credit Card Pricing Developments and Their Disclosure," Fed Discussion Paper, January 2003.

[119] National Bank Act, Section 24 (7).

[120] Mark Furletti, "The Debate Over the National Bank Act and the Preemption of State Efforts to Regulate Credit Cards," *Temple Law Review* 77 (2004), 425–456.

9

Deregulation and the Politics of Overindebtedness

The deregulation of France's financial sector in the early 1980s led to a boom in credit extension. Household indebtedness grew from 1984 to 1989, increasing from an average of 3 percent to 7 percent of disposable income per household. The share of houses with outstanding consumer debt increased from 39 percent to 53 percent.[1] By the standards of the United States, these numbers were still small. Nonetheless, the growth in the use of credit led French policymakers to question the logic of consumer-credit extension. Some saw it as a positive sign – a democratization of credit that allowed households to behave more like companies.[2] Lenders made the case that easier access to credit, and in particular to the new flexible forms of revolving credit, allowed households to behave in more "adult" ways. The dominant interpretation, however, was that consumer credit was being used in ways that would prove socially and economically disruptive.

What followed was a political backlash that was driven by a range of social and policy actors who worried that consumers were overindebted, and that the government should act to reduce their debt. Explanations for both the cause and the consequences of this overindebtedness (surendettement) differed. Some blamed the new revolving-credit accounts that had been popularized with Cetelem's launch of the Carte Aurore. Consumer finance companies accused banks of making loans without rigorous credit checks. Others blamed the lack of a central credit registry, allowing borrowers to approach multiple lenders for loans. Why exactly consumers would want to borrow so heavily was also

[1] Roger Leron, Rapport sur l'Application de la Loi No 89–1010 du 31 Décembre 1989 Rélative à la Prévention et au Réglement des Difficultés Liées au Sûrendettement des Particuliers et des Familles, 1990, 7; "Les Français et le Crédit," *Figaro-Magazine*, April 8, 1989, 94.

[2] Martine Gilson, "Crédit: Les Français Craquent," *Le Nouvel Observateur*, January 26–February 1, 1989.

up for dispute. Some applauded the fact that consumers were finally able to use credit without having to worry about the moral implications. Others argued that consumers were using credit to compensate for stagnant real wages, and that the appropriate response was higher wages, not more credit. From the American perspective, what is striking about these debates was the relatively low level of indebtedness at which they occurred. From liberalization in 1984 until a debate emerged about overindebtedness in 1988, household consumer indebtedness doubled; yet it had still only reached the level of indebtedness already experienced by American households in the early 1950s.[3]

The French overindebtedness debate set the stage for a new set of institutions designed to manage the social consequences of excessive consumer debt. Two main reforms were undertaken. The first was to create a new centralized credit-reference database that all lenders would be required to consult. The second was to provide a simplified debt renegotiation procedure for consumers that had gone too far into debt. Although these institutional innovations were seemingly inspired by American models, the reforms were debated on very different terms from the way in which they were understood in the U.S. context. The proposal for a centralized repository for positive credit data reflected this difference. The new credit database was not seen as a tool for extending credit access by overcoming the adverse selection problem associated with risky borrowers. It was proposed, instead, as a means to reduce excessive debt. The point was to make sure that lenders knew how much debt their borrowers held, not to help them manage the adverse selection problem associated with risky borrowers. The eventual failure of a positive consumer credit database ultimately reflected an administrative judgment that consumer data privacy was a more important goal than credit access.

French concern about the social impact of credit focused on the plight of overindebted consumers, and French policymakers pushed for reforms that would make it easier for consumers to gain access to bankruptcy. The surprise is not that the French were concerned about the overindebted, but how resistant French legislators were to breaking debt contracts in the interest of social justice. When the American Congress amended the Bankruptcy Act in 1978 to liberalize corporate and personal bankruptcy, consumer lenders hardly noticed, much less objected. Ten years later, as France contemplated a limited form of discharge for consumer debt, lenders balked. What emerged was a state-managed process for renegotiating consumer debt, but without the possibility of a fresh start. It took a further fifteen years for France to introduce a provision for (semi-) automatic discharge of the kinds American borrowers enjoyed. Far from sacrificing markets to social outcomes, the French showed themselves to be far more serious about contracts than their American counterparts.

[3] Jean-Pierre Robin, "Crédit à la Consommation, les Français s'Americanisent," *La Vie Française*, June 21, 1987.

Taken together, the 1989 reforms of consumer credit rating and consumer insolvency reflected fundamentally different conceptions of the rights and responsibilities of consumers in credit markets than had emerged in the United States.[4] In the U.S. model, consumers had a right to access credit, coupled with a right to relieve themselves of debt through discharge in bankruptcy should the burden of repayment become excessive. This system placed the burden of responsibility on lenders, which had both the necessary information and strong incentives to make wise lending decisions. The French model that coalesced in the late 1990s followed the opposite logic. Rather than placing the burden on lenders, it gave consumers strong incentives not to overborrow. Without accurate positive credit data, consumers bore responsibility for proving their creditworthiness. And without an easy escape from debt, consumers had powerful incentives to limit their debt exposure. If credit in America had become a consumer right, with lenders bearing the burden for limiting overextension, French credit was a consumer responsibility, with no guarantee of access and little possibility of escaping from contracted debts.

Liberalization and Retrenchment

The first sign that there might be a problem with financial deregulation in France was the rise of so-called free credit. These were sales loans that were offered without any direct interest charge. In the furniture sector, which quickly embraced the practice, 20 percent of all credit offered in 1984 was without interest. As a merchandising strategy, free credit seems to have been effective. The two furniture retailers that were most aggressive in offering credit for free – Galeries Lafayette and Castorama – were able to consolidate their position as France's leading furniture retailers. Galeries Lafayette at the time was offering 94 percent of its credit sales at zero interest.[5] For the government of President François Mitterrand, who in 1984 was struggling to rein in inflation, free credit raised the old fear that unbridled consumer credit would stoke the flames of inflation and hurt competitiveness. Laurent Fabius, prime minister under Mitterrand, attacked the practice as "pushing customers to purchase using credit they don't really need."[6] The Banking Law of 1984 responded by reining in free credit sales. Retailers could no longer advertise free credit terms outside of the point of sale. More importantly, when free credit terms were offered, retailers were required to display a lower price for goods when they were purchased without free credit. This lower price was set by a formula, based on the average interest rate plus 50 percent. For average periods of credit, typically a year, retailers were required to offer cash prices that were roughly 20 percent

[4] The 1989 reforms also eliminated the prepayment fee, which was about 3 percent for mortgages and 4 percent for other consumer credit.

[5] CHA, Direction du Développement, "Crédit Gratuit," September 4, 1984.

[6] Laurent Chavane, "L'Enterrement Discret du 'Crédit Gratuit,'" *Le Figaro*, July 23, 1984.

below the "free credit" price.[7] Interestingly, most consumer groups supported the new law, as did small retailers, who did not have the financial means to compete with the free credit being offered by large retail chains.[8]

But the restrictions on free credit did little to restrain overall credit growth in the context of liberalization. As banks began to move aggressively into consumer lending, beginning in 1984, credit growth boomed. Non-mortgage household debt in France rose from 110 billion francs in 1984 to 370 billion francs in 1989, the peak of the credit boom.[9] Part of the concern about the new credit was the form that it increasingly began to take. Consumer finance companies, undercut by lower-interest-rate personal loans from banks, responded by launching new revolving-credit products. Cetelem's new Carte Aurore, launched in 1985, grew to 600,000 card holders in 1987 and 3 million by 1990.[10]

Following Cetelem's lead, virtually every major consumer lender in France, including dedicated finance companies and large banks, launched similar revolving-credit products. In the summer of 1987, Cofinoga launched the Carte Plus.[11] That fall, Sofinco launched Prêt à Carte, which for the first time linked a Carte Bleue payment card to a revolving credit facility. Not to be outdone, France's large commercial banks responded by creating their own revolving credit products. In the fall of 1987, BNP launched Crédisponible, with revolving credit at 15.8 percent, Crédit Lyonnais launched the Crédilion account, and Société Génerale offered Crédiconfiance.[12] France's auto lenders also joined the fray. Armed with large databases of auto loan customers that had reliably repaid, they began to offer co-branded credit cards directly to customers; Sovac launched the Peugeot Carte Bleue; Sofinco launched the CB Sofinco-Fiat.[13] In the fall of 1987, Cetelem's own auto loan affiliate Cofica made an agreement with France's national automobile club, the Association Française des Automobilistes, to offer the Club-Aurore card to the group's 500,000 members.[14]

The new revolving credit appears to have been popular. Between 1986 and 1990, revolving credit doubled as a share of total consumer credit, from

[7] François Renard, "Le Crédit Gratuit Va Pratiquement Disparaître," *Le Monde*, July 25, 1984, 19.

[8] Laurent Chavane, "L'Enterrement Discret du 'Crédit Gratuit'," *Le Figaro*, July 23, 1984.

[9] Roger Leron, Rapport sur l'Application de la Loi No 89–1010 du 31 Décembre 1989 Rélative à la Prévention et au Réglement des Difficultés Liées au Sûrendettement des Particuliers et des Familles, 1990, 7.

[10] Jean-Philippe Vidal, "L'Explosion du Crédit à la Consommation," *Tribune de l'Économie*, October 27, 1987; *Figaro-Économie*, May 14, 1990; *Figaro-Économie*, June 19, 1995; CHA, Philippe Herail, "Cetelem: Une Histoire des Valeurs, un Avenir," August 2002.

[11] Catherine Rigollet, "Le Bazar des Produits Financiers," *L'Express*, March 6, 1987.

[12] Florance Pricard, "La Carte Bleue Fait Crédit," *La Vie Française*, October 12–18, 1987.

[13] Florance Pricard, "La Carte Bleue Fait Crédit," *La Vie Française*, October 12–18, 1987; *Quotidien de Paris*, October 9, 1987.

[14] *Le Matin*, October 12, 1987.

8.5 percent to 17 percent.[15] Total credit use also doubled over that time. For consumer finance companies, which moved most rapidly to offer revolving credit cards, these accounts represented 37 percent of all lending by 1990.[16] The explosion of revolving credit provoked concerns from the French public. Observers feared that it offered "easy credit" that would drive households excessively into debt. Bankers were defensive, arguing that borrowers with access to revolving credit were able to be more financially responsible because of the greater control it gave them over their spending and repayment. Lenders tended to use developmental metaphors when talking about their revolving credit clients. LaJaques Lenormand, the director of the personal lending department at Crédit Agricole, was typical in claiming that "clients with access to revolving credit are far more adult, more evolved, better informed and, in this sense, are better managers."[17] French consumers were evidently more circumspect. A survey of French consumers in 1992 found that, of those who knew what revolving credit was (30 percent), two-thirds described it as "very useful." But half – and therefore presumably some significant share of those who found it useful – also described it as "a trap from which one never escapes."[18]

Revolving credit also raised specific concerns among consumer advocates about its impact on French consumer-protection policy. One of the core pillars of French consumer protection enshrined in the 1978 Scrivener law was the linking of sales contracts to debt contracts. Under the law, installment-credit contracts were binding only with the delivery of a product. Conversely, sales contracts were binding only with the approval of a loan. The law also created a seven-day cooling-off period for credit sales that required sellers to take back their products if the buyer decided to nullify a credit contract. In practice, sellers commonly waited seven days before making a delivery to avoid having to take back used products if a customer opted to reverse a credit purchase.[19] Even after the initial cooling-off period, the Scrivener law continued to link sales and credit contracts.[20] As French consumers moved away from installment borrowing and toward revolving-credit plans, the benefits of these consumer protections diminished. Yves le Duc, general secretary of the French consumer group CSCV, wrote:

[15] Roger Leron, Rapport sur l'Application de la Loi No 89–1010 du 31 Décembre 1989 Rélative à la Prévention et au Réglement des Difficultés Liées au Sûrendettement des Particuliers et des Familles, 1990, Annex II.

[16] François Henrot, "Les Instruments du Financement à Crédit de la Consommation en France," in André de Lattre (ed.), *La Consommation et son Financement en France et dans le Monde* (Paris: Berger-Levrault, 1994), 56–57.

[17] *Figaro-Économie*, May 14, 1990.

[18] Paul Defourny and Josette Bienfait, *Données d'Image sur le Crédit* (Paris: Cetelem-BVA, 1992), 7.

[19] Law 78–22, January 10, 1978, transcribed as articles 311 and 313 of the French Consumer Code; *La Croix*, May 29, 1976.

[20] Law 78–22, January 10, 1978, transcribed as articles 311 and 313 of the French Consumer Code.

> The link between the credit contract and the sale of a product...is dissolving.... The large retailers and banks that offer their own cards no longer need to know if a good is delivered, or if it is in good condition...whatever the case, payment is required. This is an important regression with respect to the law of 1978.[21]

Beyond the impact on consumer protections, the new easy access to credit raised concerns about the social meaning of consumer borrowing. Observers argued that French families were using consumer credit as means to compensate for stagnating purchasing power.[22] Yves Ullmo, secretary general of the National Council on Credit, described the effect: "Since [1983], disposable income has increased little. To maintain a certain standard of living, use of credit has been a solution."[23] Faced with stagnating wages and new demands, households were relying on credit to fill the widening gap. The Leron Report on consumer credit, commissioned by the French Senate, reprised the view that French households were supplementing their inadequate income with credit: "French households have entirely refused the erosion in the growth of their purchasing power, and have wished to maintain a high level of consumption, which translates into a reduction of their savings and a growth in their indebtedness."[24]

Rising indebtedness raised two concerns. First, families that were relying heavily on credit could become increasingly excluded from the life of the community. For those who became excessively indebted, policymakers worried that they would become permanently marginalized in society. Second, the impact of marginalization would fall most heavily on those families that were already vulnerable. As Christine Doré, former head of the consumer lender Sofinco, warned: "The more modest the family, the more they stretch out the length of repayment, and the more expensive the credit becomes for them."[25]

Credit Information and the Problem of Overindebtedness

The first move to restrict credit access focused on the practice of credit rating. In 1988, Jacques de la Rosière, governor of the Banque de France, announced his intention to create and manage a mandatory listing of credit data on all consumer borrowers. This would reestablish a system created in 1946 in which banks reported all of their loans to the central bank. Although this process had been retained for commercial lending, consumer lending had been made exempt

[21] Philippe Lebellec, "Crédit à la Consommation: Prudence," *La Croix*, November 11–12, 1987.

[22] Martine Gilson, "Crédit: Les Français Craquent," *Le Nouvel Observateur*, January 26–February 1, 1989.

[23] Roger Leron, Rapport sur l'Application de la Loi No 89–1010 du 31 Décembre 1989 Rélative à la Prévention et au Réglement des Difficultés Liées au Sûrendettement des Particuliers et des Familles, 1990, 7; Jean-Marc Biais, "Le Piège à Mauvais Payeurs," L'Express, February 3, 1989, 62.

[24] Roger Leron, Rapport sur l'Application de la Loi No 89–1010 du 31 Décembre 1989 Rélative à la Prévention et au Réglement des Difficultés Liées au Sûrendettement des Particuliers et des Familles, 1990, 7.

[25] Françoise Fressoz and Philippe Boulet-Gercourt, "Les Français Flambent à Crédit," *Libération*, August 13, 1987.

as part of the credit liberalization campaign of the early 1950s. Consumer groups strongly supported the creation of a positive or "white" credit database. The goal was not, as with U.S. credit-rating reforms adopted in the 1970s, to ensure fair access to credit for all. The debate in France focused instead on the potential for more accurate credit data to force France's lenders to behave more responsibly. The primary target was France's commercial banks, which were seen to be expanding lending without particular attention to riskiness. Consumer representative Louis Mesuret warned: "[The banks] do not respect their obligation of prudence and offer credit willy-nilly (à tort et à travers)." The positive-credit database would allow all lenders to know the total debt held by consumer credit applicants so that they could better evaluate the likelihood of repayment.

Research into patterns of national credit extension has emphasized the role of centralized credit reference data in promoting credit access. As Japelli and Pagano argue, shared credit reference data can increase lending volumes and decrease defaults.[26] Where central credit-rating services have not arisen, they attributed this to the challenges of getting consumer lenders to share data.[27] The French case offers some evidence that their analysis might be right. When the Banque de France proposed to create a public credit reference database with positive credit information – a so-called white list – the Association of French Banks came out strongly against it. It worried that such a list, which would impose on lenders a requirement to provide data on the outstanding loans of their customers, would allow non-bank finance companies to gain access to their own clients. Of course, such a database would also have allowed banks to access information on consumer finance company customers. But France's banks, who were still new to consumer lending, assumed that they would be able to keep non-payments low because they had developed long-term relationships with their depositors. These relationships would provide the core of risk management for personal loans by banks. Ultimately, the poor repayment experience of France's bank lenders would prove them wrong. At the time of the Banque de France's proposal for a white credit database, however, banks assumed that they stood to lose valuable information and gain very little.[28] Although the details remain murky, France's large banks are reported to have used their political influence to get France's powerful data-privacy body, CNIL, to recommend against the creation of a positive credit listing of the sort proposed by de la Rosière.

With the failure of a white list, France's association of finance companies (Association des sociétés financières, ASF) launched its own debtor black list in October 1988. This list, which was voluntary to its members, included only

[26] Tullio Jappelli and Marco Pagano, "Information Sharing, Lending and Defaults: Cross-Country Evidence," *CSEF Working Paper*, no. 22, 1999.

[27] Tullio Jappelli and Marco Pagano, "Information Sharing in Credit Markets," *Journal of Finance* 48/5 (1993).

[28] *Libération*, December 7, 1988.

borrowers who were at least three months late on their payments. Members were encouraged to check applicants against this list before making loans. All but the largest lenders participated, accounting for thirty-five of the thirty-seven member organizations and 70 percent of all finance-company lending.[29] The Banque de France responded the following year by creating its own black list. Unlike the ASF list, all consumer lenders were required to check loan applicants against the official government list. And, unlike the proposed white list, it included only nonpayment information. The database, called the Fichier National Des Incidents De Remboursement Des Crédits Aux Particuliers (FICP), was accessible only to credit providers and individual debtors who wished to view their own records.[30] In practice, the FICP database became a no-credit black list for borrowers. In 1991, it included 800,000 late payers; by 2003, that number had grown to 2.3 million.[31]

New initiatives periodically surfaced in France advocating the sharing of positive-credit data, including information on outstanding loans, taxes, income, and assets. In one proposal, which came before the National Assembly in 2005, the center-right UDF party argued that a positive registry would give financial institutions a better sense of total lending and help them better assess a consumer's ability to repay. France's financial institutions were divided on the proposal. Some, including the consumer lending institution Cofinoga, argued that positive data on potential borrowers would help them avoid adverse selection in selecting customers, thereby reducing both defaults and credit rationing. But many other financial institutions, supported by France's umbrella association of financial companies (ASF), argued that a positive-rating system would only assist foreign financial firms – such as UK-based lender Egg – to identify and exploit new clients in France.[32] France's consumer groups generally agreed with this view, worrying that a positive list would become a tool for more aggressive commercialization of credit, leading to higher levels of consumer indebtedness.[33] CNIL again blocked the proposal as an illegitimate use of private data.

Credit Rating and Data Privacy

To understand France's lack of a positive-credit reference bureau, we need to understand why concerns about privacy came to trump interest in credit access in France, but not in America. In both countries, data privacy policy had

[29] *Le Monde*, December 8, 1988.

[30] Pierre-Laurent Chatain and Frédéric Ferrière, *Surendettement des Particuliers* (Paris: Editions Dalloz, 2000), 188.

[31] *Libération*, March 20, 1993.

[32] Catherine Maussion, "Crédit: Tout le Monde dans le Même Fichier?" *Libération*, October 5, 2002.

[33] Bertrand Bissuel and Anne Michel, "Les Établissements de Crédit Accusés de Favoriser le Surendettement," *Le Monde*, April 28, 2005; Sylvie Ramadier, "La Bataille du Crédit à la Consommation," *Les Échos*, 21–22 January 2005, 8.

its roots in the same technological revolution that transformed the consumer-lending business: the introduction of the mainframe computer. Policy responses to the collection and processing of mass data differed in the two countries for reasons that had as much to do with the state of consumer lending as they did with concern about illegitimate uses of data. Without an existing network of consumer-credit bureaus, French regulators opted to impose strong data privacy protections not just on state agencies but also on private companies. In the United States, where concerns about data privacy were equally strong, protections were defined in a narrower way that limited government collection of data but gave greater latitude for assembling commercial databases of the sort needed to engage in credit rating.

Concern over data privacy emerged first in the United States, with Vance Packard's 1964 best seller, *The Naked Society*, in which he portrayed a government that was using the latest spying techniques to track and manipulate its citizens. Packard estimated the total number of entries in U.S.-government databases that listed individual names at 2.8 billion. A Senate subcommittee investigation into invasion of privacy found that the FBI alone held 100,000 files on Americans, and that the Federal Housing Authority had been known to use night-vision goggles to evaluate the "amicability" of applicant-couple's marriages. The issue came to a head when Karl Kaysen, an economist who served on President Kennedy's National Security Council, proposed the creation of a National Data Center that would combine all of the government's records into a single database. The 1966 Freedom of Information Act allowed Americans for the first time to access personal data collected by the government. The Nixon impeachment case raised new concerns about the potential political corruption on the potential for political corruption based on government surveillance. The U.S. Congress responded with the 1974 Privacy Act that severely restricted the sharing of personal data among government agencies.

In France, concerns about data privacy emerged a decade later than they did in the United States. This lag was primarily the result of the later development of mainframe computer technology in France, whose withdrawal from the North Atlantic Treaty Organization military structure led the United States to block French access to American mainframe technology. When France's state-financed computing program, the *Plan Calcul*, finally generated its own mainframe, the IRIS 80, the French government became the first customer. In 1974, *Le Monde* set off a public scare when it reported that the French government had been using the IRIS 80 to create a complete database of every French citizen, called SAFARI. The SAFARI program recalled the still-recent scandal over the Vichy-era Service National De Statistique, whose comprehensive "Jewish census" became the basis for Vichy's wartime programs to deport French Jews to German concentration camps. Trade unions warned that companies with access to a centralized government database might be able to use the information to target labor activists.[34] Jean Taitinger, who was later appointed

[34] "L'Ordinateur Contre les Libertés," *Témoignage Chrétien*, June 19, 1975, 10–11.

to investigate responses to these threats, warned in 1974: "The freedoms that the French people have fought for over the span of centuries could become illusory and without substance, in the face of an excessive or disorderly growth of databases of personal information."[35] In 1978, France formed a powerful administrative body, the National Commission on Information and Freedom (CNIL), invested with authority to review and block any government program that required the assembly of a database with personal information.

Early moves to defend data privacy in both the United States and France focused on potential abuses by the government. What mattered for the consumer-lending sector was how privacy standards would be applied to privately held data. It is at this point that the organization of consumer lending in each country became decisive. In the United States, consumer lenders already had a long tradition of relying on independent credit-rating agencies to help approve loans. Small cities and even towns each had their own credit-rating office. These numbered 50 in 1900, 300 in 1918, and an estimated 1,260 in 1938, at which point 93 percent of department stores reported using credit bureaus in approving consumer credit.[36] There were at least three reasons why these local credit bureaus flourished. First, the U.S. lending sector was highly fragmented. With loans being made by thousands of unit banks and tens of thousands of independent retailers, credit bureaus helped to identify customers with multiple credit accounts. Second, high population mobility meant that lenders were unlikely to have personal ties to borrowers. Credit bureaus regularly shared information with each other as families moved from one town to another. This allowed lenders to make loans to new arrivals – who were also likely to be most in need of credit for new household goods. By the time public concerns about data privacy had emerged in the United States, these credit bureaus were already consolidating into national and regional chains. As they began to computerize their data – first to do so was the Retail Credit Company of Atlanta (later Equifax) – they also actively engaged with legislators to emphasize the value of the service they provided. U.S. legislation to regulate the private collection of personal data was shaped in part by these companies. In a political deal with legislators, they accepted giving consumers access to the data they collected, in exchange for freedom to assemble and commercialize enormous private databases that included a broad range of personal financial data. At the time, the big-three U.S. consumer-credit bureaus held data on an estimated 72 million American families.

In France, similar private credit information services did not exist at the time when national data privacy policy was being set. There are three reasons for the absence. First, most of France's large consumer lenders relied at the time on retailers to assess the creditworthiness of their borrowers; they did

35 Cited in Jean Pellandini, "Informatique et Libertés Individuelles," *Le Figaro*, April 18, 1974.

36 Arthur H. Hert, "Charge Accounts of Retail Merchants," *Annals of the American Academy of Political and Social Science*, 196 (1938), 116–117.

not initially need to assess credit risk directly. Second, the number of lenders was relatively small: roughly 100 in 1970, compared to an estimated 16,000 in the United States. With larger internal databases, they had to worry less about outstanding loans to other lenders. The largest of these lenders, including Cetelem, did begin in 1972 to share lists of nonpaying customers. This black list was never formalized, and was also not shared outside of the group. Finally, *encadrement* meant that lenders were already limiting their lending to very-low-risk categories of borrowers. What mattered about France's lack of credit bureaus was not its impact on nonpayments, which remained low, but what it meant for the regulation of privately held data. Facing no opposition from consumer lenders – nor any other economic sector – the scope of responsibility for CNIL was expanded to encompass the private as well as the public sector. By the time the idea of a centralized positive database was elaborated, ten years after the founding of CNIL, the same strict principles of data privacy were being applied to both public and private databases.

After the creation of the FCIP black list, proposals periodically surfaced concerning the potential advantages of collecting and distributing more extensive positive credit data, including information on outstanding loans, taxes, income, and assets. In one proposal, which came before the National Assembly in 2005, the center-right Union for French Democracy (UDF) party argued that a positive registry would give financial institutions a better sense of total lending and help them better assess a consumer's ability to repay. France's financial institutions were divided on the proposal. Some, including the consumer lending institution Cofinoga, argued that positive data on potential borrowers would help them reduce both defaults and credit rationing. Others suggested it would simply lead to more targeted marketing of credit by lenders. CNIL again blocked the proposal as an illegitimate use of private data.

Personal Bankruptcy

France's second major regulatory move to address the social costs of overindebtedness was in the area of bankruptcy reform. In 1987, Jean Arthuis, secretary of state for consumption, had already begun advocating for an American-style personal bankruptcy provision. The essential element of that system was the ability to discharge consumer debts that were unlikely to be collected. He explained:

> Certainly the French are behind the Americans [in credit use], but with a growth rate of 2% in the entire economy, we cannot at the same time maintain stability, privilege productive investment, free up resources for training, and at the same time "stimulate" consumption. We must consider the potential risk of non-solvency of borrowers, since inflation is no longer there to wipe out over-indebtedness.[37]

[37] Jean-Philippe Vidal, "Le Gouvernment s'Apprête à Freiner le Crédit à la Consommation," *La Tribune de l'Expansion*, January 18, 1987.

The result, enacted under Arthuis's successor, Véronique Neiertz, was the 1989 Law on Prevention and Regulation of Individual and Household Over-Indebtedness that for the first time introduced a civil personal bankruptcy procedure in France. Until 1989, French consumers had no useful recourse outside of a full, and expensive, bankruptcy proceeding of the sort used by companies. Creditors with defaulting borrowers brought their cases to the courts, which summoned the defaulting consumers, who often simply did not appear. Courts then granted creditors the right to repossess property and attach salaries, typically leading to eviction.[38] For creditors, this ad hoc response created coordination problems, with creditors of overdue borrowers rushing to secure insufficient assets. For courts, consumer cases were clogging up their dockets. By 1989, 75 percent of all cases before France's system of small claims courts, the *tribunaux d'instance*, were consumer nonpayment collections cases.[39] For consumers, the risk was permanent exclusion from society. As one family association argued: "It is financially and socially unhealthy to keep in a desperate state families that have lost everything."[40]

The Neiertz Law of 1989 created a new administrative instrument that operated alongside the legal system to help resolve cases of consumer over-indebtedness. The core of the new system was a set of Departmental Commissions for Over-indebted Individuals managed by France's central bank and to which any consumer could apply for debt restructuring or relief. The commissions had broad authorities. They could suspend payments for up to two years, restructure the payment period for loans, and modify interest rates. New repayment schedules were determined on the basis of the commission's assessment of the "minimum vital income" to meet the claimant's most basic needs, and repayment plans could last up to but not longer than ten years. Formally, the commissions could only propose repayment solutions. If both parties to the negotiation did not voluntarily accept it, the case went before a judge, who, from 1995, had the right to enforce the recommendations of the commission on both parties (or, in rare cases, to design a new repayment scheme).

Two features of the 1989 law were distinctive. First, the commissions included no formal requirement for credit counseling, although in practice consumer and family associations often helped indebted households navigate the administrative procedures. Second, private credit intermediaries were banned in France, although credit-consolidation loans remained legal.[41] In assessing cases, the commissions distinguished first between "active" cases of overindebtedness, in which consumers had simply taken on too much debt, and "passive"

38 "Un Peu d'Oxygène pour les Familles Surendettées," *Nous* 103, March–April 1990, 9.

39 Quotidien de Paris, May 4, 1989.

40 Laurent Grisel, "Surendettement: Ce qu'il Faut Changer," *Cadre de Vie* 66, October–December 1989, 1.

41 *Familles de France* 664, September 2000.

cases, in which external causes had made it impossible for the borrower to continue paying. In 1990, active cases accounted for 48 percent of all cases. By 2004, active cases accounted for only 27 percent of all cases. Because the total number of cases had grown substantially, the number of active cases was nearly the same – approximately 50,000 cases per year. In 2004, the most important sources of passive cases were unemployment (30.8 percent), divorce or separation (14.7 percent), and sickness or accident (10.8 percent).[42] As the number of cases seen by the commissions each year rose, the share of active cases consistently fell.

Consumer lenders were initially highly skeptical of the Neiertz procedure. Cetelem's director of risk management called the Neiertz proposal "a source of irresponsibility, laxism, and bad faith."[43] The AFB, representing France's banks, proposed instead that creditors provide borrowers with insurance against "life risks" – unemployment, ill-health, divorce – that might lead to non-payment.[44] Initially, lenders were not especially responsive to the proposed repayment schedules. In 1990, only 45 percent of solutions proposed by the commissions were accepted by creditors. In 1992, Cetelem president Paul Defourny attributed one-third of cases seen by the commissions to instances of borrower cheating. He estimated that the Neiertz Law had cost the lending industry 1 billion francs in its first two years. As he described it, "The [Neiertz] law . . . moralized our profession by creating a sort of deontological code."[45] But as cases of overindebtedness rose, and as the commissions showed that they were able to produce workable solutions, industry acceptance of commission proposals rose to 75 percent by the end of the 1990s.

Initially, the system seemed to be working. A series of studies conducted in the 1990s showed that most cases had their debt restructured to the maximum of 10 years, interest rates were reduced on average from 13 percent to 9 percent, and average monthly payments were reduced from 6,000 francs to 3,800 francs.[46] Within certain limits – business-related debt was excluded, and consumers had to show good faith in presenting their cases to the commission – nearly all cases were accepted. The number of cases filed with the commissions grew considerably, from 90,000 at their founding to 190,000 by 2004.[47]

[42] INC, Le Surendettement en Chiffres (internal document).

[43] Françoise Blind, "Crédit à la Consommation," *Quotidien de Paris*, March 30, 1989.

[44] *Quotidien de Paris*, May 4, 1989.

[45] Renaud de la Baume, "Surendettement: Un Banquier Dénonce les 'Tricheurs'," *La Tribune à l'Expansion*, March 19, 1992.

[46] Hubert Balaguy, *Le Crédit à la Consommation en France* (Paris: Presses Universitaires de Paris, 1996), 106–107.

[47] The commissions were administrative bodies. Each had four members, representing the Banque de France, the Treasury, a consumer association, and a representative of a lender association. In 2003, two nonvoting members were added: a social worker and a lawyer. Archives of the Institut National de la Consommation (INC), Paris, France, *Le Dispositif Juridique* (internal documents).

By the late 1990s, however, it had become clear that the new procedure was not accomplishing its social goal. A growing number of cases that had already been renegotiated were returning to the commissions. The Neiertz legislation had been intended for debtors who had simply fallen behind. Increasingly, however, the commissions were seeing cases in which the debtor did not have the means to repay at all, even at no interest over the full ten years. For these cases, debt restructuring was not enough. Increasingly, financial firms came to accept that, at least for the direst cases, a full discharge of debts might be necessary. Indeed, finding a fresh start for over-indebted consumers could ultimately help lenders. A survey by the family association Familles de France in 2000, for example, found that 66 percent of the debt taken on by consumers applying to the FICP was going to pay interest on other loans.[48] A tentative reform in 1989 allowed for a three-year moratorium after which, if the consumer was still not in a position to pay, all debts could be removed. A further reform in 2003 created the possibility for automatic discharge. It allowed for a complete discharge of debts for debtors in good faith (i.e., absent fraud) in cases when they were judged to be "irremediably compromised." Because the procedure involved breaking debt contracts, it could only be decided by a judge. It also added a social worker and a lawyer to each commission.[49] Consumer group reactions to the civil bankruptcy procedure were mixed. Whereas most family groups saw it as a positive step, trade unions and other groups felt that it was overly harsh in its requirements to liquidate all property.[50] In fact, only 5 percent of all cases were discharged under the new procedure.

Why was France's approach to the clear distress of overindebted consumers seemingly so harsh? The contrast with U.S. law is especially stark. The U.S. Bankruptcy Reform Act of 1978 gave consumers access to a procedure under Chapter 7 by which the courts would liquidate current assets (with some exemptions) and then discharge remaining debts. Moreover, U.S. consumer lenders appeared to accept the procedure as reasonable. Why was France, a country putatively willing to sacrifice market efficiency for equality of outcomes, acting so strictly in the case of consumer contracts? Why, for that matter, was the efficiency-oriented United States so willing to abrogate credit contracts?

One possible explanation of France's tough legal stance toward debtors rests on the country's civil law tradition and its lack of legal flexibility. Another explanation is that, unlike in the United States, the French constitution explicitly embraces sovereignty of contract. But these sort of legal objections were never a serious impediment. Early legal proposals did include a provision for automatic discharge that was later removed over objections by lenders. In fact, there was even a precedent for automatic discharge in consumer bankruptcy in France. This took the form of a special legal procedure employed only in the

48 INC, Familles de France, *La Lettre* 156, June 2000.

49 INC, *Le Dispositif Juridique* (internal document).

50 INC, "Les Débats sur le Surendettement Continuent," *INC Hebdo*, March 28, 2003, 2.

departments of Alsace and Moselle. While under German occupation between 1871 and 1918, both had adopted the German law of 1877 providing for discharge in bankruptcy. With the region's reintegration into France, the German bankruptcy provisions were retained as a provision of local customary law.[51] Under this provision, courts in Alsace-Moselle could force creditors to accept partial repayment tied to a discharge of all remaining debt. Consumer advocates pointed to the German model as a workable French institution. It was not adopted, not for reasons of legal propriety, but because of opposition from France's lenders, in particular the commercial banks.

Three other factors help to explain the harsh French response. The first two have to do with timing. First, American bankruptcy reform came at a time when consumer lending was in any case hardly profitable. French reform was taking on what had already become a highly profitable sector. Second, French banks in particular were looking to consumer credit for new growth in profitability, and opposition from the AFB weighed heavily against more liberal reform. The third reason was driven by the broader context of France's social system. In important ways, the U.S. bankruptcy provision was an integral part of the vision of consumer credit as a private-sector welfare regime. Households were encouraged to use credit to help themselves. For those who did not succeed, liberal access to discharge of debts allowed them a fresh start. In France, the social contract had been written differently. For those in need, the state provided direct supports. The goal of private credit had never been to help families help themselves. Hence, the point of bankruptcy law was never intended to harness credit for social welfare.[52] The point of reform was simply to restructure debts in a way that private lenders were seemingly unable to manage.

Credit Controlled

The reforms of the late 1980s did not generate the institutions, including positive risk data and a path to automatic discharge of debts, that could have pushed France toward the American model of consumer credit. The failure to establish a centralized repository for positive-credit data of the sort provided by private credit-rating agencies in the United States was important because the lack of credit-rating agencies has commonly been seen as an explanation for low credit extension. This was not the way French policymakers thought about the role of credit rating. Rather, it was proposed as a tool to manage the problem of over-extension of credit due to multiple lending. Studies in France showed that the most heavily indebted consumers tended to borrow from five lenders or more. Advocates of a white list argued that better

[51] Dominique Dagorne "La Faillite Civile en Alsace et en Moselle," in Michel Gardaz, ed., *Le Surendettement des Particuliers* (Paris: Economica), 1997.

[52] Françoise Blind, "Crédit à la Consommation," *Quotidien de Paris*, March 30, 1989.

knowledge about actual borrowing levels would allow lenders to know when a particular borrower was overextended. Hence, the French debates over credit rating had little to do with credit access; debate concerned whether it would help limit overindebtedness. Rather, the domestic struggle over indebtedness pitted consumer-finance companies against banks. Banks worried that credit data collection would give consumer-finance companies access to their customers. And, critically, the French data privacy agency argued that collecting positive-credit data would infringe a fundamental right to privacy.

French debates over the introduction of consumer bankruptcy procedures clearly show the priority that French policymakers placed on the enforcement of debt contracts. In this way, French lawmakers were more serious about credit markets than their U.S. counterparts. In the U.S. market, a liberal policy for breaking debt contracts of the overindebted was simply a cost to be paid if debt was to be made widely accessible. The goal of market access had social consequences that called for a liberal provision for the breaching of contracts. For French lenders and policymakers, this cavalier approach to contracts was unacceptable. They worried deeply about the incentives that a liberal bankruptcy regime would create for borrowers. Ultimately, France's 1989 initiative to promote debt renegotiation was sold as a means to overcome a market failure. By helping manage the problem of holdouts when multiple lenders sought to renegotiate consumer debt, the new scheme was understood to promote market efficiency. For households whose needs could not be met with their current income, France provided alternative sources of social support.

By 1990, France's credit boom had dramatically slowed, from an annual growth of 30 percent in 1987 to 20 percent in 1988, 16 percent in 1989, and 2 percent in 1990.[53] Some attributed the reduced growth to the effect of the first Gulf War; others thought that it was simply an artifact of France having "caught up" after years of credit restraint.[54] The most important cause, however, was the failure of France's large banks in consumer lending. Crédit Agricole closed its dedicated consumer-lending group, called Unibanque.[55] In May 1991, Citibank sold its French consumer-lending affiliate, Citifinancement, to Crédit Lyonnais.[56] The biggest winner from these exits was Cetelem, whose stock increased 60 percent in 1992.[57] Flexing its financial muscles, Cetelem acquired 49 percent of Cofinoga in 1993, as well as a growing set of consumer-lending companies across Europe.[58] This shifting of fortunes accompanied a change in the French public's attitudes toward credit. By 1992, public opinion had soured on consumer credit. Asked in a 1989 poll whether they

53 *Le Figaro*, May 30, 1991.
54 La Tribune de l'Expansion, April 8, 1991.
55 *Le Figaro*, May 30, 1991.
56 *Le Figaro*, May 30, 1991.
57 Roland Laskine, "Au Mieux de sa Forme," *La Vie Françedilla*, January 9–15, 1993.
58 *Figaro-Économie*, June 19, 1995.

agreed with the statement "I am completely opposed to short term credit. It is preferable to save first when you need something," 45 percent responded yes. By 1992, 53 percent of French responded yes to the same question.[59] A survey conducted by a private polling company for Cetelem regarding public attitudes toward overindebtedness showed a similar shift. In July 1990, 52 percent of overindebted borrowers blamed the debtor for their overindebtedness, compared to 26 percent who blamed the lenders. By December 1991, 44 percent blamed the lenders, and only 32 percent blamed the debtors. Among the general public, 80 percent in December 1991 reported feeling that overindebted consumers were the victims of lenders, and 60 percent also thought that consumers must have lied in order to take on so much debt.[60] Whichever interpretation one emphasized, credit markets were clearly not the tool for economic prosperity or social mobility that American households perceived.

A set of events in the mid-1990s emphasized this shift in attitude. In 1996, the UK-based Thorn group launched its first rent-to-own store, called Crazy George's, in Bobigny, France. It followed with a second site in Le Havre. Doing so pitted two different credit cultures against one another. The Crazy George's store format was based on the company's highly successful Rent-a-Center chain, launched in 1992 in the United State, and the equally successful Crazy George's rent-to-own chain in the UK. The idea of the store was to offer goods under a rental contract that would eventually lead to consumer ownership. Their French stores targeted communities with high concentrations of poor and elderly, and where credit was not readily available. The effective interest rate on the rent-to-own purchases ranged up to 56 percent. Because the rental was not formally a sale, it did not fall under France's usury restrictions.[61] Thorn went out of its way to portray the rent-to-own format as an American import. Initially, it had envisioned offering the rent-to-own service through its existing French consumer electronics rental company, Visea. Beginning in 1994, Visea began posting billboards with slogans that read: "If we lend only to the rich, why did we invent credit?" and "If we deny credit to those who are unemployed, what good is solidarity?"[62] The reference to solidarity was a direct attack on the French idea of equal citizenship without equal access to credit. Thorn finally opted to introduce the rent-to-own (*location avec option d'achat*) format as a new brand. To launch its first Crazy George's store in Bobigny, it paraded around town in convertibles festooned with balloons and American flags. The French media quickly focused on the new format as an

59 *Le Point*, June 13–19, 1992.

60 Paul Defourny and Josette Bienfait, *Données d'Image sur le Crédit* (Paris: Cetelem-BVA), 1992, 10.

61 Crazy George's forty outlets in the UK operated on far lower effective interest rates, ranging between 20 percent and 25 percent. This was likely because of the more highly competitive consumer-lending market in the UK, which gave Crazy George's customers other borrowing options.

62 *La Croix*, January 18, 1994.

"Anglo-Saxon" import. Public interest heightened when the first store was shut down by France's commercial police on the grounds that it was not accurately reporting the final total price on its goods.

For Crazy George's customers, many of them retired, on a pension, and without access to traditional consumer credit, Crazy George's provided their only possibility to purchase large household goods. Unlike consumer lenders, Crazy George's accepted social payments as income to qualify for a loan. In fact, a third of all customers reported no household salary income. To facilitate repayments, the stores sold only to customers within a 5-kilometer radius and insisted that customers drop off their payments in person and on a weekly basis. All applicants were required to give the names and telephone numbers of three friends and two relatives, so that application information could be confirmed.[63] These measures kept default rates below 1 percent.[64] A survey of Crazy George's customers found that 66 percent were first-time buyers of basic household goods such as televisions and computers.[65] Yet critics of Crazy George's were vociferous, arguing that it was wrong for the poor to pay more than twice as much for products. Behind the opposition was a familiar coalition of the Christian right and labor left. France's Catholic newspaper, *La Croix*, took a hard line: "Consumer lending... is to be condemned, and the old Christian tradition of usury, meaning a total prohibition on the charging of interest, not only abusive interest rates, should be retained."[66] The union-affiliated consumer group Confédération Syndicale du Cadre de Vie (CSCV) brought a lawsuit against it for exceeding France's usury cap.[67] The view seems to have been shared by the general public. A public poll at the time found that 70 percent of French opposed the rent-to-sell format.[68] This cultural experiment ended too soon for us to know which attitudes would have won. In 1998, Thorn shut the French Crazy George's stores in preparation for an acquisition by the Japanese private-equity firm Nomura Investments. But it suggests that distinctive French attitudes toward credit persisted even in the wake of financial liberalization.

[63] Odette Terrade, "Projet de Loi de Finances pour 1998 – Consommation et Concurrence," 87/9, French Senate, 1997.

[64] "Crazy George's Déclare Forfeit," *LSA* 1594, August 27, 1998.

[65] CSA, survey of 157 customers, October 1997.

[66] Hugues Puel, "Crazy George's met l'Éthique au Défi," *La Croix*, December 11, 1996.

[67] Crazy George's à Contrecourant, *L'Humanité*, February 20, 1998.

[68] *Le Monde*, November 25, 1996.

10

Credit and Welfare

Over the course of almost a century, American households were taught to approach consumer credit as socially progressive and economically virtuous. By the 1990s, household credit was viewed on both the left and right of the political spectrum as an effective tool for improving poor households' access to economic prosperity. The idea that free access to financial markets could play a role in generating social equality dominated the third-way politics of the Bill Clinton presidency, and carried through seamlessly to the George Bush presidency under the new label of the ownership society. To some degree, the focus on financial markets as a boon to the working poor simply made a virtue of necessity. As tax rates fell, rising social demands met declining government revenues, and the political left turned to the markets to finance its social goals. It legalized gambling so that the winnings could go to support education. It embraced housing and financial assets as a means to invest for future retirement – an approach that came to be known as asset-based welfare. Expanded access to consumer credit was one piece of a broader societal project that included home ownership, private retirement funds, and stock market investments.

The surprise of these market-welfare policies of the Clinton and Bush administrations was that they did not generate a strong backlash. Household debt increased dramatically through the 1990s, and poorer households no longer enjoyed those benefits that had softened the financial costs for earlier borrowers. Above all, the cross-subsidy for poorer households had disappeared; in fact, they had reversed. From the late 1980s, new risk-based pricing schemes meant that it was the relatively modest borrowers who were helping subsidize generous credit terms for the more affluent.

This shift in the direction of subsidy was driven by changes in the economics and technology of lending. As consumer lending became profitable, and especially as it became more profitable than merchandizing, lending shifted from a cost center to a profit center for most retailers. Freedom to charge higher rates made it possible for lenders to distribute the costs of loans more proportionately. For smaller borrowers, this meant higher interest rates, quite apart from any risk premium. To the extent that poorer borrowers also represented greater repayment risk, they had to pay even more. At the same time, the rapid decline in inflation over the 1980s and especially the 1990s drove up real interest rates for all borrowers.

That the American political left was able to ignore the rapid growth in liabilities taken on by the country's working class and poor is in part a consequence of the even more dramatic appreciation of assets in the housing and stock markets in the late 1990s. Household debt at the time was rising as a share of income, but it was declining as a share of wealth. The wealth effect from the run-up in housing prices in the late 1990s was especially dramatic for relatively poor homebuyers. With low equity and high debt, they enjoyed the benefits of highly leveraged investments. Rapid increases in housing assets created a feeling of wealth that made growing household debt seem manageable. By refinancing, consumers were able to roll over expensive credit card debt into relatively inexpensive refinanced mortgages. Most homeowners that refinanced their homes to pay off consumer debt continued to borrow on their credit cards. In retrospect, this process laid the foundations for economic crisis. The U.S. housing crisis that would precipitate the 2008 financial crisis started as a consumer debt crisis with its roots in the 1990s.

The bursting of the American housing bubble in 2007–2008 severely strained the American narrative linking market access to prosperity. The depletion of housing equity had made families especially susceptible to even modest drops in house prices. The leverage that had amplified their investments as housing prices rose had the opposite effect as housing prices fell. Far from promoting social welfare, the rapid decline in home values revealed that markets could be deeply regressive in their consequences. Access to financial markets had not helped America's low-income and poor families. It had instead placed them in deep financial crisis. This reality posed a fundamental dilemma for the American narrative linking credit and prosperity. If consumer credit was bad for the poor, how had Americans come to believe that it would make everyone better off?

Constructed Interests

The history of consumer lending in France and America gives a comparative perspective on an answer. The heavy use of consumer credit in postwar America and the relatively light use of consumer credit in France are hard to explain by reference to either national regulatory traditions, national cultures of consumption, or views about the welfare state. For much of the twentieth century, American credit markets were if anything more highly regulated than their French counterparts. And, although both countries deregulated consumer credit in the 1980s, only France experienced a backlash that led to reregulation. It is also hard to attribute American credit use to a culture of consumption. On the one hand, that culture was itself facilitated by easy credit. On the other hand, French lenders never offered sufficient credit to drive a consumption boom that could have mirrored American consumerism. Finally, there is little basis for linking credit access to differences in the generosity of the welfare state. One problem is that France embraced – indeed virtually invented – the idea of credit as welfare, in the form of the charitable pawn. The other problem is one of timing. Consumer-credit use grew most rapidly in the United States in the 1950s and 1960s, at the same time the welfare state was growing. Although credit use did surge again in the 1980s, this was fully a decade after American workers first experienced wage stagnation and welfare retrenchment.

More generally, the case of consumer credit belies the way political scientists have traditionally interpreted French and American approaches to the trade-off between market efficiency and social equality.[1] The United States embraced consumer credit not primarily because it was efficient, but as a means to achieve social welfare. The French opposed credit not on welfare grounds, but primarily because they thought it was economically inefficient. To understand the evolution of these different interpretations, we must look to the economic logic of consumer credit from the perspective of lenders and the political logic of consumer regulation from the perspective of the state. By combining empirical analysis of industry interests with the politics of regulation, this book offers a framework for explaining how similar economic actors came to understand their interests in very different ways.

The root of the national differences we see trace to the political construction of very different interpretations of the economic and social role of consumer credit in industrialized society. Consumer credit emerged from the nineteenth century deeply tarnished by the exploitative lending practices of small informal lenders. How credit was rehabilitated as a legitimate financial practice shaped the politics of consumer credit throughout the twentieth century.

In the United States, an evolving coalition of lenders and nongovernmental groups drove a narrative that linked credit to social welfare. During the interwar period, social welfare advocates and consumer lenders came together to support small-loan laws that provided higher allowable interest rates in exchange for transparency. They shared a common vision that even relatively expensive consumer loans offered on fair terms were an improvement over the usurious rates and aggressive collections used by loan sharks. With the end of World War II, a new coalition emerged between labor and manufacturers who perceived that liberal access to credit would help jump-start demand for manufactured goods. This seemed to create a virtuous cycle of increased scale, productivity, wages, and further growth in demand. As an added benefit, early gains to

1 See especially Gøsta Esping-Andersen, *Three Worlds of Welfare Capitalism* (New York: Polity Press, 1990).

scale seemed to have reduced product prices sufficiently to allay concerns that liberal access to credit would drive inflation. In fact, many consumers were both saving and borrowing at the same time. Moreover, caps on consumer-lending rates meant that lenders were in practice cross-subsidizing smaller loans to working-class families from profits on larger loans to more affluent consumers. This cross-subsidy hid the inherently regressive cost structure of consumer lending.

As this pro-credit productivity coalition dissolved in the 1960s, and organized labor became increasingly critical of consumer credit, the political basis for liberal consumer credit extension again shifted. Beginning in the late 1970s, a new set of coalitions emerged to promote continued credit access, but for quite different reasons. Arguments for extending consumer credit no longer tied credit access to the material aspirations of the working class. They instead emphasized the rights of previously marginalized groups – especially blacks and women – to achieve equal access to financial markets. Moreover, the new extension of credit in the 1970s failed to generate a backlash in part because the high inflation associated with the first and second oil shocks dramatically reduced the real interest rate charged to consumers. Consumer credit in the 1970s was inexpensive credit, and the effect of inflation weakened the impact of interest payments for poorer borrowers. At the extreme, credit became a means for those with modest means to hedge against the impact of inflation. Like a deus ex machina, inflation helped to preserve the myth of credit as a social virtue.

In France, the legitimation of consumer credit occurred through a different coalition – one between consumer lenders and state regulators that emphasized the importance of regulation in defining the bounds of acceptable practice. Prior to World War II, France mirrored the United States in embracing the idea of credit as a form of welfare. The *monts-de-piété* were emblematic of this emphasis. So accepted was the linking of credit and welfare that France's growing welfare state absorbed formerly independent social lending institutions into its apparatus. One consequence was that consumer lending was seen as being linked to welfare only insofar as that credit was facilitated by the state. It was an arrangement that did little to resurrect the reputation of private, and especially doorstep, lenders.

From the early 1950s through the end of the 1970s, the French state limited growth in credit volume for consumers. This policy was supported by labor, which feared that excessive credit use by workers would reduce their purchasing power and lead to a de-radicalization of the workforce. It was also supported by industry, which worried that excessive credit use by consumers would crowd out industrial investment and drive inflation that would hurt exports. In the wake of financial liberalization in the early 1980s, a brief experiment with liberal credit access generated a new debate about the risks of overindebtedness. French regulators responded to these new concerns, not by restricting markets, but by enforcing debt contracts and limiting the provision of public-credit information. Under these reforms, consumer credit was not interpreted as a right, as had occurred in America, but instead as a serious financial responsibility.

The French and American histories emphasize how core economic interests with respect to consumer credit came to be constructed in different ways in the two countries. For Americans, credit access provided a path to social welfare, at the same time driving manufacturing scale and productivity. For the French, credit access reduced workers' purchasing power and crowded out industrial investment. What mattered about these arguments was not that they were empirically true – in fact, nobody at the time was certain what impact credit might have on workers or households. This empirical uncertainty left sufficient latitude for coalitions of actors in both France and America to advocate nearly opposite interpretations of the role of consumer credit in the modern industrial welfare state.

These differences highlight the ways in which the perception of basic economic interests can be highly contextual. Policy outcomes cannot be imputed in a mechanical way to the underlying economic interests of workers or lenders. How banks in the two countries approached consumer lending, for example, depended partly on the structure of the sector and partly on the public perception of consumer lending as a legitimate activity for banks. How consumer lending was transformed from an illegitimate to a legitimate economic activity therefore proved critical to differences in national outcomes. In the United States, a coalition of lenders and social activists worked to promote the idea of consumer credit as a private-sector alternative to aggressive government welfare programs. In France, these sorts of social activists did not exist. Instead, it was a close alliance of regulators and lenders that ultimately transformed consumer lending into a legitimate economic activity. From these two different legitimacy coalitions emerged very different views about the role of consumer credit in society.

The Liberal's Dilemma

The story of American consumer credit matters not just because of its economic and distributional consequences, but also because of what it implies about the trajectory of American liberalism more generally. European liberalism was built on a strong conceptual separation of freedom and social welfare; the American liberal tradition as it emerged in the twentieth century blurred that line.[2] On the

[2] For European liberals, for whom markets were understood to be socially neutral, societal goals would have to be addressed directly through active redistributive policies that must necessarily infringe on liberal principles. Whether this active redistribution occurred through labor policy, and thus infringed on the freedom of corporations, or through the welfare state, and thus infringed on individual freedoms, would define the major divide between corporatist and liberal versions of social democracy.

left and right, American policymakers and social activists came to see markets and social justice as profoundly interconnected.

In its conservative variant, American liberalism of the kind associated with the Chicago School of Economics insisted that market access was valuable not in its own right, but for the social and political benefits the market would confer. Rather than accentuating the boundary between state and market, the Chicago School's approach was to blur it by promoting a radical reengineering of government-business relations.[3] On the one hand, the Chicago School idea was to claim for markets some of the functions that had previously been seen as belonging to the state. On the other hand, one of the important functions of their political project was to harness the state for the construction of free markets. This explicitly political project set American liberals apart from their European counterparts. Milton Friedman's *Capitalism and Freedom*, which would become a manifesto for the American liberal project, emphasized the link to politics: "Economic freedom is... an indispensable means toward the achievement of political freedom."[4] Friedrich Hayek, who had been invited to America to help found the Chicago School, was turned down for tenure in the University of Chicago Economics Department in part because his views on liberalism were seen to be insufficiently political.[5]

The move on the right to marry markets and politics was quickly followed by a response on the left. Although profoundly different in inspiration and approach, John Rawls's *A Theory of Justice* also explicitly connected economic freedom to progressiveness of economic outcomes.[6] Rawls's vision combined the ability to choose one's own economic fate, what he called fair equality of opportunity, with a basic level of redistributive justice defined by the difference principle, in which the position of the worst off in society would be maximized. In *Justice as Fairness*, Rawls reemphasized that fair equality of opportunity was integral to the functioning of the difference principle: the requirements of the former had to be met before satisfying the latter.[7] Tellingly, this melding of markets and justice that would come to dominate liberal ethical philosophy in the United States was greeted with confusion in Europe. Whereas European neoliberals saw it as an affirmation of markets, besieged social democrats saw it as a reassertion of redistribution.[8] For the American left, however, the embrace

[3] Rob Van Horn and Philip Mirowski, "The Rise of the Chicago School of Economics and the Birth of Neoliberalism," in Philip Mirowski and Dieter Plehwe, eds., *The Road from Mont Pèlerin: The Making of the Neoliberal Thought Collective* (Cambridge, MA: Harvard University Press, 2009), 161–163.

[4] Milton Friedman, *Capitalism and Freedom* (Chicago: University of Chicago Press, 1962), 8.

[5] Rob Van Horn and Philip Mirowski, "The Rise of the Chicago School of Economics and the Birth of Neoliberalism," in Philip Mirowski and Dieter Plehwe, eds., *The Road from Mont Pèlerin: The Making of the Neoliberal Thought Collective* (Cambridge, MA: Harvard University Press, 2009), 161–163.

[6] John Rawls, *A Theory of Justice* (Cambridge, MA: Harvard University Press, 1971).

[7] John Rawls, *Justice as Fairness: A Restatement* (Cambridge, MA: Belknap Press, 2001), 43.

[8] Cécile Laborde, "The Reception of John Rawls in Europe," *European Journal of Political Theory* 1/2 (2002), 141.

of markets as a tool for achieving social justice became a politically feasible way forward in the absence of an expansive welfare state.

One reason may be that, for much of the postwar period, the impact of financial markets on welfare outcomes *was* benign. Until the mid-1980s, greater market access did seem to generate welfare-improving outcomes that were compatible with social democratic aspirations. Consumer credit is one part of that broader story. Even relatively high levels of consumer credit were not unduly harmful, and frequently helpful, to American workers. In a variety of ways, working-class credit was subsidized. Retailers used profits from cash sales to support credit programs. Profits from larger loans helped defray the costs of more expensive smaller loans. Inflation in the 1970s dramatically reduced the real interest rate for all borrowers. Only in the 1980s, as inflation fell and credit pricing was liberalized, did the true cost of credit begin to be borne by the working classes and poor. By then, a new coalition built around economic access for marginalized groups hid the potential social costs of household debt.

The relatively benign interaction of market access and social welfare that characterized consumer-credit markets also characterized other financial markets. In insurance, the practice of risk pooling meant that even privately run general insurance schemes provided a cross-subsidy to the most vulnerable members of the risk pool.[9] Programs to promote home ownership allowed workers to take a leveraged position in an appreciating housing market. The democratization of stock holdings through private retirement plans appeared to deliver the impossible, allowing everyone to enjoy investment returns that were superior to the overall rate of growth in the economy. In each of these cases, greater access to financial markets appeared to benefit everyone. So successful was the marrying of market access to social-welfare goals that advocates of financial liberalization in the 1980s and 1990s, on both the right and left, saw the two projects as essentially complementary.

Under the new third-way liberalism of the 1990s, the embrace of markets as a tool of public welfare policy extended well beyond consumer credit. Markets became the means for administering previously government-run social policies ranging from education to health care. State governments embraced lotteries to raise funds for scholarship programs. School choice initiatives were implemented to raise the level of underperforming primary and secondary schools. Welfare-to-work programs created incentives for the unemployed to find new jobs quickly. A move toward individually contracted health insurance was meant to increase competition and lower costs. Ultimately, as was the case in consumer credit, many of these efforts to marry markets to social goals would eventually prove counterproductive. Outcomes from school-choice programs favored the wealthy. Welfare-to-work programs left many poor with inadequate support. State lotteries turned out to be highly regressive in their

[9] Isabela Mares, *The Politics of Social Risk: Business and Welfare State Development* (Cambridge: Cambridge University Press, 2003); David Moss, *When All Else Fails: Government as the Ultimate Risk Manager* (Cambridge, MA: Harvard University Press, 2002).

outcomes. And health insurers invested in keeping out high-risk categories. Just as the left was embracing markets, markets seemed to be betraying the goals of the left.

This new tension, in which markets seemed to be working against social welfare, posed a dilemma for American liberals. The credit crisis in America pointed to a new class of issues in which private freedom and public-welfare goals appeared to increasingly conflict. Traditionally, Americans had called on government to regulate in cases of market failures – to ensure better information, provide more complete contracting, and help overcome principle agent problems, adverse selection, and moral hazard. The new tension between markets and social welfare suggested that governments that retained aspirations to social-democratic outcomes would have to regulate not to fix markets, but to block them. Access would have to be restricted. Products would have to be regulated – not because they were inherently dangerous, but because they would be used by American households in ways that would make them worse off. If these dilemmas proved to be pervasive in economic and social policy, Americans were entering a post-Rawlsian world, one in which a new liberal consensus would have to be constructed.

Index

NOTE: Page numbers followed by *f* indicate a figure; those with *t* indicate a table.